With Best Wishes
Robert Hugh

# LIFE'S CHALLENGE

# LIFE'S CHALLENGE

## A GUIDE TO SUCCESSFUL LIVING

BY

ROBERT HEAP

PSYCHOLOGY MAGAZINE LTD.

MARPLE, CHESHIRE

# CONTENTS

# PREFACE

SINCE the publication of *Successful Living*, the first volume of essays by Robert Heap, Editor of the ever-popular *Psychology* Magazine, the publishers have received numerous requests for a second volume. They now have pleasure in presenting *Life's Challenge*, in which a further selection has been culled from the extensive repertoire of editorial chats appearing in the pages of the Magazine.

The Editor chose to call these essays "chats" for a special reason which will appeal to the many readers who each month have been inspired and uplifted by the thoughts he has penned. He wanted them to feel that he was talking intimately with each one of them in a face-to-face conversation, as it were, and his and our hope is that this is the spirit in which this new compilation will be read.

In the present volume we place before an eager public fifty-six essays or chats which have never been published elsewhere except in *Psychology*. We believe that those who approved of the choice made in the first volume will welcome with equal enthusiasm this further collection.

*Life's Challenge*, then, may be regarded as a second volume of *Successful Living*, and, like its predecessor, it has been brought into being by the insistent demand both here and overseas of those who have admired the Editor for his plain speaking and acknowledged the power of his sustaining message.

While many believed that the essays in Volume One would never be surpassed, our experience of the inspirational needs of men and women has encouraged us to gather together what we are convinced is an even more finely representative and stirring a group of personal chats.

We believe that readers of this volume will agree that Mr. Heap has preserved the sureness of touch, the positive approach, which have invariably marked his work in the past. Here one finds as deft a skill in handling words as can be met anywhere in the field of inspirational literature. The penetrating understanding and maturity of concept reflected in these essays are typical of what readers of *Psychology* have come to expect from him.

THE PUBLISHERS.

# LIFE'S PRICELESS TREASURE

WHAT is the expressed aim of the large majority of men and women? What does nearly every human being seek from the cradle to the grave? What is the motive force behind the greater part of human endeavour? What is the master quest of life?

The answer is happiness. Man is drawn towards the illusive mirage of happiness as the infinitesimal particles of moisture are drawn towards the sun. But the majority of men and women are mistaken about the lure of life. They think it is in the accumulation of wealth, fame, popularity and power. But each of these in itself is impotent to create happiness.

If we ask those who seek power, wealth, success or fame, why they do so, their answer will indicate that they seek these things because they believe that they will find happiness in their achievement.

One man believes that power is the key that can open the golden portals of happiness. Whilst he is still conscious that his striving for power is only a means to a larger end, he will probably come to no great harm—even though happiness may elude him.

But once let him pursue power as an end in itself, once let him seek power as the means of gratifying that inner craving for dominion over his fellow-men, then he becomes a Napoleon or a Hitler. The pursuit of naked power ends in damnation and destruction.

In either case, however, the pursuit of power will not bring happiness. It is like looking for heaven in the terrifying loneliness of empty space. Heaven, as well as happiness, is not a place, but an *inner harmony*.

He who pursues wealth is also chasing a mirage, for gold is not the magic substance that can transmute leaden existence into vibrant life. But as long as Man pursues wealth as a means to a larger end, then all is not lost, even though happiness may elude him. It is when wealth—and wealth alone—becomes the only end in life that the spirit shrivels up and Man becomes that pathetic object—a miser.

But let us note well, that in the early stages at least, whatever goal Man may set himself, the larger purpose is the achievement of happiness. Later his objective may become distorted; he may pursue unworthy ends, such as naked, ruthless power. Yet that does not invalidate the argument that the first objective was to secure happiness.

## A State of Mind

Judged from this standpoint, the majority of men and women pursue happiness as an ultimate objective. And in so doing they mistake the mirage for the well of life! After years of feverish effort they may achieve some measure of wealth, fame, popularity and power —only to find that the possession of these is not necessarily coincident with happiness. For happiness is a state of the mind—pursued by everyone—but rarely attained.

We should not decry wholesome ambition nor eulogise inaction or indolence. But we should stress the fact that happiness is not to be gained through achieving power, wealth, popularity or fame. These may or may not aid, according to whether an individual is wise in understanding the true nature and values of life.

Chasing happiness is like looking for gold at the rainbow's end. If we pursue happiness as a goal we shall find it merely a will-o'-the-wisp.

The goal of life is self-fulfilment and service, the ultimate good of all human endeavour. Happiness is the by-product of the well-balanced, well-spent life; it is the *result* of successful living.

Man is given worthy opportunities and he has large resources at his command. His goal should be not only to live but to live fully, realising his personality to the utmost, in the attainment of some noble ideal that will be of service to his fellow-men.

Happiness comes upon him unawares. It is the calm beauty of the evening when the day's work has been done.

We do not live in order to be happy; we *are* happy when we live fully. We should give the utmost weight to these remarks. There are many letters received at Psychology House that tell the same story, time and time again, of men and women asking us, in effect, to show them how to be happy. They do not realise that theirs is the wrong approach.

What would we think of an individual who searched for wine in the soil? True, wine is a product of Mother Earth. But it is the result of cultivating the vine, of pressing the grapes in due season. Wine is the by-product of Man's toil and co-operation with Nature.

So, too, is happiness!

What would we think of an individual who dug deep into the earth to find modern machinery? All he would find, at best, would be iron-ore—the basis of iron and of steel. But the machinery he requires is the result of Man's labours upon the raw material dug out of the earth. Machinery—man-manufactured things of iron and steel—is the result of Man's efforts to improve upon the raw material.

So, too, is happiness!

We should not seek happiness direct but seek first the full life.


### Acceptance of Life

Many and various are the ways in which men and women seek happiness. Many are the objectives they aspire to in order to be happy. With some, the pursuit of happiness is a conscious urge, a drive to make a direct assault upon the fortress of contentment; with others, the aim is an unconscious motive in their lives. They seek wealth, fame, fortune, power or popularity either as substitutes for happiness, or as the means to be happy.

But though there are a thousand different things for which people may strive in order to find happiness, there seem to be only two routes that men and women follow. One is an acceptance of life—making the most of things; the other is the road of retreat from harsh reality into the inner shell of make-believe.

Those who seek to be happy by accepting life on its own terms are, in the main, the Extravert type—the "hail-fellow-well-met" individuals —who find it easy and pleasurable to mix with people. They find their fun in community existence and in the pleasures and recreations that society offers.

They like people, overlook their faults and are at their best when mixing with the crowd. They are restless, dislike quiet, chafe at inaction and want to be up and doing.

The Extraverts accept life with the best grace possible, make the most of their opportunities, hoping for a "lucky break", but seldom completely cast down except by some major catastrophe. They adapt themselves to circumstance, take delight in simple physical pleasures, are happy-go-lucky and make the most of each day as it comes along.

A sensible approach, we might say! And so it is. But it is not the best way of getting the most out of life. For it is acceptance of life on a plane not much higher than that of the animals. The Extravert asks little but the satisfaction of creature needs and does not satisfy that inner urge towards self-perfection that is within the soul of all of us.

The second type—the Introverts—are ill at ease in social gatherings. They often try in many ways to escape from life's hard realities. They distrust life; they are abnormally sensitive to its cruelties and injustices.

The Introverts are easily discouraged in the hustle and bustle of life; they long for perfection and, not finding it in the outside world, seek it within themselves.

Living largely with a self-centred outlook on life, the Introverts often have a great capacity for feeling sorry for themselves. They believe they are misunderstood and wronged. Their feelings are easily hurt and they feed their hurts with copious draughts of self-pity, carefully nursing their resentment.

It is they who find it easy to follow the philosophy that if men and women discipline themselves to need nothing, they will find contentment. If people are content with what they have, then certainly they suffer no unhappiness from unsatisfied desires. They will find contentment but not happiness. This is another life-pattern with a certain amount of logic to support it.

But again—that is not the rich, noble life of effort, achievement and service to mankind which should be the true goal of life.

Both these roads can lead to disillusion. Practical Psychology points to the high road of endeavour as the right road for Man; the road that means a life of labour and service, a life dedicated to a noble purpose, a life of expansion, progress and self-fulfilment.

Admittedly, upon that road we find hardships and discomforts, adversities and trials. But it is along that road that we would also find successful living; it is upon that route that we will often be attended by happiness.

We now come to the third type—the Ambiverts. These are part Extravert and part Introvert, and whilst they are usually reasonably well-balanced people, it does not follow that Ambiverts find happiness. The characteristics of either the Extravert or the Introvert frequently predominate.

Let us now sum up the three types of men and women—the Extravert, the Introvert and the Ambivert.

The Extravert leads an exciting life, he is the life and soul of parties; he is the popular man in the office or works. He finds a thousand things to do. He fills in every minute of every day—and sleeps soundly at night. Whilst things go smoothly he finds a great deal of pleasure in existence. There is no denying that. To the outsider he seems to be the completely happy man. And to some extent, perhaps, he is—for he asks so little of life.

But he is absolutely dependent upon material things. Deprive him of these and he is helpless. He is the child spoiled with an excess of toys. Whilst the toys retain their novelty, he is moderately content. Once they lose their novelty—and all toys do in time—then he is miserable, afraid, irritable and dissatisfied.

What does the Extravert find when he looks back over the years that have gone? He discovers that his triumphs are empty, that life seems to be without meaning. His life has lacked a fundamental purpose; he has lived on one plane alone and has never satisfied the hunger of the spirit.

He may have found *some* happiness; he may have led a blameless life, be an excellent citizen and a good neighbour, but life is still incomplete, unfulfilled—for Man cannot live by bread alone.

### The Inner Life

The Introvert is the other side of the same penny. He may be moody, emotional, lacking a social personality, courage and quick decisions. He feels handicapped in the battle of life and retreats from the battle-front into a world of fantasy. He may fail to find any happiness in the inner life, and the best he can hope for is that attitude of mind that finds contentment whatever his circumstances.

The Introvert tries to dodge the hard realities and exigencies of life. Yet however much a man may keep reality at bay with day-dreams, he still has to learn his daily bread—he still has to have some communion with his fellow-man. It is this reality that breaks down the shell of the retreating Introvert. He is forced to face the real and hard facts of existence. Those who seek to escape the challenge of life are the more seriously battered by the exigencies of existence. For there is no escape!

The Ambivert is very rarely *evenly* balanced and harmonised between the opposing interests and tendencies of the Extravert and the Introvert.

There are infinite gradations among the Ambiverts. For instance, one Ambivert may have too much of the Extravert traits of aggressiveness and carelessness, whilst another may be troubled by the timidity and the emotional tendency of the Introvert.

Yet the Ambivert is the type to which we should aspire. We should try to blend the combined Extravert—Introvert tendencies into our personalities. But even when we have effected this transformation, it requires more than the characteristics of the Ambivert to help us along the road to happiness. It calls for *complete* men and women, *realised* men and women, who are prepared to develop themselves fully, to live nobly, to cultivate Mind, body and spirit; to face life courageously, to dare, to do, and to achieve.

The tragedy of life seems to be that so few are happy. How many happy faces do we see in a crowd? There are thousands drawn, weary, envious, tragic, sensual and discouraged. Only here and there, like rare jewels resplendently shining forth from a dismal setting, do we behold a face reflecting tranquillity and happiness.

Why is it that the majority of men and women fail to pass through the gates of happiness? The answer to this profound problem seems to be that the curse of life is ignorance. People are blinded by false estimates and values. They build their hopes upon non-essentials and sacrifice practically all for that which gives no satisfaction.

Happiness is not dependent upon external occurrences, upon outward order and harmony. It is not the person, event, circumstances or conditions without that determine the degree of happiness or misery, but the spirit within; not what happens but how we react to it.

If we are undisturbed by the jangling disharmonies which assail us from the outside world, if we refuse to be crushed by adversity or let external conditions disturb our own tranquillity of mind, then we will have found the Key to the Golden Gates of Happiness.

# REACHING FOR BETTER THINGS

HAVE you ever thought in your most serious, solitary moments—what is the purpose of life? Why do we all struggle and strive and battle on to survive? But it is not just racial survival that counts or even interests most of us. Why do *you*—why do I—live on from year to year, working and playing, seeking always to extend the length of our sojourn on this earth and often fearful of its ending? *What* is the meaning and justification of life? *Why* do we carry on? *What* do we live for? *Where* are we going?

Yes, of course, these questions have come into our minds. And what replies do we get from our Inner Mind, our Greater Self? What answers do we get from other people, if we get so far as to discuss such matters with them, or to express in words our doubts, our fears, our sense of uncertainty?

We seem to get no satisfactory answers to these questions. Is this because most of us have not even the courage to look the questions squarely in the face, let alone discuss them with others? Consciously or unconsciously we give ourselves no time to think about such matters. Life for all of us rushes by, but it does so with terrifying speed as we get older. *If* we have time to think, we find some legitimate excuse, such as a social engagement, some voluntary work, a hobby or duty which *must* be done. Another opportunity of answering questions, solving problems, facing up to the meaning of life has escaped, driven away by our own fear and inability to face the deeper, more serious problems of existence.

What it all seems to amount to is that most of us live from day to day, for we do not know where we are going, and are fearful of facing up to our own ignorance and lack of vision.

When we were young, some of us did ask ourselves the questions outlined above, urged on by our inquisitiveness, and thirst for knowledge. But even then, these questions of the purpose of one's individual strivings, of the meaning of life created a feeling of uneasiness. It wasn't pleasant or satisfactory. During those early days, life stretched before us for forty or fifty years; it was full of promise and hope; the lure of the unknown future beckoned us on to win and claim the prizes of success, achievement, adventure, knowledge, happiness. But all too soon we were caught up in the whirl of life as we strove for one or more of these glittering prizes; responsibilities followed, and there was little or no time to question one's final goal. And up to a point this is as it should be, for "we grow by doing, not by thinking of our thoughts and feeling of our feelings".

6

Then we reach the "fifty mark" and the tempo of our lives slackens. Or does it really? Life still appears to rush hectically on—towards what? There is still not time to do everything that should be done, and certainly not time to do the things we would like to do. Suddenly we find ourselves asking again—what is it all about? Where is all this rush and bustle getting us? Is it just a habit acquired over the years? For it now seems, not to be a matter of living twenty-four hours a day, but striving to cram in twenty-six. Nevertheless, now and then, one's Inner Self manages to get a few thoughts through to the surface of the Conscious Mind: "What's it all about? Why are you rushing and scurrying and striving like this? Where is it leading you?"

Every now and then these thoughts crop up in our minds, often at our busiest moments; it is really quite disconcerting. So persistent do these thoughts become, that at last we decide to give them room; we give something up and make time, in the evening or when out walking, to consider our mode of life, the use we are making of our time, where our hurried journey through life is taking us.

"Shall I," each one of us may wonder, "in ten years' time, look back and regret the manner in which I have spent them? Shall I come to the conclusion that my hard-driving, busy way of life was foolish; find that my values have all been wrong; that I have missed the spice and savour of later life, the adventure, the leisure?"

## Facing Up to Vital Questions

And why are we apt to think along these lines? Is it because most of us have got into a *habit* of rushing; because we *think* we cannot be done without; because we *must* have the money? But *why*? Where are we going? *Why* all this struggle to get things done? What will it benefit us in the long run? Couldn't we ease up a little and find time before it is too late to do some of those things we always wanted to do and never had the time or opportunity before? Perhaps if we did this we should not find the question "What do we live for?" quite so persistent and nagging, for we should be satisfying that inner hunger to express ourselves.

Why is it that so many of us wait until we reach the early fifties before we face up to these vital questions? Wouldn't it be wiser and better to face up to them earlier on in life, to take stock, to think about what is good in the things we are doing and what is pointless and stupid; to decide where we are going—what our goal in life is to be? For surely a guided life is better than one without a plan. Many people do set a goal—make a materialistic plan—of what they are going to do, what they want to achieve, and where they hope their lives will lead them. A very small percentage make an idealistic

L.C.—2

plan with a long-term policy; a plan which involves knowledge of the good and evil in life.  Of course, their plan involves a job, a trade or profession, but behind it and with it and in it, they believe that the world can be made into a happier and better place in which to live, and they go on working towards that end.

Just believing is something.  Somehow we have got to banish the gloom and pessimism which there are in the world to-day regarding human affairs.  Conditions and circumstances for the human race have looked bad before, but out of the tragedy and the suffering and the muck and mire of life, there has always arisen something better.

The world is full of beauty and wonder and the miracles of nature; these are the triumphs of millions of years of progress.  Are we to believe that the evil or foolishness in man is to destroy all this?  Perhaps it will help us to banish this pessimistic doubt if we remember that all progress in life means initial trials and tribulations, difficulties and setbacks, before all the good things that progress brings along can fully mature.  We should also keep in mind that the "quest after ideals is the central reason of life; it is the geometry of life".

## Urge to Achieve

When an individual asks himself: "What shall I make of my life?" he must set himself a goal—an ideal—towards which he can work. Every young man and woman, worthy of the name, must have a goal. They must decide where they are going.  They must be imbued with the restless, impatient energy which comes from the insistent urge to achieve.  This urge, this striving towards our goal may be likened to a man upon our backs, driving us forward relentlessly, never letting us give up, for ever luring us on towards the goal.

Life is a continual fight—a perpetual struggle.  There are some who refuse to take part in life's dramatic struggle and go down to defeat. Others, beholding the seemingly overwhelming odds, shrink from the fight and supinely surrender.  They see other stout-hearted, invincible men and women press on towards their triumphant goal.

Thousands of years ago, the life struggle was chiefly on the physical plane; the battle went to the strong and it was imperative to develop physical skills.  As man developed, mental and spiritual qualities took prominence, though physical skills were still necessary.  But whatever progress man may make, life will still be a struggle.  And it is necessary that it should be so, for only through effort, activity and struggle will any progress be made by the individual or the race.

Those who endeavour to slip out of the struggling procession of life and rest permanently by the roadside might just as well give up at once, for life for them is finished.

## Accepting Responsibility

We cannot, however, much as we try, avoid the ups and downs of life; they are not the result of a fickle fate, but part of the Infinite Plan; it is our reaction to them which matters. "All good things require difficulty" and the struggle can be a struggle to achieve some progressive step for the good of humanity. Elbert Hubbard expressed this essential struggle of life very neatly when he wrote "The only real neutral in this game of life is a dead one". And he went on to illustrate the drastic effect of people suffering from inertia and endeavouring to become neutrals in life's struggle—"If enough employees in a business house are neutrals, the whole concern will eventually come tumbling down about their ears."

If we would achieve anything worth while, we must set a goal and not be distracted from it by any petty or less worthy aims, emotions or thoughts. We must wage relentless war against discouragement; be prepared to face and overcome many of life's adverse circumstances. Whatever goal we may set must be a very clearly defined one. It must also be the predominant desire which overrules every other desire—one intense desire we want above everything else, one single purpose held in the mind with firm resolve. Then a definite plan must be created for carrying out our desire, and we must begin *at once* to put the plan into *action*.

We should not be afraid to tackle new problems or refuse to accept responsibility, for it is responsibility that develops character and helps to bring achievement and success. Many people, even young people to-day, shirk responsibility. They can never get far in any walk of life, nor can they hope to wriggle their way through life in that heedless way. The individual who succeeds is the one who goes ahead and gets things done without being told or being mollycoddled every step of the way.

There is far too much pessimism abroad to-day, too much stress laid on the dangers to which men, women and children are prone. But we need to know only a little of the history of our country and of the human race generally to realise that the risks of to-day are infinitesimal compared to what they used to be. Even one hundred and fifty years ago, the average individual could only hope for a life span of forty years. The dangers from war and disease were far greater that they are to-day, and because life was so insecure people did not probe too far into the future. They lived more in the present—from day to day—about which they were more or less sure and which they held within their grasp. They lived more intensely. They lived and loved and laughed almost with abandon, for they knew not what the morrow might bring.

Perhaps because of this, the people at that time enjoyed life more. Certainly they were more like children living for the day. But now we have taken things to the other extreme. We are so intent looking into the future, preparing for the years that are to come, the positions we are to hold, the retirement we are to enjoy, that we forget to enjoy the simple pleasures which come our way day by day. They pass and we are hardly aware of them, or we miss them altogether. Time gets short and still we try to cross all our bridges before we come to them.

True, to-day we face the threat from nuclear war, but there have always been wars, sudden and violent. The threat from disease is becoming less and less. So why should we, or at least the young men and women, spend so much time and effort trying to make themselves safe?

## The Call of Adventure

Many years ago numerous young men were often forced away from home to earn their livings, owing to work not being available in their own localities. There were others who sought adventure, owing to the drab, poverty-stricken conditions which existed; they fought on land or sea, and although many survived and came back as heroes, life was cruel and hard. Only the rosy side of the story of those early days is told in fable and song. There were no paid holidays, sick pay or pensions in those days.

Then along came the industrial age, when machinery and commercialism ruled people's lives. Adventure, except for the few, became practically non-existent.

To-day, the pendulum has swung to the other extreme. The fear of hardship and poverty, unemployment through ill health or bad times, and the encroaching spectre of old age, bring in their train the cry for security which now seems to be the aim of practically everyone.

Yet, in spite of this almost general search for security, such is human nature, the call to adventure will not be silenced or denied. What opportunities are there for the majority to adventure forth? They are many and varied, but it requires unusual courage and fortitude such as the youth from the Far East possessed when he cycled over two continents in order to reach England and have an English education. Such was the adventurous spirit of this young man with a most worthy aim foremost in his mind.

Some people seek adventure in their leisure hours by sailing, rambling, pot-holing or mountain climbing. The more hazardous adventures, however, are still for the few and are accompanied by all the attendant risks and hardships; some may climb hitherto unscalable mountains or explore the unfathomed and unknown depths of the oceans; some are privileged to sail to Antarctica and winter there. But for the majority of us, we must find adventure in our everyday lives. We can create a spirit of adventure in our jobs or careers provided we do not allow so-called security to be first and foremost in our minds. The jobs that bring worth-while rewards do not come to those whose main concern is pensions and other benefits. The prizes come by sheer hard work, individual effort and by *taking risks*.

British merchants used to be called merchant-adventurers. This explains why they were so successful. They didn't regard commerce and trade as drudgery, they didn't play for safety, but looked upon trading as great daring adventures, and they made Britain the greatest trading nation of the world.

Life may be compared to a game and we must take one side or the other; there are no neutrals, no passive standing on the sideline, wavering and dithering. So many men and women are afraid to adventure, to take risks. "Safety-First" is a good slogan to keep in mind when driving a car or crossing a busy street, but such precaution leads nowhere in life. We've got to get into the full-blooded excitement of the game—take chances—if we would succeed.

Yet life to many people to-day seems to be a vigorous search for security. But security can very often mean boredom. And boredom can lead to neuroses, to vice, to crime. Many are lured along these paths, seeking the excitement and variety which life and living itself should provide.

Many a youth, in considering what his life work is to be, bases his choice of a career upon security and the assurance of a pension.

### Taking Risks

Then there are others who are apathetic and content to remain in easy jobs. They cannot hope to succeed for they have chosen the easy road that leads downhill. It is the road crowded with people who live in unaspiring ruts and die without the realisation of any splendid objective. But it is the hard road, filled with adventures and risks, that leads to the lofty heights of achievement and success. And it is a road that is never crowded.

Surely it is better for young people to cultivate the spirit of adventure and daring than to be satisfied with so-called security. For achievement and success always begin with one word—*dare*!

The majority of men and women seem to be imbued with this false sense of security in one form or another. They think that it is what they want and crave for. They believe it is the panacea for all ills; that if they had it they would be happy and contented.

Yet, by seeking this so-called security, one of the basic laws of life is being defied, because *life is insecurity*. It has always been so, for life is surrounded by risks—those unknown factors. We can never abolish risk for it is the warp and weft of life—the scales of evolution.

The individual who plays too much for safety, who is over-cautious, who tries to remain neutral, belittles himself and all his efforts. He must have faith in himself—believe in himself and use this faith factor by taking advantage of all the opportunities that life offers to him. He cannot remain neutral, he cannot stand still, he must for ever be moving ahead, reaching for newer, greater and better things.

# THE POWER OF ATTRACTION

WHEN we try to understand Life, with all its ramifications, it appears to be so complex and baffling that one's head begins to spin if we try to sort everything out. There are so many things we do not know; so many we fail to understand; so many that seem to be unjust, or the result of mere chance. Yet, although the material affairs of Man can become chaotic, the Universe itself is governed by immutable laws. Everything in Nature obeys these Universal Laws without question—except that human rebel we call Man. The reason for this is that Man has been given reasoning power, and a free will to exercise as he wishes. This is often where the trouble starts.

Man, with his ever-growing knowledge, his remarkable conquests over land, sea and air, his insatiable ambitions, seems to have become too big for his shoes. He has to respect the *physical* laws of the Universe, for they are as plain as the nose on his face, and if he tries to ignore them he knows that he will suffer.

For example, Man knows by experience that he must breathe, drink and eat in order to exist at all. Therefore he obeys these laws of self-preservation. By similar reasoning, no person but a lunatic would step off the roof of a high building expecting to be able to walk on air. He knows enough about the Law of Gravity to realise that it *works*, and that if he attempts such reckless defiance he isn't likely to live very long.

Yet, with all their knowledge, experience and intelligence, the majority of people disregard completely the spiritual, mental and psychological laws of the Universe, and then wonder why their affairs are in a chaotic state. There is no excuse for not knowing about these important laws, for they have been expounded and disseminated by all the greatest thinkers of the world for generations.

The unhappy fact is that most people are grossly materialistic. They want to grab all they can out of life for their own selfish ends. They want money, power, prestige, pleasure—all the wonderful things that the material world has to offer. With all these attractive things within sight and almost within reach, why should they bother their heads about psychology, spiritual progress, mental culture and the rest? Surely only cranks are interested in such high-faluting stuff!

Now the very fact that you are reading this book proves that *you* are not one of those blind, out-and-out materialists referred to above. Nor are you a crank. You are intelligent enough to want to know

13

more about yourself, more about Life, more about the laws that govern it.

We do not profess to know all there is to know about Life. Far from it! We are fully conscious of our own limitations, and we are always learning. But we do know a few important facts about successful living which so many people have overlooked, or deliberately ignored. And we want to share our knowledge with you, which is the living purpose of this book.

## The Human Magnet

Now we shall deal with the Law of Attraction. One seldom hears anything about this Law, yet it is of supreme importance in the life of every one of us.

First we must remember that although there is plenty of trouble and misery in the world, there is also plenty of good. This fact is obvious enough. What many of us do not realise, however, is that Man is a living magnet, and he has the power to attract towards him almost whatever he desires.

Right away, some readers may suspect a serious flaw in this statement. Surely *nobody* desires failure and misery. Everybody in his right mind must desire success, happiness, peace of mind and all the other precious treasures of life. Why, then, do some of us appear to have more than our share of unhappiness, while others sail through life from one triumph to another? There must be something wrong somewhere, these readers may say—and, of course, they are perfectly right.

The Law of Attraction is that "like attracts like". Man, like a human magnet, draws to himself in likeness to his internal mental and emotional impressions, irrespective of whether they be good or evil, constructive or destructive. It is true that we can attract towards us all the good we desire—*when we know how*. It is equally true that we can and do attract towards us much misery and unhappiness that we do *not* desire, because we don't realise that we *are* attracting it! Now we see why it is so important to learn as much as we can about this psychological law.

Just let us think of the things various personalities seem to attract towards them. Knowledge, power, love, money, success, health, friends, for example. Others seem to attract envy, hatred, poverty, sickness, accidents and unhappiness. Some appear to have almost a flair for failure, while others acquire the touch of success. Why is this? It is because of what we might call "the magic of belief"; that if we expect failure we shall fail, and if we expect success we shall succeed. When we whole-heartedly *expect* certain things or conditions, a magnetic force is released from the mind, which, by the Law of Attraction, tends to bring these very expectations into being.

## How the Law of Attraction Works

Let us study a few typical examples which demonstrate how the Law of Attraction works for our benefit—or backfires against us.

Suppose a person is desperately lonely. His heart aches for friendship, yet in spite of his ardent expectations and his strong desire he cannot attract friends towards him. The Law says that he *can* attract what he expects and desires. Therefore there must be something wrong with such a person, or with the methods he adopts.

In order to attract friends the individual must do something about his expectations and desire for friendship. He must deserve and earn it. There is no other way. Well, how does he set about deserving and earning friendship? First he must develop a pleasing personality. If he is lonely and unhappy, this isn't easy. Nevertheless, no matter how sorry he may be for himself, *he must not show it to the world.* Instead, he must put on a brave front, raise a smile, offer some little service to others, especially to those he most desires as friends. Above all, the individual must avoid moaning about the miserable, friendless existence he is trying to endure.

As we know, many lonely, unhappy people use exactly the opposite tactics to those we have mentioned. There they sit, with a long miserable face, and in conversation they pile on the agony. "Nobody bothers about me. I could sit here and die in this chair for all the neighbours care. You'd think at least the vicar would visit me to cheer me up a bit. After all, I am one of his parishioners!"

Of course, the idea of this catalogue of calamity, is to gain sympathy. The long face is intended to illustrate the misery more convincingly. Unfortunately for such a person, it has the reverse effect in most cases. Let's be honest. Suppose we visited an individual like that. Would his or her attitude *attract* us and make us want to visit that person frequently and become a friend? Not likely. Unless we are unusually fortunate, we have quite enough troubles of our own, without being depressed by having to listen to nothing else but a moaning recital of somebody else's troubles. This should be crystal clear to anybody, yet thousands of lonely, friendless people act exactly as described, and wonder why nobody bothers about them. They *desire* friends badly enough, but their attitude repels friendship instead of attracting it. They have not learnt how the Law of Attraction works.

In giving this example of some lonely people, we are not overlooking the many hardships and heartaches with which many of them have to contend. But we do want to emphasise that everything possible should be done to avoid allowing these to control the mind to such an extent that they become the dominating factors in the thought pattern.

Let us look at another example from a different angle this time. Here is an ambitious and conscientious foreman, employed in a factory, anxious to create a good impression upon the boss. In order to run his department efficiently, that foreman desires, above everything, the loyal co-operation of the workers under him. So what does he do? He goes around snapping at people, looking for trouble, "cracking the whip", being as aggressive and offensive as he imagines befits an efficient foreman. Then he wonders why everybody slacks off directly his back is turned, and why they all hate the sight of him.

Any executive worthy of his position doesn't need to bully and chase people around. Instead, he is ready to praise, where praise is due; he offers advice in a friendly manner; he is always tactful in his approach; he invites trust and confidence. Such an executive will get the very best out of those under him. They will work with a good heart because they respect and admire him. In business, as elsewhere, the Law of Attraction pays rich dividends to those *who know how to use it*. Similar examples could easily be given in home life and everywhere else.

### Impressing Others Favourably

It has been said that one should not judge a person by appearances only, and if we do, our judgment may be quite wrong. It is possible that some brute of a man might attack a slim and delicate-looking young woman who turns out to be a judo expert and has him flat on his back in no time. We know of big, muscular men who are surprisingly kind and gentle, and insignificant little men who are vicious hooligans. In spite of this, we *are* judged largely by our appearance, and while human nature acts in this way, we must bear it in mind and make full use of it to our advantage.

If we attend for an interview in the hope of being selected to fill a business vacancy, it would be very foolish to present oneself shabbily dressed or in otherwise unsuitable attire. We may have all the necessary mental ability to handle the job with distinction, but that first impression we create in the mind of our prospective employer will be most unfavourable and damaging. The Law of Attraction demands that we first *appear* to be what we are or wish to become.

This is an extremely important point to remember, for it goes much deeper than the above simple example. People who doubt their own worth create doubt in the minds of others; by placing a mean valuation upon their ability, they find that others accept their estimate. Those who appear to be less than they are, never receive as much as they deserve; they are never given credit for their true ability; they are generally overlooked when the opportunity for promotion arrives, and they are left behind in this highly competitive world.

People who have a naturally modest disposition resent the individual who is always telling everybody how good he is. Admittedly, the inveterate braggart or egotist is not an attractive personality, for he overplays his part and becomes a shocking bore. But many of us would be better off if we cultivated enough self-assurance to impress others favourably. The habit of self-depreciation is a negative one; therefore it interferes seriously with the Law of Attraction. No matter how many excellent qualities we may possess, they will never be acknowledged and rewarded if we hide them from the world beneath a cloak of self-depreciation.

In many respects we must sell ourselves to the world before we can hope to attract success, respect, friendships or even due credit! No good salesman expects to sell his wares if he points out all their faults and disadvantages. How, then, can we expect to attract towards us all the good things our merits deserve, if we do not appreciate our own good qualities? It's no use having any ambitions at all unless we know how to *attract towards us* the things we desire.

So far we have discussed only how other people can be attracted towards us, but the Law of Attraction doesn't confine itself to personal relationships. Its amazing power is extended to every other sphere of life. It can, for instance, attract the things and conditions we require.

What do we want more than anything else in the world? Whatever we want, we may be sure there is plenty of it. The problem is now to attract enough of it towards ourselves.

Suppose we want a lot more money—surely a popular desire, for good or ill. Well, we may believe it or not, there are as many ways of getting money as there are ways of spending it. Unfortunately it is much *easier* to spend money than to obtain it—and there's the rub. Any fool can spend money, but few indeed can attract money towards them, and fewer still can make wise use of it when they have got it.

We can earn money, steal it, win it by chance, or find it—usually in the form of some precious mineral, by prospecting. We recommend the first method as being most reliable and satisfying. We should never expect something for nothing but should be prepared to earn what we want. If we wish to earn money, we can sell our time and skill to an employer, or we can start up in business on our own account. Whichever way we choose we must, above all, give good, reliable *service* if we want to attract money into our pockets.

Nowadays most of us can at least earn enough to live reasonably well by either of the above methods, so long as we continue to offer *good service* and honest value. But suppose we want money *more than anything else* in life? Then we must be prepared to sacrifice everything else to get it. We do not advocate this lust for money to the exclusion of everything else that makes life worth living, for most of life's greatest blessings *cannot be bought* with all the money in the world. However, it is possible to attract more money towards us without sacrificing our finer instincts and the blessings which are worth far more than money. To do so, we must adopt a *positive attitude* towards money.

### The Inner Creative Power

We must first realise that there is within us a tremendous, creative, producing power if we focus the mind upon the object of our desire. Mind is the creator, builder and organiser of all human endeavour. Thought creates. Mind is the builder. Only by a realisation of this mighty mental process can we attract money—or anything else. We must become a conscious, living magnet for money. We must appreciate the value of money and learn how to use it wisely to make more. We must study the methods used and the results obtained by competitors in our particular line of business. We must select the best methods for our own use and improve upon any faulty methods that we discern. We must be confident, positive, inwardly *certain* of success. We must arouse all the powerful vibrations within us and key them to our desires. We must hold the thought of money to such an extent that we can picture it flowing in to us in ever-increasing amounts. We must feel that we are the *centre* towards which all the money we need will flow.

If and when we develop this money-making *habit of thought* we shall discover that *new ideas* about how to earn more money will also flow into our mind, and thus increase our potential money-earning powers. We shall become more persuasive and clever at attracting money from others towards us—always in return for honest service, of course. In the beginning this will be very laborious work, but in time we shall develop a kind of "sixth sense" where money-making is concerned. Our judgment will become more reliable. We shall be able to use the Law of Attraction to our advantage.

Perhaps, however, when we realise all that it entails, we shall decide that although we would like more money, we don't want it that much. Very well, the Law of Attraction can be used for many other things. The principle remains the same.

Many of us do not feel the desire for wealth. We are content to have enough money for our modest needs and a bit extra for little pleasures and luxuries on occasions. But most of us desire *something* important which we lack in our lives. We may not want riches or power. Instead we may desire knowledge, wisdom, virtue, love, social success, self-confidence, or any one of a number of other things. The principles of the Law of Attraction are the same in every case.

### Positive, Optimistic Attitude

It is essential that we adopt a positive optimistic attitude in the first place, to obtain our greatest desires. It is fatal to dwell upon our misfortunes, our disabilities, our disappointments, our ignorance— or whatever else is holding us back from the fulfilment of our ardent desires. We should never succumb to pessimism or self-pity. We should also *refuse to listen* to all the moaners and groaners and "wet blankets" we may meet; refuse to allow their negative influence to swerve us from our fixed purpose or to quench our indomitable determination to reach the goal we have set.

We may not be clever or handsome, or possess any of the qualities we may admire so much in others, but we have some talent, faculty or quality with which we will be able to accomplish a great deal. Instead of being despondent and reacting irrationally and emotionally to our present circumstances we should accept them for the time being, then reason things out rationally and dispassionately. Probably we have greater abilities than we have been able to exercise fully; or we have abilities that even we haven't yet discovered. We should search for them; display them; *know* that they will earn their own rewards—perhaps rich rewards if we use them with an optimistic and positive frame of mind.

We should never allow others to discourage us, but decide on our own purpose and stick to it tenaciously. It doesn't matter what other people think about our ambitions as long as they are wholesome and constructive.

We *are* what we think we are. If we believe ourselves to be only among the mass of mediocre individuals, that's all we are, or are ever likely to be. If we believe we are a reservoir of inner power waiting to demonstrate, and that our fundamental abilities are far greater than anyone else suspects, we must go ahead and prove it. We must believe in ourselves because we cannot expect others to believe in us if we do not believe in ourselves.

We can neither be happy nor successful unless we have a reasonable confidence in our abilities and powers and acquire a positive mental outlook.

By following, conscientiously and persistently, the simple yet scientific principles and techniques we have outlined, we can develop creative faith in ourselves, acquire new powers, more popularity, increased efficiency and greater happiness and success.

# LET'S VANQUISH DISCOURAGEMENT

EVERY life should have a definite aim. Yet there are countless drifters in the world—men and women whose lives seem to lack meaning and purpose. They follow the line of least resistance and drift through life on a plane of dull, drab mediocrity. They have no challenging objective, no splendid ambition, no definite goal in view—they are like ships without rudders, floundering along through life's sea.

If we are to live successfully we should decide what we wish to do with our lives, what our aims are and how we intend to reach our goal. Then we should map out a campaign and bend every effort and all our energies towards the determined realisation of our aspiring hopes and ambitions. As we journey along through life, pressing forward towards a fulfilment of our aims, we shall, of course, need many assets to help us on our way.

The most valuable assets are those we build and accumulate within our own characters. These virtues need not be listed here in their entirety, but they include faith and courage, self-confidence and persistence. We shall, of course, meet with many bitter experiences and disappointments along life's road and there will be many occasions when we shall feel despondent and discouraged.

This feeling of discouragement when things go wrong is nothing to be unduly concerned about, for it is the common lot of men and women everywhere. *No one has ever achieved anything worth while without frequently being greatly discouraged while travelling along the road to achievement and success.* The annals of history are crowded with individuals who overcame every discouragement and climbed from obscurity to greatness.

Arkwright was scorned and discouraged at every turn. His wife smashed his first model of the spinning machine and later burned other models—the products of many years of unremitting toil. His fellow-townsmen banished him from their city. Not a voice was raised on his behalf. Yet Arkwright refused to be discouraged and carried on, and his inventions were the beginning of all modern machinery and brought about the industrial revolution.

Charles Goodyear faced every conceivable discouragement and opposition as he struggled to perfect his invention for the use of rubber. People called him crazy but he persevered and made the world his debtor.

Columbus, meeting discouragement from every source, steadfastly pursued his campaign of exploration and through his discovery altered the subsequent history of the world.

20

And so it is of nearly every great benefactor. In spite of every possible discouragement and hardship they fought their solitary way and eventually emerged triumphant.

Without detracting any credit from these famous personalities, we *expect* such a display of courage and tenacity from men and women who have already proved their fine calibre. They are already great, each in his or her own sphere, and we cannot imagine *them* giving in to discouragement. But what about all the rest of us who are *not* famous? How do we react to discouragement?

### Refused to be Discouraged

Here is the true story, in brief outline, of a man who is not famous or even well known. In fact, he was only a branch manager in the shoe trade. He now has his own prosperous little business; but he achieved this only after a long and difficult fight.

This man left school during a period of economic depression when jobs were not easy to find. He had received a reasonably good education, but he was not at that time sure what he wanted to become in life. Moreover, he had to take almost any work that was offered to him. After many unsuccessful applications to various firms he obtained work in a small engineering factory. The wages were ridiculously low, and the general working conditions and environment were most distasteful—especially to this boy, who was refined and sensitive. However, he worked hard and conscientiously for three months, and then—the firm got into financial difficulties and closed down.

After this first discouraging experience he eventually found similar employment in another local factory. Once again he put his best into his work and was soon training a girl to run his machine. When he told his parents how well he was progressing, they shared his satisfaction and encouraged him to carry on earning promotion. It wasn't long before the girl he was training could run the machine efficiently, and with understandable pride he reported this fact to his employer. What happened then? The management gave the girl *his job*—at a lower rate of pay—and "regretfully" gave him notice to quit as "redundant".

Again this unfortunate lad searched for work, but all he could find was a job as shop-boy in a shoe shop. As he scrubbed the steps, washed the windows and cleaned the brass name-plate, he felt deeply ashamed of his menial tasks. He dreaded the possibility that one of his former grammar school masters might walk past and see him doing *this* after all their efforts to educate him.

As you can guess, this boy had no intention of remaining a shop-boy for any longer than he could help. He had visions of becoming a salesman, then a window-dresser, then a manager—and eventually of having a shop of his own. While working in the shop and delivering shoes to customers, he learned all he could about the trade. He also listened to the sales-talk of the shop assistants and he watched the window-dresser most carefully.

Unfortunately—for him—he was such a good shop-boy that the manager would not entertain the idea of allowing him to try his hand as a salesman. After all, where would the firm get another shop-boy as smart and conscientious as *he* was? The manager advanced all kinds of excuses to prevent him from becoming a salesman—including the appearance of his clothes. So the boy saved up and bought a new suit, but he was still refused the chance he so badly wanted.

### Became Keenly Interested

Then, one day, a traveller called at the shop to introduce a line of famous arch-supports. They needed to be expertly fitted, and the manager was offered the necessary training as a "Pediopath" (fitter of foot appliances) plus a certificate if and when he qualified. The manager wasn't interested—but the shop-boy, who had overheard the conversation, was so *interested* he could scarcely control his excitement! When the traveller left the shop, the boy ran after him and enquired if *he* could be trained to fit and sell these foot appliances.

The traveller after some hesitation eventually agreed, but informed the boy that the training would cost five guineas, and that an examination would have to be passed to earn the certificate. Only qualified fitters were allowed to sell these appliances, or more foot troubles would be created than remedied!

The shop-boy managed to scrape together five guineas from his slender savings, studied the Course and was awarded the precious certificate.

The shop manager had no idea what was going on until the traveller called again and told him that as his shop-boy was now a qualified "Pediopath" there was no reason why he should not buy a stock of foot appliances and so give a boost to the business. The manager was *furious*. He refused to stock the appliances, so the shop-boy approached the owner of the shop direct, and told him the whole story. The owner bought £100 worth of foot appliances, and gave instructions for a special window display. Whenever a customer wanted expert advice on any foot trouble, the manager had to call the shop-boy "Pediopath", who fitted the necessary appliance and drew the commission—much to the manager's annoyance.

Even then this spiteful manager would not allow the young man to sell shoes, nor would he allow him to help the window-dresser. The youth's further ambitions were discouraged by every possible means, but his determination remained unshaken.

Within a few months, while still in his late 'teens, that boy went straight to a high-class shoe shop in the West End of London as a salesman and window-dresser. Before he left his previous employment the manager taunted and ridiculed him for even aspiring to such an ambition and told him that he wouldn't last more than a few weeks in his new post.

But not only did this ambitious youth prove highly satisfactory in his new job, but he eventually became a branch manager. The next time he met his former manager, who had done *everything possible* to discourage him, he was at the Shoe and Leather Fair, buying footwear for his own shop!

This may not be a spectacular success story, in one sense, but it is a convincing example of the way to overcome discouragement— by determination, self-confidence, initiative and courage. Fortunately, this boy always received encouragement and good advice from his parents. Their faith in him supported his faith in himself.

In order to overcome disappointment and the possible aftermath of discouragement, we must have faith in ourselves. That is the first and most important requisite. We cannot expect others to believe in us if we do not believe in ourselves. In life's struggle countless men and women are defeated by themselves. Doubting their own worth, they create doubt in the minds of other people. They place a small or mean valuation upon their own ability, and others accept their estimate. A feeling of inadequacy and a sense of inferiority are the great barriers to self-realisation and achievement, but the spirit of self-confidence points the way to successful living. Having faith in ourselves, however, does not mean egotism or being blind to our own faults, but a calm, dispassionate conviction in our own possibilities and in the performance of our tasks.

### Encouragement and Appreciation

If we receive encouragement from others, including encouragement from our own family, we are extremely fortunate. Even the best of parents often find difficulty in feeling much enthusiasm for the particular ambitions of their children. Parents have probably outgrown the enthusiasm of youth. Often they are not even interested in the same subjects that appeal to the younger folk. Parents, in the light of their wider experience, also see the snags and dangers of certain ambitions of youth. Therefore they may be inclined to be sceptical, to voice criticism or to remain depressingly apathetic to the ambitions of a son or daughter. Naturally this parental gloom is very disappointing to young people, and unless they are very careful, the rot of discouragement sets in.

Young people should always be *encouraged* to go ahead with their dreams, desires and efforts towards their *chosen* careers—not discouraged or sidetracked into channels preferred by their parents and

L.C.—3

elders. Young people are entitled to build their own lives in any legitimate direction *they* wish. Too much "cold water" is poured over the ambitions of youth. They should be offered kindly advice and guidance by all means, but not deliberately discouraged from following the careers they desire.

Lack of appreciation can also bring about discouragement. It can cause people to wilt—wilt actually in ability and in spirit. The majority of men and women thrive on appreciation, become better personalities and can rise to great heights if their efforts meet with genuine appreciation.

## A Good Philosophy

Sometimes the discouragements we encounter eventually turn out to be the stepping-stones to our subsequent achievements. So we should not bewail the discouragements that assail us for they can be the promise and pledge of ultimate triumph. Nobody, since the world began, ever succeeded without opposition. Discouragement lurks everywhere, and the higher we aim the more disappointments we are likely to suffer on our way to the top.

Yes, discouragements haunt us from childhood to old age. As children we are frequently discouraged by parents, teachers and others. Although there is not very much we can do at the time of these child-hood discouragements, we can learn lessons from them which can stand us in good stead later on in life. As young men or women we are often discouraged in love and later in marriage and parenthood. It's no use trying to escape from these discouragements. *The only way to deal with them is to stand and face them, then put forth our best efforts to try and put things right.*

In old age we may be discouraged by our failing physical powers. The physical machine may slow down but the mind and spirit can go on from strength to strength. When time marks our faces with deep lines of care, and our temples glisten with the frosts of life's autumn, we can still refuse to grow old in spirit. We shall, of course, have to relinquish some physical activities but there will be others ready to replace them. We should modify our goals in accordance with what we can reasonably expect to accomplish. And we may find the new goals finer and better than those of previous years—goals that can bring us greater happiness, satisfaction and contentment.

# THE IMPORTANCE OF PERSPECTIVE

DURING the last fifty years, life for most of us has been transformed almost beyond recognition. In this comparatively short period more drastic changes have been introduced than in the preceding century.

Poets have often reminded us of the ever-changing pattern of life. "Naught may endure but mutability," wrote Shelley. Longfellow expressed a similar observation in these words:

> *"All things must change*
> *To something new, to something strange."*

Of course, in this world nothing remains static. Life itself is energy, movement, rhythm, growth, transmutation. The world itself is turning upon its axis and circling in its own orbit, and everything in the world is always changing, including Man himself. Nothing remains constant. The seasons change through spring, summer, autumn, winter and back to spring to complete the cycle. The face of Nature continues to change according to each season. Plant life grows, blooms, withers, dies, and is reborn from the seeds which have been shed or planted in fertile soil. There are extremes of heat and cold. Light follows darkness in endless succession. Movement and change all the time.

And so it is with Man. He is born to breathe, think, move, create and progress. If he neglects to perform his allotted task, he perishes quickly enough and before his natural time. If an individual should strap a limb in one position for a long enough period, the limb will atrophy, wither and become useless. Muscles must change their position frequently: they need exercise. Tools that are allowed to stand idle, soon grow rusty. The best way to keep a spade bright is to dig with it. If we leave a spade idle, exposed to the elements, what will happen to it? We may say it will "rust away". Certainly it will no longer be recognisable as a spade, but, as a heap of rust and rotten wood, it will ultimately become absorbed into the earth itself. Actually, all that has happened to the spade is that it has *changed* from one form to another.

## Changes Bring Problems

These simple and homely illustrations remind us that although change is essential, for it is according to natural law, all kinds of change are not necessarily for the benefit of mankind. The spade that rots away may play its humble part in fertilising the soil, but it will be of no further use *as a spade*.

This brings us to a very important point. The course of Nature is set by the Creator. It moves in rhythmic cycles. It is orderly and efficient. There are a Divine Wisdom and Purpose in every natural change as it takes place, and the result is always good.

Man has the urge and the power to make changes in his environment, his circumstances and in *himself*. Unfortunately he is not at all as *wise* as his Creator, nor are his *motives* always impeccable. Consequently, although Man's way of life must change, one way or another, the changes Man himself makes are often bad instead of good. Within certain limits Man is his own creator. He alone is responsible for many of the changes he makes. He will earn the rewards for the wise changes he introduces, but he must also pay the price for his mistakes. Man can and does create harmony or chaos, joy or sorrow, good fortune or disaster. It is Man's heavy responsibility to decide *what kind* of changes he will make, and whether they promise to be beneficial for the human family. His whole future depends upon the wisdom of his choice.

We have mentioned previously the dramatic and astonishing changes which have taken place during the last fifty years. And with these changes have come the inevitable problems. Life in the modern world presents numerous perplexities.

To what extent have these man-made changes benefited mankind and the world in general? Is Man any happier? Is he any more secure? Is he healthier in mind and body? Is he living a fuller, richer life in the true sense of those words? Is he any nearer to Perfection—which many of us believe is his ultimate destiny?

Within the confined limits of the space available, let us examine these questions and discuss them.

Perhaps the most dramatic change during the last fifty years is the vastly increased tempo of life. As a boy, I remember spending some of my school holidays on a farm. Everything was so peaceful and leisurely. The farmer, in his stout hob-nailed boots, strolled across the farmyard to the barn, and the roaming chickens hardly bothered to move out of his way.

The farmer's boy, having fed the pigs, leaned over the sty wall and patted a fat sow on the rump as she ate. In the meadow the cattle grazed contentedly, wandering at will. In the orchard one could hear, occasionally, a ripe apple fall with a gentle plop on the soft grass.

At the end of the week, as a special treat, the farmer used to drive me into the nearest market town in his pony-drawn trap. The leisurely clip-clop of the pony's hoofs and the rhythmic motion of the vehicle are as fresh as ever in my memory. How pleasant life seemed to be in that peaceful world of yesterday.

## Modern Craze for Speed

The scene to-day is quite different. Fast cars roar along still-narrow, twisting country roads. In dry weather the once-fresh hedgerows are covered with dust thrown up by motor vehicles. In wet weather unlucky pedestrians are sprayed with mud from spinning car wheels. Drivers and passengers in fast cars miss all the intimate pleasures and wonders of the beautiful countryside. In fact, they have even been known to pass through a village without recognising it!

Quite apart from this aspect of speed plus the din created by many motor-cycles, there is the appalling toll of road deaths and injuries.

Our travelling habits have changed from a leisurely jog-trot to almost a mania for top-gear speed. Speed saves time, and time means money—so far as trade and industry are concerned. We travel from one point to another in less time. But are the advantages of faster travel worth anything like the shocking price we pay, as a nation, in loss of life, personal injuries, material damage, nerve strain, taxation, respiratory diseases (aggravated by petrol and diesel fumes), and working hours lost by victims of road accidents? And so far as speed for pleasure is concerned, who derives more, the driver of a fast car or the humble hiker tramping over moors and the wild countryside?

These are the questions we should consider before we decide whether this *change*—this modern craze for speed is a *wise* change in our way of life.

What else has changed a lot in the last fifty years? Working conditions and methods of production. A revolution has taken place in this sphere, and we must admit that in many respects this change is for the better. The days of sweated labour are over in this country. Machines maintain production, while workers enjoy far more leisure and a much higher standard of living than ever before.

Any elderly or even middle-aged man will tell you what *his* working conditions were like, only thirty-odd years ago. Old people can tell an even more depressing tale. For example, an old lady being interviewed on the radio recently, explained that she couldn't read, because she never went to school. Why? Because as a very young girl she had to work in the fields, picking up potatoes. Well, we don't want those days ever again.

There are, however, one or two other points to consider before we declare the modern industrial methods to be an altogether good change.

## Impersonal Relationships

Modern methods of manufacture, amalgamation of larger businesses and the almost total absorption of small business units have had a few unfortunate effects.

First, the intimate, individual personal interest of too many workers has been curtailed or has disappeared altogether. In the old days of small industrial units, the handful of workers in each little family business had a more *personal* interest in the job. They were in close contact with the boss. They knew his history, his character, his family, his problems, his ambitions. They also knew his local competitors and the kind of work they turned out. Consequently, most workers had a strong sense of loyalty to a good boss. They were keen to help him to beat his rivals. These workers, in the old days, took real pride in their work, and healthy competition was the breath of life to them. Moreover, the methods of business and manufacture in those days were such that each craftsman enjoyed the satisfying thrill of *creating* something. He could point to a magnificent piece of work and claim, with justifiable pride, "I made that, from start to finish."

How different things are to-day. The machine has gained ascendancy over individual craftsmanship. The satisfaction and personal pride in doing a complete job have entirely gone under to-day's new production methods. The individual now is only one of thousands working in factories almost as big as towns. Day after day all that one factory-worker does, to quote one example, is to dab white spots on toy rocking horses; his every moment is time-checked, and he seldom, if ever, sees the boss.

Recently I heard a man say he was a "chocolate marker". All he did all day was to put that little "squiggle" on the tops of chocolates to indicate their flavour. He couldn't even do a *different* squiggle for a change, for he marked only the coffee creams!

Other factors relevant to modern working conditions include the amount of money being earned by some youths, and the amount of leisure they have in which to spend it. Authorities and the general public are puzzled by the increase in crimes and misdemeanours committed by teenagers. The chief reason might be explained in two words: sheer boredom.

Many of these young people earn high wages for monotonous work. During their ample leisure hours they just "let off steam" and make themselves a nuisance for a bit of excitement. The trouble with these young people is that they have not adjusted themselves to a wise pattern of living in this modern world. If only these teenagers would spend some of their leisure and money in *creative hobbies* there would be less chance of their getting into mischief.

So much for modern working conditions. In the old days most young people were too weary at the end of each long day even to enjoy a meal—much less to roam the streets looking for trouble. Furthermore, there was very strict parental and police discipline to curb the unruly ones, before they got out of hand altogether.

Whoever dares to criticise modern methods, beliefs, styles, art, morals, music, ways of life, is to-day promptly labelled "a Square" and treated with contempt. The "Squares" are the so-called "old-fashioned" fogies of this modern world. Their experience of life counts for nothing among the younger set—and anybody who criticises *them* must have one foot in the grave, or, at least, in modern idiom, must be a "nut case". Of course, every new generation criticises the older generation, it always has been and always will be so, but to-day it seems to have been taken to extremes.

There is little point in condemning youth or even advising them unless they are ready to listen and consider the voice of experience. It would be foolish and unfair also to condemn any odd behaviour or style just because it is modern. Time marches on, and nobody can stop drastic changes from taking place, even if he would. So perhaps we should not take too seriously the behaviour of modern youth.

## A Sense of True Perspective

Some of to-day's drastic changes could almost be called upheavals. Coal is being pushed out by oil; cotton is being threatened by tough synthetic fabrics; metal is being largely replaced by plastic. Nobody wants to hinder progress—but we should be sure we are moving *in the right direction*. That is the crucial point.

In the entertainment world, there are some changes taking place which are endangering our sense of true perspective. A lad with a guitar, the idol of an hysterical teen-age "following", can earn more than the Prime Minister.

Amid the swirl of life's many and varied changes, we are apt to be influenced by false estimates—to lose our sense of true values. The importance of "perspective" in measuring the frequent changes and factors in life cannot be over-emphasised. We should not be duped into accepting every modern change without question, even if it may be considered "old fashioned". We should guard against false influences and blind prejudice. We should keep our balance, think constructively and logically, be discriminating, cautious, adapting ourselves to the best of the new, while clinging to ideals which have stood the test of time.

# CHANGE THE PICTURE

*We need not be fettered by circumstances or environment. We can break through our prison-house by the force and creative genius of Mind. We need not walk the dark and dreary lane of humdrum living, for the awakened Mind can set us on the highway to the richer life.*

\* \* \*

SUPPOSE a well-known reputable firm were to claim to have discovered a new drug, something that would expand and heighten ordinary experience, something that would make life more vivid, more vigorous, more zestful; something that would end the petty pin-pricks of ordinary living and give men and women a new grasp of a new and thrilling life.

Then suppose that this new wonder drug were advertised in to-morrow's papers, don't you agree that millions, all the world over, would flood the manufacturers' offices with requests for samples? Humanity would hail the dawn of a new era in human life; mankind would rejoice in this, the greatest discovery in all the history of Man, and human life would be transmuted from the drab and mediocre to the sublime and satisfying.

But, of course, no such drug exists!

Yet there is something that can produce almost similar effects to this mythical drug. It has been used, to some extent, at least, by all the men and women who have made their mark in the world—whether in business, in science or in the arts. All the choice and master spirits of the ages, from Shakespeare to Dickens, from Faraday to Marconi, have invigorated their lives by an injection of this incredible "something".

But perhaps some people may think it is unfair to consider the exceptional men and women in history. It would be more to the point to consider what effect this unique "something" would have on the lives of ordinary men and women.

Well, let us then ask what would the average man or woman expect from this remarkable "something"? What would they want it to do? Here are some of the things that perhaps the majority of people would ask from this miraculous "something".

### Lifting Life's Burdens

They would want to feel better, in health and in spirit, to feel on top of the world, to feel each new day to be a golden opportunity and not the burdensome, drab, sordid thing it so often is. They would require this "something" to give them an inner radiance that would transform the workaday world into a brighter, happier place; to make life's perplexities seem easier and life's major problems not so difficult to overcome. They would wish that this "something" would rid them of the complexes and inferiority feelings that drag them down to mediocrity; that it would untangle the emotional disturbances that shadow their lives. They would want it to help them to savour life more fully, to live more richly and more successfully.

Success, health, happiness and achievement would be the keystones of their hopes and desires. They would crave for a richer, nobler, happier, more satisfying way of life.

It's a lot to ask for, isn't it? Certainly, it is more than can be expected from any chemical invention. For we must admit that what is asked for is, basically, some *creative* process within the personalities of men and women.

Although this magical "something" may appear to be an unrealisable dream, nevertheless, science confirms that it actually does exist.

It is not sold in bottles. It is not swallowed in tablet form three times a day. Then what is this wonder-working "something"? Practical psychology provides the answer. It reveals that this great "something" is—*MIND*.

Mind is the vital factor in life. It is the creator, builder, organiser and perfecter of human destiny. Without the directive energy of mind, the will is impotent, the imagination loses itself in the labyrinth of fantastic reverie, the emotions turn to anarchy, and life becomes meaningless.

### A Typical Example

Let us look a little closer at this magic that is mind. It can be illustrated very well by the following story:

John was an executive with a very large firm of exporters. He got up one morning feeling that he had the whole weight of the world on his shoulders. His wife was short-tempered, the children difficult, and his morning mail consisted entirely of a number of substantial bills.

He glanced at the newspaper. International crisis was headlined right across the front page! Lower down on the same page was an announcement about petrol rationing. Turning over the page he read about a threatened strike at a factory which concerned him closely. His work made him familiar with the damage caused by such strikes, delays in fulfilling overseas orders, orders cancelled, all making it more and more difficult to secure the level of exports upon which our very existence depends.

The newspaper also gave prominence to the general unrest in the social atmosphere, riots by empty-headed youths, more crimes of violence, all adding up to a very miserable state of affairs.

"What a rotten world!" was John's silent comment.

On the way to work he saw further evidence of a world out of joint to add to his gloom, and the day's news deepened his depression even more. He spent the midday break strolling in the city park, meditating on the condition of the world in general.

His own life left a good deal to be desired. He was hard pressed financially, and being past the first flush of youth, he was not as fit as he could wish to be to cope with the problems that beset him. The outside world seemed, to him, to have gone mad. In the workaday world there was nothing but rising costs, unrest and threatened strikes. In international affairs, nothing but trouble and more trouble, with Great Britain reviled, hated and despised where previously her prestige stood high—not a happy augury for future peace.

The more he thought about things, the blacker the outlook seemed. He could see little hope of bettering his personal affairs; he saw small grounds for believing that the country's economic position would improve, or that international upheavals would settle themselves in his lifetime. He cast nostalgic glances at the happier and more stable pre-war years and seriously wondered whether it was worth carrying on.

It was in this frame of mind that John returned to work and tackled his routine in a desultory fashion. After an hour or so, he received a message that the Managing Director wished to see him.

It was rather an unusual occurrence for him to visit the Chief, and he wondered what it could be all about.

The Managing Director soon informed him.

"Mr. ——," he said, "I've been watching your progress for some time, and you have proved yourself able, conscientious and loyal. I am offering you the appointment as manager of our Midlands office."

John stammered his appreciation and thanks, and discussed in some detail his proposed move.

He returned home jubilant.

Few of his worries had actually been removed. The world was still in a mess. But now he felt that his domestic happiness was probably higher than average. The pressing bills would be met somehow. The threatened strike, the social unrest, the country's adverse economic condition—well—there were answers to all these if they were tackled in the right spirit and with a will. And the problem of international upheaval, he felt, could also be sorted out by the use of a bit of common sense.

### A Change in Mental Outlook

This story has been told at some length in order to emphasise that the John who came home that night was, in every way, a different John to the one who set out that very morning. And it was all due to a change in focus of his mental outlook.  For, except for the stimulus of promotion, his affairs were in no way altered.  But the jolt that had re-focussed his mental outlook gave him a far rosier, optimistic picture of the world.

A case of self-deception, the cynics may say!  But is it?

If the mind is given a chance to focus in its true perspective it will see opportunities where pessimism sees only adversity; it will see hope where dejection can know only despair.

Although it was an item of good news that jerked John's outlook into focus, what I want to emphasise is that we can, all of us, give ourselves that mental jerk that will make us more optimistic, hopeful, courageous, fortify our faith, renew our strength and enhance our wisdom.

Admittedly, it is not always easy to look on the bright side.  Our spirits may be dampened each day by contact with some set-back or other.  But we can still *select* the thoughts we entertain.

Of course, depressing thoughts will come unbidden to the mind. We may, for instance, think of all the things we need and how far we are from getting them.  The train of thought leads us on to the question of our financial position in general.  We think further—perhaps about how hard we have struggled to attain our present position and salary; of all the sacrifices we have made—and yet we see others who, without a tithe of the effort or sacrifice we have made, are in better positions and earning more.  And we begin to wonder is all the struggle and sacrifice worth it?

We cannot help, occasionally, having these thoughts flash on the screen of consciousness, and it is not easy to turn them off.  *But we can change the picture!*

We can change our thoughts from negative to positive.

We ourselves determine whether our thoughts shall be good or bad, constructive or destructive.  And the results will correspond in the long run to the kind of thoughts we entertain.  Our thoughts can lead us to the summit or to the abyss, to happiness or despair.

We should, therefore, guard the character of our thoughts; cultivate the building up in our mind of thoughts that are wholesome, positive and constructive.  And if we make these thoughts more and more our daily habit of mind, we shall find that our thinking can be the rudder which can guide the barque of our lives over life's tempestuous sea, past all dangers, shoals and jutting rocks into the harbour of tranquillity and calm, into the port where the larger, richer, fuller life can reign supreme.

# SPRING-CLEAN THE MIND

*"The eyes of the mind are as
important as the eyes of the body."*

\* \* \*

AS I write we are at the beginning of March; from my window I
see a brilliant blue sky, contrasting sharply in the frosty air with
the mountains of white clouds, piled like fairy castles over the distant
sunlit hills. The keen air sharpens their outlines; the birds sing and,
but for the delicate black tracery of the bare branches of the trees,
standing out so sharply against the still, blue sky, I might almost be
persuaded that spring was here. It is a promise of things to come if
we will but have faith and patience to wait.

### Windows of the Mind

Life is like that. We all have our troubles and our worries as a
part of life. But there is another part—there are joys and pleasures,
food to eat, sleep to enjoy, friendship and conversation and the beauty
of the earth around us. That is the kind of life upon which the eyes
of our minds often gaze.

In general, we are not much different from the "other chap".
We may look at him and think he has no worries or very few. He
laughs or jokes and passes by on his way through life, and we watch
and may envy him his happiness, his job, his money, house, position,
in fact everything he has and which we think we have not.

The majority of us have the gift of sight. Through these physical
eyes, a hundred people may look out on the same streets or fields,
the same crowd in the morning rushing to work, the same sky. But
hardly two people will see the same scene with the mind's eye. Physical
conditions make some more aware of the effects of light and shade,
of contrasts and the various hues of colouring. Others, by training,
have developed the powers of observation, so that they perceive the
little things, the detail which is always there, the often absorbing
charm and interest of human behaviour and of Nature.

Many people, unfortunately through inability to observe, through
lack of training, guidance or of knowledge, fail to see what goes on
around them. How many walk along with downcast eyes, rarely
looking up at the bright skies, or notice the few species of birds which
are to be seen even in towns and cities?

Have you ever watched the flight of birds over the countryside

34

and noted with what precision they fly in perfect order across the sky? For example, have you ever noticed geese as they go like this, seven in number, flying in slanting line, following the leader, all equidistant the one from the other; or in perfect Air Force V-formation, the leader at the head, three on either wing? The many wonders of Nature are portrayed all around us everywhere, yet we often fail to see them.

Then again, many of us pass through life with the "windows" of the mind grubby and grimy. Of course we could clean them, but the pathetic part is—all too often we don't even realise that our mental windows are blotchy and blurred. Consequently we go through life partially blind to its mystery, wonders and beauty. Yet the remedy lies in our own hands.

Fear seems to be the main reason for the "windows" of the mind becoming smudged and smeared, thereby giving a distorted vision of life. This fear appears to be a fear of life generally. There are many people who have little or no faith in life; they constantly doubt and worry and fret. They set their goal in life and work towards it; they are usually hard-working, conscientious men and women. But here is where they so often go wrong—they get the wrong perspective on life through thinking only of work and their goal. They miss the fun and adventure of things, the richness of leisure and companionship; their standard of values goes hay-wire. They take themselves too seriously and from the fire of their burning anxiety to succeed comes the smoke to smudge the "windows" of their minds, so that their outlook becomes clouded over, their judgment unbalanced, and they are in danger of missing the joy of living long before they reach their goal.

From then onwards, the course such people follow is steadily downwards; they fear people; are afraid of poverty and dread old age. Even autumn to them is a season of decay, denoting coming death rather than a period for rejoicing at the fruitfulness of Nature, the final crowning and reward of the work of spring and summer, for autumn means "to increase"; it is the herald of a well-earned rest preparatory to renewed life in the following spring.

So as their mind becomes overburdened with fear, doubt and depression, it gradually ceases to think straight; its perspective becomes distorted as it peers at life through its grimy windows.

### One Step at a Time

We would do well to wash the "windows" of our minds now— to-day, then peer through these mental windows not at the whole of life which lies before us but at one day at a time. Life is big—life is vast. But we can cultivate a faith in life and make our plans accordingly, taking one step at a time, living from day to day. Each day well lived, with good work done, will prepare us for the next day, and the direction in which we should take each step will become clearer and clearer to us as we journey along through life. Perhaps part of that grand, old hymn will help us to remember this:

> ". . . *I do not ask to see*
> *The distant scene,*
> *One step enough for me.*"

## Be Positive!

We can be pessimistic or optimistic. It comes more naturally to some people than others to be bright, cheerful, confident and hopeful, but much of this attitude is the result of example, circumstances and outlook in childhood. To be too optimistic can, of course, be a danger, but, on the whole, optimism is a constructive attitude of mind. Some men and women almost enjoy their pessimistic view of life, but it is destructive, both to themselves and to those with whom they come in contact.

A great deal of this pessimism is due to a habit of negative thinking, which can be altered by mind training and self-discipline. The more positive attitude of life helps in the climb to success and happiness. The use of will-power alone, however, is not sufficient if we would live more successfully. Imagination plays a dominant part. These two great powers—will and imagination—must become close co-workers in the building of the successful life.

Will and imagination are not only the masters of all our thoughts and acts, but they rule our moods as well. And our outlook on life and our attitude towards it not only influence our own lives, but the lives of those we contact, as is so simply shown in the following lines:

> "*I met a man. He said to me,*
> '*The news is very bad, I fear.*
> *We're heading for destruction, and*
> *The outlook's very dark and drear*'.
> *At once the morning seemed to be*
> *Less fair because he'd talked to me.*
> "*I met a man. Said he to me,*
> '*Well, Francis, things are bad, but still,*
> *We'll win through somehow, never fear—*
> *I'll bet my boots we can and will!*'
> *At once the morning seemed to be*
> *More fair because he'd talked to me.*"

## Inner Tranquillity

Life for most of us is a very mixed experience—full of contrasts. Life is neither all beautiful nor all ugly, all good nor all bad, all kind nor all hateful, all sweet nor all bitter.

Of course, there are trials and troubles, difficult conditions and adverse circumstances, which we have all got to face at times. But does worrying about them do any good? Are any of these problems better solved by tensed nerves, bottled-up emotions, by loss of sleep, by the aches and pains that are the companions of worry? Surely worry only makes all problems tougher and harder to solve? Worry makes clear thinking virtually impossible; the mind is apt to become clouded; there is the tendency to think in circles and the mind often jumps to irrational conclusions.

Fear and worry are indeed the twin parasites that prey upon people everywhere. These remorseless enemies of the human race can blight happiness, break up homes and marriages, smash careers, and cause needless physical and mental illnesses.

The number of men and women who live under the grim shadow of apprehensions is countless. There are, for example, those who fear and worry about old age. Some worry that age may bring poverty and want; others are afraid of being unwanted and fear loneliness as old friends and dear ones fall away or pass on before them. Many, especially those who have led active lives and been full of vitality and held positions of usefulness, leadership or authority, worry and fret as their stamina and physical powers begin to wane and their places in the world become of less importance, as younger men gradually take over the reins. But worrying and fretting over such things are useless and lead nowhere; they certainly won't prevent the encroaching of old age. Surely the common-sense acceptance of the inevitable time-table of life is the first step towards inner tranquillity and peace?

The possibility of loneliness in old age can be largely overcome if the shadows of self-pity are replaced by the bright light of adventure in meeting new people and making new friends.

The modern world may shrug its shoulders at those in the late fifties and call for people who are younger. But even if there may be tasks that are too much for people who are near or past the sixty mark, there are other tasks that are too much for those who are *under* that age. Some of the greatest contributions in the lives of men and women have been made in these later years, for they have acquired many valuable assets, maturity, experience, more understanding, patience and knowledge.

So if old age is accepted as a process of maturely "growing up", the promise of later years may be truly realised, just as Robert Browning expressed it in the poem: ". . . the last of life, for which the first was made".

## Mutual Understanding and Tolerance

We all look out on the same world—yet to each individual it is a different world. How surprised we should be if, even for a few moments, we could see the world through the eyes of another person.

This is one of the secrets of mutual understanding and goodwill between individuals. Only when we have understanding can we have sympathy; and we can understand only when we can look at life with a perspective similar to the other person's.

It is extremely difficult, however, for us to see the other person's point of view, because our outlook on life is so different one from another. But much can be achieved in the way of understanding by pausing awhile during the rush and bustle of life and turning our mental or spiritual eyes in a different direction. It will help us to understand better why an individual thinks differently from us; why there is such a wide variance of viewpoints. By exercising a little patience, a little restraint, by looking closer at the other person and trying to put ourselves in his place, we may come to appreciate why he thinks as he does; why he holds certain opinions that are different from ours. And whilst we may not agree with his thoughts and opinions, our demeanour will lead us to a better understanding of human nature.

This tolerant attitude and respect for other people's opinions, and their right to express them, can not only bring about understanding and co-operation between individuals, but can also bring harmony, peace and goodwill throughout the nations of the world.

# THAT "SAFETY-FIRST" COMPLEX

HAVE you ever wished to be a king? No, perhaps not since you reached an age of discretion and cast off childish things.

A child's life is made up of wishing. What it cannot achieve or obtain in actuality, most satisfactory to itself, it acquires by wishing and pretending. Nothing in a child's dream world is impossible.

If you have come closely in contact with children, you may, on occasions, have been amazed at their imaginative power. They will describe people, animals, conditions and events in such detail and with such assurance, that you hesitate for a few moments, being almost convinced that their descriptions are true. It is a wonderful gift, though one which requires to be wisely directed, if the child is to learn to differentiate between fact and "let's pretend".

Then there is this habit of wishing—wishing for the things and conditions which don't exist or are out of reach; then the child's imagination is used to realise in a "make-believe" world those things which are unattainable. Poets have been quick to pick on this trend in childhood, and many delightful poems for children have been written as a result, one of the best known being R. L. Stevenson's:

> "I wish I lived in a caravan
> With a horse to ride,
> Like the pedlar man."

In ancient days many people were fatalists. Some are to-day. They believed that the individual's whole future was fore-ordained, predestined. What was the good of *doing* anything about one's life, since it was already written in the stars what the future held? Others believed that they were at the mercy of the gods. As long as they could cultivate the goodwill or favouritism of the gods, so long would their wishes—or prayers—be granted.

The child has some of this superstitious faith in the power of some unseen being; hence the belief that a wish, if wished hard enough, may be realised. The wishing becomes a habit, part of the child's existence; games are played, based upon the childish wishes; folk-lore and fairy-tales are built up around the wish—"I wish" being the theme of the final realisation and with very little genuine effort on the part of the hero or heroine. This habit of wishing in the child fantasy period has to be re-educated or redirected into action or the doing phase.

## Wasting Mental Energy

But have we entirely cast off these childish habits? Have we matured or have we formed a habit of wishing? From childhood onwards, even the most practical, self-controlled person will use some energy in wishing. There are the spontaneous wishes we know are impracticable such as: "I wish the sun would shine", "I wish it were summer", "I wish it would snow"—all wishes entirely beyond our control. Even adults give way at times to this useless occupation— a waste of valuable time, of mental and spiritual energy.

Then come the more practical or materialistic wishes: "I wish I were rich", "I wish I could go abroad", "ride a horse", "own a car", "speak French", "play the piano"—and a thousand and one other wishes. So we wish away our time, our energies, our opportunities. Time slips away unheeded and unused:

> *"Time, you old gypsy man, will you not stay?*
> *Put up your caravan just for one day!"*

Perhaps only in the winter of our lives do we look back and realise how we have mis-spent our powers, missed our opportunities and wasted the precious, fleeting days.

Stop this waste of time *now*! Don't wait until it's too late. See the red light ahead pulling you up as you make your next wish. "I wish . . .!" There you go again. Stop now and examine your wish. Is it futile, childish, useless? Do you *really* want that wish? Is it worth while? Hold it up to the light and examine it honestly and frankly. If it is worthless, cast it away at once.

But if it is an oft-repeated wish, an ardent desire, something worth while, the achievement of which would enhance your personality, enlarge your mental abilities—why, then examine it more carefully.

## Dreaming and Doing

Everyone has troubles and difficulties. At some time in life each one of us comes "up against it". But some people do seem to have the dice loaded against them more heavily than others. Some are handicapped by poverty, ugliness, unhappy homes, but perhaps the greatest handicap is ill health. But Life or the Great Spirit, when handing out the talents, gives everyone some gift; somewhere it is balanced out, each one has compensations—*but* each individual must first seek his talents and then *use* them.

Dreamers play a big part in life—a very big part. There are, however, two kinds of dreamers: dynamic dreamers, who are also doers, and idle dreamers, who are mere visionaries and do nothing about their dreams.

Life's master accomplishments are the achievements of the dynamic dreamer. Without the power to dream, there can be no creative evolution, no improvement in the status of life. Behind every revolutionary departure in the upward march of Man is the vision of some dreamer who beheld glimpses of reality during ethereal flights of fancy, brought his vision down from Olympian heights to be materialised and adapted to the needs of Man. This is the history of each new invention which has lightened the loads of toilers and multiplied happiness, comfort and well-being for mankind.

Music, art, literature, painting, sculpture are but the materialisation of dreamers' dreams. Every vast organisation, reaching to the ends of the earth, has been first a dream of its creator. In every laborious upward climb, socially, politically, economically, the race has advanced step by step with mighty dreams.

It is, however, only by relentless physical and mental effort and unceasing labour that dreams can be brought into splendid materialisation.

But for every dreamer-doer there are thousands of idle dreamers— smokers of mental opium pipes. They are pregnant with ideas which are never born. They never seek the materialisation of their dreams. They content themselves with unproductive flights from reality. Shrinking from contact with the world that is, from the hardship of combat, from purposeful struggle, they withdraw into a world of vain dreams.

This is the reversion to infantile consciousness. So complete is the spell of imaginative dreaming to the child, that the real seems unreal and fantasy alone is clothed in the robes of reality. And so it is with the idle, neurotic dreamer. He gets a morbid thrill from the unceasing circles which his flight of fancy describes, circles that lead to no constructive accomplishment.

Every dreamer must learn to be a doer. We must retire for a while to dream, not for merely morbid, sensual self-satisfaction, returning to barren, unaspiring mediocrity of actual accomplishment, but rather must we drive ourselves to some form of objective expression. We live in a practical world in which we must deal in objective values.

### Wishful Thinking

There was a man who became a cripple. He had education, training and mental ability above the average. Yet he allowed his disability to possess him entirely; he filled his mind with bitterness and resentment against a fate which condemned him to physical inactivity. Nothing his friends could say or do could shake him out of his attitude of mind—he had a "chip on his shoulder". The life of uselessness which he deplored was fast becoming his, and more, for his irritability, cynicism and sour temper were making him a burden to all around him.

One day a friend of his youth returned from abroad, visited him, and finally spoke frankly to him about the futility of wishful thinking —the waste of gifts, of mental energy, the loss of friendship and affection, and finally the lack of achievement in a life which still had much to offer.

The man sat in silence and listened. The struggle was on. Finally he stirred and said: "I've been spending my time wishing—wishing for a miracle; wishing others would cure me, instead of trying to help myself and making the best of my life. Now I see that others can only *help* me—can only point the way. I must still *do* something about it myself. *I* am the most important factor in carving out my own life and future. I'll just have to stop wishing and start doing. I will draw on my storehouse of faith. There I will find the first step I am to take." Here is a first-hand example of the way in which wishful thinking can be harnessed to action with excellent results.

## Taking Risks

So very many of us to-day spend our time looking for the *sure* things in life. This may be excusable and understandable in those well past middle age, who maybe are looking ahead to the years of old age and retirement. But for the young, who should be go-ahead, ambitious, full of the zest and spirit of adventure, the idea of playing only for safety is wrong. Surely it is almost a disgrace for young, strong, competent men to look for safe, easy jobs.

Security—there's no such thing. For all of life is a risk. There is nothing *sure*. Even being alive is a risk. Going about the house, walking the streets, carrying out our daily tasks—always a risk is present. There always has been, and always will be, an element of risk in business, in trade and commerce. The only thing any person concerned can do is to minimise the risk by ability and forethought.

The majority of people to-day seek safe jobs with sick pay, holiday pay and pensions; then they sit down and wait for old age! But there is no need to wait for it. They are dead already, not just old! Life for them has lost its zest, its savour, its adventure, its impetus. These are the people who fool themselves that they are *safe—safe*— the word that is the spiritual rot to the people of Britain to-day—for they can never be safe; political changes or war may sweep away their security—then they learn, perhaps too late, that there is no absolute safety except in death.

So if I were a king—an old-fashioned king who could make his own uncurtailed proclamations, I would start off by appealing to the young men and women of this country, and urge them to a life of adventure by their willingness to take risks.

The restrictions and regulations, the interference and the dullness of so-called security, which is sending our young people abroad by the thousands, could perhaps be cast on one side, if they would kick over the traces against these things that are imposed upon them from so many quarters.

## Life is Like a Game

Life is very much like a game. We cannot always win. But therein lies the spice of existence—the prizes, the victories are there for the adventurous. From a nation of pioneer adventurers in Elizabeth I's days, we later became a nation of merchant adventurers, of tradespeople; but now we appear in great danger of deteriorating into a nation of Civil Servants with a slogan of "Safety First".

Is it any wonder that young men and women, overpowered and well-nigh strangled by frustration and red tape, find that the only escape is to emigrate? For with a big, wide, wonderful world waiting to welcome it, youth does not depend on Britain. It's Britain that depends on youth—the life-blood of the future of a nation which was once the greatest power in the world.

Isn't it time for some plain and straight talk? Isn't it time we cast off the life of wishful thinking, stopped fooling ourselves and faced the hard facts? Isn't it time we cast away the "Safety First" slogan and recaptured some of the old, pioneer spirit of our fore-fathers? A welfare state is an excellent ideal—*but* it is made up not only *of* the individuals in the State but *by* them. If we want these ideal conditions, we cannot just accept them: *we must make them*! We must *work*, and work together, or the future of the children of to-day may be one of *want* and Britain will sink lower and lower until only the memory of its greatness remains.

We need a new, national change of outlook in regard to work, to get rid of the work-dodgers, the clock-watchers, the time-wasters. We need real, conscientious, individual effort, to give the best possible return for the pay we earn. We need a revival of that old, daring, adventurous spirit that made this nation great. These are some of the things that could make Britain's great prestige of the past appear dim compared with the prestige of the future.

## A Golden Rule

Finally, let us keep our heads out of the clouds—our feet on the ground; take our dreams and wishes in hand and banish the useless, unattainable ones.

So many people have aspired to the unattainable heights only to become nerve-wrecked and disillusioned men and women in a frenzied and futile struggle to become what they are not logically fitted to become.

We cannot all be the owners of successful businesses, company directors, film stars or politicians. Each one of us must find our niche in life and then be determined to be the best in that line, for:

*"If you can't be a pine on the top of the hill,*
*Be a scrub in the valley—but be*
*The best little scrub by the side of the rill;*
*Be a bush if you can't be a tree.*
*We can't all be captains, we've got to be crew,*
*There's something for all of us here,*
*There's big work to do, and there's lesser to do,*
*And the task you must do is the near.*
*If you can't be a highway then just be a trail,*
*If you can't be the sun be a star;*
*It isn't by size that you win or you fail—*
*Be the best of whatever you are!"*

# DYNAMIC DREAMERS

*"It is difficult to imagine anything more dreary and destructive to self-respect than for a human being, born with divine capacities, to drift through life, unstirred by any heroic objective, motivated by no superb ambition, with no goal in view, like a ship without a rudder, a play without a plot, a song without a melody."*

\*     \*     \*

I WONDER what school or creed is mainly responsible for the dangerous idea that Man is moulded by circumstance; that men and women are made or marred by the twin devils of heredity and environment.

For whoever is responsible for this prevalent habit of thought will have a great deal to answer for at the bar of history.

True, men and women are greatly and vitally influenced by parentage, upbringing and environment. Some "have all the luck", as we say. But that doesn't imply that life is altogether a matter of luck, that the favourites of fortune get all the jam and the unlucky, sometimes not even bread. It is good to be born rich, but it is better to grow up in wisdom.

Admittedly, if we could order such things, a man would be wise to choose a good mother, a good home, comfortable circumstances; he would be a fool if he didn't select a good school, and make contacts there that would help him immeasurably in later life.

If we understood enough of the mystery of heredity, a man would also be wise to choose to be born of sound, healthy stock. But alas, we are given no such choice. We may be born in a palace or in poverty, but there is nothing we can do about it.

Must we then accept our lot meekly, submissively, fatalistically? Of course not! It is up to each one of us to break free from "birth's insidious bar".

We have no say in where we are born, when we are born or in what circumstances we are born. But from birth onwards it is up to us to decide, more or less, what we become.

All life is a *becoming*. All life is a growing, creative process. We may originally have none of the advantages which would help us along, but we make our fortune from day to day.

All this would not be worth the space devoted to it, were it not that there is a tendency for the twin devils of heredity and environment to be regarded as shackles from which we cannot free ourselves. Carried to its logical conclusion, the argument is self-evidently

45

ridiculous. A man is born to poor parents—therefore he must be poor all his life. A woman's parents are "unsound"; therefore the offspring must inherit the father's vices and the mother's weaknesses.

If this theory is right and we are the products of the forces of heredity and environment, over which we have no control, then all incentive to ambition and determination is swept away. We are merely puppets of forces that can elevate or crush us, and we may as well submit to the inevitable.

## A Disproved Theory

What a gruesome, melancholy and devastating philosophy of life! Whilst the theory may seem to have been substantiated by painstaking experiments in the laboratory, it is disproved by thousands of heroic examples of men and women who, by sheer force of will, imagination, unremitting effort and right thinking, have surmounted every obstacle, dominated an unfavourable environment, scorned hereditary limitations and pushed their relentless way to the summits of achievement and success.

If humanity had accepted this "heredity and environment" doctrine ten thousand years ago, we should still be living in caves and our lives would be empty, brutish and short. But the march of civilisation affords further evidence on a grand scale, of Man's triumph over heredity and environment, of humanity's will to triumph over misfortune and march ever onwards and upwards to the larger life.

We should reject this pernicious dogma, and assert that the handicaps of heredity and environment can be overcome, and that men and women can realise their potentialities to the full.

We must accept the fact that, in the main, we make—or mar—ourselves. We rise by our own efforts or we sink deeper into the slough because of our inertia; we aspire and succeed or we despair and fall by the wayside.

Thousands of men and women everywhere are defeated in life's struggle not so much by heredity and environment as by themselves.

> *"Not in the clamour of the crowded street,*
> *Not in the shouts and plaudits of the throng,*
> *But in ourselves are triumph and defeat."*

## The Self-made Man

I had an unusual experience the other day. A man came to see me and, during the course of our conversation, he told me that he had lived his life in accordance with the major principles of Practical Psychology, and could vouch for the soundness of the philosophy. He had not, however, read *Psychology* Magazine until a few months previously. He had discovered the principles of Practical Psychology by trial and error, and he was delighted to find a magazine in existence that preached the gospel of self-realisation, the principles which had governed his own life.

"I wish I had known of *Psychology* years ago," he said. He was a youngish-looking man of vibrant personality. I was rather surprised at the range of his experience for one so young, until he confessed his age to be over forty, not, as I had guessed, the early thirties.

"Nothing like the active, positive life for keeping one young," he asserted. And then he told me something of his life-story. He was born in the North of England, of poor parents, and had to leave school at an early age in order to help the family finances. But he was by no means uneducated. He was a cultured man, largely through self-education.

His first job was a "blind-alley" one. He did not choose it. He had to take what was available at that time. He changed jobs a number of times, always for a pathetically small increase in wages. Many of the jobs he undertook he thoroughly loathed. But all the time he was absorbing experience, educating himself, seeking that opportunity which, he felt confident, existed somewhere.

During these early years he wanted, above all things, to become an executive of a large wholesale concern in a neighbouring town. He could give no logical reason for this particular desire, nor could he trace when the desire first came to light. All he knew was that he would very much like to get on the staff of this firm and eventually to hold an important position within it.

The man's dream seemed very unlikely to come true. Especially in the lean years of the world trade depression the chances of a regular job seemed remote enough, let alone the opportunity of joining a particular firm of one's own choosing.

Yet he did not despair, although he admitted to himself that this particular ambition was likely to remain a dream. He plodded on at his menial tasks from day to day, doing each job to the best of his ability; he constantly sought ways of improving himself, studying a great variety of subjects in order to give himself a broader education.

Gradually he worked up an excellent connection as a salesman for a small concern. It was from this post that he volunteered for service in the Forces in 1940.

At the end of the war his old job was still open to him, and his prospects seemed exceptionally good. Whilst on his "Demob Leave", he saw his employer, who gave a very pointed indication of promotion to come. But despite the attractive prospects offered, he elected to join his "dream" firm—on the Accounts Staff—at less than half the salary offered by his previous employer.

He admitted that he would find it hard to explain the reason for this decision. True, he had always wanted to work for that particular wholesale firm, but accountancy was something new to him; it would take him years to arrive at any senior position, and he was not particularly interested in accounts.

Nevertheless he started his new job with enthusiasm, performing his duties conscientiously, learning as much about the business as he could, and worked hard on rather uninteresting tasks for two or three years. He sometimes wondered if he wasn't a fool, and wished he was back at the more interesting, better-paid job he had left.

And then, the position of Assistant Sales Manager became vacant. He applied for it and was successful—*mainly because his accountancy experience was considered a great advantage in that particular post.* A year later, he was promoted to Sales Manager—the very "dream job" that he had recognised in fantasy so many years ago. His dream had come true.

But stranger still, perhaps, was the man's more recent experience. Long before the war, before he was married, he had pictured in his mind's eye the house of his dreams. He had conjured up in imagination a detached house in Tudor style with a large rose garden in the front, the view of a distant river with cool hills in the background. In his own words, he almost knew the number of tiles on the roof—knew even the knots in the woodwork and a slight defect in the pane of one of the windows.

Just a week before the man had called to see me, he had seen the very house, practically a replica of his dream picture. The house was for sale. He had bought it and would move in within a month.

"Not all according to my dream, perhaps," he added with a smile. "Houses have to be paid for, and if you haven't the money, mortgages arranged. Buying this house will mean some sacrifices, but I am prepared for that. Everything worth while demands effort."

"So all your dreams came true?" I queried.

"No—not all of them—not yet, anyway," he replied. "But a substantial part of them have done so. And I do not seem to have made any direct attempt on these particular objectives. My job with my present firm appeared to offer no prospects of the work I wanted —yet it was transformed into that. I did not know this house existed— yet it's now mine—and it's within reach of my office, too."

"Mind you," he went on, "not all the things I imagined have come to pass exactly as I thought or hoped they would. Sometimes the reality is better than the dream; sometimes the realisation is not quite so satisfying as the dream promised. Sometimes, the achievement is merely a finger-post to another objective."

## A Plan of Life

I have dealt in some detail with this man's experience for a particular purpose. It is such a splendid example of determination, triumph over difficulties, and the realisation of an ideal. It is an object-lesson in Practical Psychology.

The man we have been discussing was unaware of the principles of Practical Psychology. By happy accident he stumbled upon the great truth, that an idea steadfastly pursued, an objective vigorously attacked, a dream constantly fought for—can become reality.

An idea firmly planted and persistently held in the mind can work seeming miracles. The Conscious Mind cannot conceive how the gap between idea and actuality can be bridged. The Subconscious knows, however, and even directs one's steps, perhaps by devious routes and unrecognised paths, towards the ideal. Once plant a thought, idea or desire in the Subconscious and the result is inevitable. We act, as it were, under the control and guidance of another power, directing us towards achieving the objective of which we have dreamed.

"Then why do all dreams not come true?" is the logical rejoinder.

There are two kinds of dreamers—dynamic dreamers, who are also doers, and idle dreamers, who are mere visionaries and do nothing about their dreams.

The dynamic dreamer sets out to crystallise his dreams in untiring effort. He knows that great achievement requires not only aspiration but perspiration.

The idle dreamer is one who dreams and never seeks the materialisation of his dreams. He dissipates his energies in fruitless reverie, in dreams that never accomplish anything, in ideas that never find expression. While Life's accomplishments are, in fact, the achievements of those who dream, the dreamer must also learn to be a doer—to drive himself to a definite form of objective expression.

The desire must be isolated to the exclusion of everything else. It is no use wishing at the same time for a hundred other incompatible things.

Practical Psychology asserts that if we have *one* intense desire which surpasses *all* others, if we have a real concrete plan, a definite fixed purpose, which we vigorously and steadfastly pursue, then the Subconscious will bring about conditions favourable to its attainment.

Practical Psychology says, in fact, that if we wish for success in some particular sphere, make the desire the dominating one in life, put forth every effort towards its attainment and bend all our conscious energies towards its realisation, then we will succeed.

The first essential is an intense desire and a clear, definite plan, purpose or goal. It is not enough to wish to become successful in a general sense. We must be specific. We must know what we wish to succeed at. Just like the man we have met in this Chat, we must have an idea of the actual firm for which we wish to work, the actual business we want to own, the very tiles of the house in which one day we hope to live.

At first, of course, especially in the case of young men and women, their ambitions are not likely to be absolutely clear-cut. But, as the years pass, they should make up their minds and be sure of what they want.

When we know our objective, we have discovered more than half the secret of achievement.

When we are really sincere about our objective, it will generate a force of its own that will drive us to make mighty efforts towards its attainment.

The fixing of our objective with absolute certainty is the means whereby we impress our predominant desire upon the Subconscious. But we must be sincere about it and this sincerity implies effort. We must live and work and strive in such a way that we fit ourselves for the ideal at which we aim. Then, if we follow this dual plan, success will crown our efforts.

## To Those who Doubt

There are many men and women who cannot accept this truth. And to doubt is to invite failure. What can Practical Psychology offer them?

*Psychology* does not despise those who doubt. The "doubting Thomases" are often a safeguard against the false philosophies and the miracle-workers! So to such doubters, *Psychology* can answer: "Put your doubts to the test."

Think of some limited objective and whatever your doubts, do your best to impress upon your Subconscious the desire to attain this objective. Give the principles expounded a fair chance—even if only a week's trial.

There will be no doubt as to the result or the doubter's final verdict.

In the larger national sense, too, the same principles apply, for no country is better than the people who make up its citizenship. We have heard and read a great deal about the New Elizabethan Era. The very thought that we are again entering upon an era of achievement has given a new spurt, a new zest to the community. Let us make no mistake about this—if we truly desire greatness, we shall achieve greatness; if we sincerely wish to wrest from adversity the fruits of achievement, we shall succeed.

In spite of the ominous problems and perplexities of our age or the dark clouds of confusion and discordance that loom so large on to-day's horizon, we seem to be witnessing a prelude to a new and splendid age for Man.

For Man must not entirely be considered for what he superficially is, but for what he may become, not for what he has achieved but for what he may yet achieve.

Man will yet press onwards and upwards to even greater progress and accomplishment—undaunted, undiscouraged and unafraid!

# ARE WE TOO COMPLACENT?

ONE of the most precious qualities we can possess is enthusiasm. It has been described as the breath of genius; the intoxication of earnestness; the element of success in everything. Enthusiasm puts a sparkle into life; it lifts us out of the common rut and makes life *worth living*!

All children possess enthusiasm. But very few adults have it. Perhaps the reason for this is that the majority of men and women lose their enthusiasm because of the drudgeries, cares and responsibilities of life.

If we view the general trend of modern life, we can hardly fail to notice one depressing factor—an insidious, ever-encroaching apathy, which is, of course, the exact opposite of enthusiasm.

Apathy is evident everywhere. In fact, if a Society for the Promotion of Apathy were formed, it would probably fail—through lack of interest; an ironical situation if ever there was one.

Too many people seem to have lost the zest for living. They exist in a kind of mental, emotional and spiritual oblivion. They are "human cabbages". They live in a cramped little sphere of their own and display complete indifference to practically everything else around them. Very few are particularly concerned about their mental and spiritual welfare and progress.

These people are indifferent even to the most important issues in world affairs—unless their own sluggish, complacent lives are disturbed. If the attention of the "couldn't care less" brigade is drawn to any personal, social or political danger, a typical reply would be: "So what! I'm all right!" Such apathy is shockingly selfish.

In an era of almost full employment, social welfare services, canned entertainment and hygienic living conditions, we are inclined to take too much for granted. We are lulled into the belief that there is *no need* to get enthusiastic about anything!

In the long-past, ugly days of trade depression and mass unemployment, we *had* to show a spirit of enthusiasm to lift ourselves out of the mire. During the war, when all that we held dear was being threatened by a ruthless enemy, our enthusiastic devotion to duty and our unwavering belief in a just cause enabled us to do the "impossible"—and in the end our way of life was preserved. What a pity that we do not whip up more enthusiasm to make the best of a hard-won peace and prosperity!

## Avoid Mental Stagnation

As we grow older and gain more experience of life, our enthusiasm is apt to slow down. It is natural for us to slow down physically, but there's no need to slow down mentally. Perhaps our experiences over the years have made us unduly cautious and timid. Very likely we have come up against the toughness of the world, been buffeted and battered about and deeply scarred. The enthusiastic adventurous spirit in us begins to fade and is likely to be replaced by complacency and the desire for more security. But we can do a lot to combat this common danger that threatens us all as we grow older. We should reason things out. Haven't the years that have gone only been preparatory for the work we are now ready to begin? Haven't we got the experience and aren't we better equipped mentally to do certain jobs than we were at twenty-five? Isn't it true that our experience of life can enable us to do more in certain directions during the last part of life than we did in the early years? Hasn't most of the world's most useful work been done by middle-aged people? Our mental powers do not come to an end as we grow older! We should rake out the cinders and ashes and stoke up the mental fire. We should do all we can to stop the smouldering period that begins so often in later years.

We should mix more with the right type of young people. We should be less censorious and more teachable and not be unduly influenced by tradition. We should listen to their point of view and realise that they, too, have the right to express their opinions. We should not undervalue them. The world needs the steadying influence of the experience of old-timers as well as the ardent enthusiasm of youth.

Not all young people possess enthusiasm. Far from it! There is plenty of evidence available of the apathy and boredom which exist among many young people to-day.

Perhaps we older folk have no ground upon which to feel self-righteous about the apathy and boredom of this section of modern youth. Maybe the fault lies with us. We may feel justifiably proud of the educational facilities we have provided for young people, and also of the attention we have paid to their social welfare. But have we taught them *how to live*? As a recent newspaper editorial pointed out, "Our young people to-day have better conditions and living standards, more money and latitude than any generation before them." Probably this is *why* so many people are so bored and apathetic.

## The Magic of Enthusiasm

"Nothing great was ever achieved without enthusiasm," said Emerson, and we know this to be true. History shows that men of great enthusiasm have shaped and moulded the lives of countless millions since time began. They knew nothing of so-called secrets of success and its techniques. Instead, they possessed something vastly greater—a flaming enthusiasm so unquenchable that multitudes were drawn to bask in its strong and steady light.

Enthusiasm! It is indeed a magic word. It overcomes difficulties and set-backs. It smashes down obstacles. It creates opportunities. It sees the possibility of improvement. It doubles efficiency. It looks towards the future with eyes of hope and moves forward with an inspiration that compels success.

Why are there so few people who are really enthusiastic about their jobs? It is surprising, and somewhat alarming, to discover so many people who regard their daily work as a penalty—an evil necessity. They work because they must, but they are far from enthusiastic about it. They do as little as they dare, for to them work is only a burden, a compulsory drudgery and a downright nuisance. How can they hope to progress at their work with such an attitude towards their jobs?

It is possible that some of these people who dislike their work are merely in the wrong jobs. They are not in the least suited to the work they are doing. If they are unable to seek and find anything satisfying about their work, they should get out of it at the very first opportunity and find a *suitable* alternative. If we detest the kind of work we are doing, we shall never succeed at it. Besides—why allow our work to make us miserable? Unless we are actually work-shy, surely there is *some* occupation, particularly in these days of full employment, which we can become enthusiastic about. It is up to us to find it.

If we take a reasonable, positive view of life, we shall realise that work isn't an imposition, but a privilege. Anybody who has witnessed the soul-destroying effects of prolonged unemployment will be in no doubt about that.

Nobody in his right mind would wish to return to the bad old days of depression, dole queues, soup kitchens and abject poverty. Nevertheless, much of to-day's general lack of enthusiasm may well exist because everything has become *too easy* for most of us. We seem to have lost nearly all our enthusiasm. We seem to take too much for granted and we are neither shocked nor thrilled very much about anything. What we need is a spur that will arouse us, give us more enthusiasm and drive, more zest and zeal for life.

Just think of the enthusiasm many of us put into a chosen hobby. What about those keen anglers who spend hours fishing in the rain or cold, when they could be at home sitting by a cosy fire? What about the active sportsmen, rock-climbers, pot-holers and similar enthusiasts? What about the match-modellers who patiently glue thousands of matchsticks into position until they have built a beautiful model cathedral? How could anybody do any of these things without enthusiasm?

The first requisite is to become deeply interested in *something*, no matter what. Once a chosen subject absorbs our interest, we cannot fail to become enthusiastic about it. Later, with increased knowledge and practice, we can become experts in a particular field. We have something to talk about, something to occupy our minds, something to *live* for.

*The fortunate few who can regard their daily work as a profitable hobby, and who are so enthusiastic about their jobs that no one can shake their belief in the worth and value of them, can hardly fail to be happy and successful.*

### Belief and Purpose

It has often been said that for a woman to express her personality to the full and to fulfil her destiny, she must become a wife and mother. No doubt motherhood is the finest role that any woman can fill— but let us remember all the unmarried women who are denied the joy and fulfilment of motherhood. What are they supposed to do about it? Are they doomed to become useless misfits in society? Not by any means!

Among the ranks of unmarried women, past and present, are some of the noblest characters that the world has produced. Joan of Arc, Florence Nightingale, Edith Cavell—their splendid records will live eternally in history. Living to-day are many unmarried women whose praises remain unsung. They may not have done anything spectacular, but they are devoting themselves to a cause for the benefit of humanity, or even for animals. Nurses, Nuns, Veterinary Surgeons, Church Workers, Probation Officers, Welfare Workers, Marriage Guidance Counsellors. They are all sincere *enthusiasts* for something in which they *believe*. Where would they be without their enthusiasm —and what would become of those in their care?

The sense of the word enthusiasm as used by the Greeks is a good definition: enthusiasm signifies God in us. This is no exaggeration if our enthusiasm is well-placed.

Enthusiasts are often ridiculed or criticised for the *object* of their enthusiasm. We may not understand the enthusiasm of pot-holers, rock-climbers or even stamp-collectors. This may be because we are not interested in their pursuits and activities—perhaps we consider them foolish, dangerous or time-wasting. If we recognise and admit any such prejudice, however, we must admire the spirit, courage or sheer persistence of these various enthusiasts. At least they do not belong to the apathetic, "dumb-bell" brigade. They have a *purpose* and they are, therefore, vitally *alive*. We have the enthusiastic pioneers to thank for all the amenities of this age.

## Ideals and Principles

If we find ourselves lacking in enthusiasm, we should study this quality as displayed in any normal child. Healthy children bubble over with enthusiasm for anything they have set their hearts on. In my schooldays we had bouts of enthusiasm for the simplest things, like gathering "conkers". All the boys competed to acquire the best and biggest collection of conkers. The prize specimens were threaded, singly, on a string, ready for our "conker fights". Friends of both opponents stood around to watch the "battle", and a rousing cheer went up for the winner. A simple, harmless bit of fun, but what *enthusiasm* went into it! Always there was something to be enthusiastic about. This brought so much happiness into our young lives.

Isn't it a pity that as we grow older our youthful enthusiasm is inclined to wane, often almost to vanishing point? By losing this faculty we miss so much in life.

When we "fly from the shelter of the nest" and face the harsh realities of the bleak outside world, we are bewildered and even shocked by much that is happening around us. Gradually we come to accept the grossly materialistic state of affairs. We are inclined to become hardened and cynical in order to keep our heads above water. No wonder our early enthusiasm is dampened and depressed. At all costs we should stand by our ideals and principles, and do everything to maintain our enthusiasm for all that we know to be good, progressive and beneficial to humanity. It should be easy enough for us to work up and hold enthusiasm for our own pet interest, *if we have any*.

It is the duty of all parents to foster enthusiasm in their children. They should be encouraged to enjoy such an *abundance* of enthusiasm, that when they go out into the world, enough of it will remain to support their efforts towards success in any endeavour.

Above all, children should be prompted in their enthusiasm for *spiritual* knowledge and wisdom, for upon this a great deal depends. They should be taught that material progress, however desirable, isn't *everything*. In fact, it is usually precarious, and unless we possess a fundamental appreciation of spiritual values, we shall discover that even material success fails to satisfy us. "A man's possessions are only as great as his own soul," says one philosopher. "If his title-deeds cover more, the surplus acres own him, not he the acres." This profound truth is well worth remembering. It brings home to us the importance of enthusiasm in the right direction—in spiritual as well as temporal affairs.

Without enthusiasm we merely vegetate. With it, we can move forward into the unknown future with faith and fortitude and do useful work in the world with zest and confidence.

L.C.—5

# THE MEANING OF FREEDOM

*"There are two freedoms—the false, where a man is free to do what he likes; the true, where a man is free to do what he ought."*

\*　　\*　　\*

FREEDOM is regarded everywhere as one of Man's most treasured possessions. Nation has fought nation for it; countless thousands have died for it. Serfdom belongs to the forgotten past, and in most respects the "under-dog" is entitled to a fair hearing and treatment.

To-day, too, we are witnessing a universal and unprecedented clamour for national independence. Freedom is the privilege of self-determination, the Utopia about which men dream.

Wise men have told us that Freedom is the aspiration of our time; a treasure more precious than Life itself; that the human soul cries and struggles for freedom from the time of its first conscious moments; that it is Man's natural birthright. We can imagine the old wiseacres nodding their heads in solemn agreement with these beliefs.

Suppose we try to analyse these widely held beliefs about Freedom. First of all, let us consider the long-term convict in his prison cell. The thought of eventual freedom must dominate his mind, day after day, year after year. Freedom is the golden promise of the future that makes the convict's grim life more bearable. Convicts have a certain amount of work to do in the prison workshops; they have to exist on a monotonous diet; mix with men or women whose characters are, perhaps, much worse than could be expected; the environment and conditions generally are bleak and depressing. Yet the worst aspect of the convict's prison life is, without doubt, his loss of freedom.

Now let us consider all the workers of the world. There they are, day after day, cooped up in their factories, offices, shops, coal-mines or other work-places. Our social system is such, that almost every-body is forced to sacrifice a great deal of freedom in order to live a civilised life. How often do we glance out of the window and envy the freedom of the birds as they fly from tree to tree?

Millions of working men and women invest a few shillings every week in football pools. Why? Not *only* for the big money prize itself, but for the "freedom" such a fortune seems to represent— a fortune which would enable them to escape from the soul-destroying daily grind; to follow the sun and enjoy a life of unfettered ease!

Then there is the harassed wife and mother tied down to her heavy responsibilities. Only her love for her husband and children could give her the strength and determination to endure the many irritating

56

restrictions imposed upon her by her arduous duties. Yet there can be very few of these devoted women who do not, at times, feel like running away from it all—to live their own lives in *freedom*.

### Illusion or Reality?

The idea of freedom has often been expressed in beautiful words by many poets. Wordsworth, for example:

> *"How does the meadow flower its bloom unfold?*
> *Because the lovely little flower is free*
> *Down to its root, and in that freedom bold."*

Freedom, however, is not only the dream of poets and philosophers —it is the dream of all mankind. But is Freedom a dream only or is it a practical possibility; a mirage, an illusion or a reality?

We speak of "free nations", the "freedom of the Press", "free speech", "free-lance" writers and artists, "free will" and even "free love". Yet *who or what is entirely free materially, or ever likely to be in this life?*

To-day we are witnessing a universal bid for freedom from colonial rule by many nations. Some of these nations have at last gained their so-called freedom. But are they as free as they imagined they would be? By all accounts, it doesn't seem that they are. They have done away with restrictions formerly imposed upon them, but they appear to be burdened by their own self-imposed responsibilities. They now find themselves having to stand on their own feet and compete against the rest of the "free world". This will be a very good thing for the wisest of these now independent nations in time. By trial and error they will discover their strength and their weaknesses. In the end they will either win the respect and admiration of the world, having lifted themselves up by sheer merit and determination, or they will face utter chaos, in which case they are likely to find their affairs controlled again by some other great power. Either way they will never be free from responsibilities to themselves and to the rest of humanity. So where is Freedom in this instance?

Let us return to the convict, whose term of imprisonment is drawing to a close. One day the massive gates of the gaol will open for him and he will be "free". But how free will he be? He will no longer be confined within four walls, and he will be able to go where he wishes, but will he find true freedom? The man will be hampered by his prison record. He will be seriously restricted if he searches for honest employment. He may even be pestered or threatened by his former associates, and he will remain a "marked man" in police records. Even if he does succeed in reforming, his past is likely to haunt him and he may feel somewhat inferior to the majority of his fellow-men. His freedom, therefore, will not be the satisfying experience about which he had dreamed for so long.

### From Freedom to Boredom

The workman who is perhaps sick and tired of the necessity of earning a living, and frustrated and irritated by the petty rules and irksome regulations of his workaday life, may one day win that football pools fortune. In his first flush of victory, this "lucky fellow" will feel like a millionaire. He can now get away from the "daily grind". No more will he have to get up early every morning and travel to work in crowded buses or in stuffy railway carriages. No longer will he have to put up with the unpleasantness and strain of going to work in fog, rain, snow, or ice. He will be *free*!—free to lie in bed in the morning when he feels like it and to get out into the fresh air and sunshine whenever possible. Isn't that glorious freedom, the freedom for which he longed and yearned?

Yes, it is—for a time! Soon, however, this "lucky fellow" is to be oppressed by new taskmasters—boredom, restlessness, discontent. He may become irritable, moody and depressed. He begins to look back to the days when he was a working man—one of millions in the same category. He thinks about the lost comradeship of his fellow-workers; he misses the pleasurable anticipation of receiving his wages every week; the little treats of relaxation and entertainment he used to plan for himself and his family, and how he *treasured* those hard-earned pleasures.

Now that he has plenty of money and plenty of leisure, the chances are he isn't sure what to buy next, where he wants to go or what to do with the almost endless time on his hands. Moreover, instead of being able to share the companionship and the joys and problems of his fellow-workers, and all the interesting conversations they used to have together, he feels lonely and lost. He is the "odd man out" among his neighbours. If this is his new-found "freedom", he decides, it doesn't come up to his expectations. It is more boring, frustrating and irritating than his working life ever was!

So what does this "lucky fellow" do next? Perhaps he buys a business, so that he can be his own boss. Is that freedom? Ask any boss in any business! What with labour difficulties, production and distribution problems, awkward customers, bad debts, overhead expenses and taxes, the proprietor of any business is by no means a free man, even if he does take an occasional long week-end off from work or the odd half-day for a game of golf.

Let us now consider the wife and mother who feels sometimes that she would like to run away from all her responsibilities. She cannot be blamed for this occasional desire to "escape to freedom". The children test her patience to the limit; her husband comes home often tired and despondent; the cake was a failure and the mud is continually being trodden indoors and she has forgotten to buy any cheese. These troubles are not always evident, of course, but they all seem to happen on the same day. No wonder her nerves are on edge and she thinks—"to blazes with everything and everybody. Oh, to be free!"

Just suppose this harassed wife *does* run away from it all? How long would she be able to stay away? If she is anything like most wives and mothers she would be worrying and fretting during the whole of her absence. Are the children safe? What are they doing about meals? How can her husband possibly manage without her? What sort of "freedom" would her temporary escape mean to her?

## Can Anybody be Truly Free?

So in spite of all this longing and yearning for freedom and all the delightful thoughts and words in praise of it, the vital question remains: Does Freedom really exist for any of us, outside our imagination?

In this connection perhaps our thoughts may turn to gypsies and their life on the open road. Is theirs a life of freedom? Not at all. True, they can practically wander at will about the countryside, but the restrictions imposed upon them in a civilised society are many and varied. Ironically, one of these restrictions is that they have to *keep moving*. Yet they are required to send their children to schools "en route". Again, no matter how honest these gypsies may be, they are usually among the first to be suspected if any robbery or assault happens to occur within the vicinity of their encampment. They have to produce things and sell them in order to earn a little money for food and clothes. They have to maintain their means of transport and perform other essential menial tasks. Their freedom is in fact very limited.

The lonely tramp is probably the only person who can claim any semblance of freedom, for his only responsibility is to look after himself.

In these days, however, the genuine tramp is almost extinct. There is no need of his existence—and who wants to be a tramp, anyway, except the odd eccentric individual?

We must conclude, therefore, that Freedom, in the form that we have examined, is practically impossible in a civilised society. It is no more than a dream, an illusion, a mirage. Whoever we are, whatever we do, wherever we live, we are restricted in a number of ways. We must observe the laws of the land, or pay the inevitable penalties, probably with further loss of freedom. We must obey the Laws of Nature or take the consequences. We have certain responsibilities to ourselves and to others.

Yet, at times, there is within us all, this unquenchable yearning for Freedom. Is there *nothing* we can do that would give us a greater measure of freedom to make life more attractive and satisfying?

Fortunately, there is a satisfactory answer to this persistent question; there is a way by which we can lead happier and more contented lives. But there are very few people who have discovered the way, and even some of those who have found the way refuse to travel along it because it demands effort and initiative; calls for a re-education of all the faculties, for self-understanding, for a new, deeper understanding of life itself.

So if we would travel along the road that leads to more successful living, first of all, we must decide to *accept* the fact that freedom, in the material sense, is for all practical purposes merely a pipe-dream; that even if material freedom were possible, it would do us more harm than good.

Then having taken this first step of accepting mentally this material fact, we must learn to make the best of our physical and material limitations. We must make up our minds to be as happy as possible in spite of the inevitable infringements upon our freedom, just as an animal born in the zoo has to live in its cage or compound and submit to its restrictions for the sake of self-preservation. What would happen if these zoo animals were all transported back to the jungle and released? They would never be able to compete against their own wild species or protect themselves adequately against their numerous enemies. Their new-found "freedom" would be their death-sentence. Perhaps this may be a good analogy—even if it is somewhat crude—to remember in relation to ourselves.

Mankind, however, exists on a higher plane than the animals of the jungle, though sometimes people and events may appear to contradict this. Civilised Man, especially, has a much higher degree of intelligence, imagination and reasoning power than subjects of the animal kingdom. Man has also developed a philosophy of life and is instinctively aware of some Higher Power directing the Universe. Man is aware of some Great Purpose in life and he has a conscience— an ability to discriminate, to a great extent, between right and wrong.

## What We really Need

These facts suggest that when we are conscious of our desire for more freedom, it is not material freedom we need, but spiritual, mental and, to some extent, emotional freedom—a very different and more important kind of freedom. When we recognise this difference in regard to Freedom, then we begin to discover that our *material* and physical restrictions, are not so detrimental after all. For these material restrictions, often irritating and frustrating as they may be, can act as spurs of incentive urging us on towards mental and spiritual progress.

Let us think for a few moments of all the inventions which have been created with the idea of minimising or overcoming many of the material restrictions and inconveniences. Railways, motor-cars, aircraft, labour-saving gadgets, improved methods of production, man-made fibres, are just a few of *thousands* of examples.

*Just as the irritation of a grain of sand within the oyster can produce a pearl, so the irritations which beset Mankind can stimulate the highest, noblest ideals that lead to the greatest ultimate benefits.*

So it seems that Man must learn how to gain greater freedom of action for his mental powers, how to acquire wider knowledge of the Laws of Cause and Effect, how to become psychologically emancipated. Only in this way can Man gain a more clearly understandable insight into the true meaning of Freedom as it relates to the vital business of more *Effective Living*.

# THE SWING OF THE PENDULUM

*"In childhood to a little church,*
*My footsteps found their way.*
*Life was not then the weary search*
*For Joy it is to-day.*
*A simple sermon—simple song—*
*An understanding creed,*
*I found—when Life was right or wrong—*
*Sufficient for my need.*

*"To-day before a greater shrine,*
*Within a larger place,*
*I seek again for words divine*
*To give me peace and grace.*
*But there is something missing now—*
*The fault, the church or me*
*I cannot tell—It seems somehow*
*That God is hard to see.*

*"I think someday I'll search it out*
*—It's fifty years or more—*
*The church with lilacs all about—*
*An oak tree at the door;*
*For men and churches both may grow*
*Too great, too rich, too wise.*
*Perhaps when roofs and men are low,*
*They're nearer to the skies."*

DOUGLAS MALLOCH.

\* \* \*

THROUGHOUT the world there are many religions, but it is surprising how similar are the basic teachings of most, if not all of these various religions. They possess certain common features which may be regarded as essentials.

Broadly speaking, religion is deeply concerned with human behaviour and our relationship with the Deity. Religion not only helps to give us a sense of greater security in a crazy, materialistic world; it develops Man's spiritual consciousness and helps him to appreciate the things that really matter in life.

During the last fifty years, religious faith has begun to wane, with a gradual and lamentable drifting away from religion. The horrors and misery of two world wars, with people bitterly disillusioned by the threat of a third, may be one of the reasons for the big decline in Church attendance. Another reason may be that as a result of the world to-day placing such great stress on material values, almost to the exclusion of spiritual ones, numerous men and women are beginning to doubt their basic religious beliefs.

At the time of writing we are told that there are at present 370 *empty and redundant* churches in this country and a further 420 are expected to become redundant during the next fifteen years or so—a total of 790 churches. Not all of these churches are old; some of them are modern buildings, like a certain church near Liverpool for instance, which is only eight years old and is being offered for sale because *it is unable to find a congregation*! The majority of these redundant churches will be demolished or sold; a few, of architectural or historical interest, may be preserved—if enough money is made available for this purpose. If this trend continues and *if* Mankind survives for a few more generations, the day may come when the few remaining Church buildings may be no more than interesting relics of a bygone age and of a so-called obsolete social custom.

## A Question of Motive

Our suggestion that church-going is a fast-diminishing "social custom" points to one great weakness in religious activity. This isn't a weakness of all that the Christian Church stands for; but it has been for too long a weakness among many of those who attend Church regularly. *Why* do they go to Church every Sunday? That is the all-important question.

There is every reason to believe that when most of our Churches could boast of large congregations, a considerable proportion of those congregations attended for personal reasons often remote from the worship of God. An astonishing number of people used to go to Church simply because it was then considered to be the respectable and fashionable thing to do every Sunday. After all, how *could* Mr. and Mrs. P—— expect their neighbours to respect them *unless* they were regular churchgoers? And without the respect of one's neighbours, life could then be made almost unbearable for the social offender.

Again, there is little doubt, that countless unmarried women and old ladies used to (and possibly still do) attend Church regularly simply because they were (or are) attracted to the vicar—or his handsome and eligible curate. This form of hero-worship is certain to boost a congregation, but it gives a false picture.

Many a church has been known to lose half its congregation because the new preacher delivers almost interminable and erudite sermons. Or perhaps the vicar is too forthright and pricks too many consciences?

The most *apparently* devout members of a certain Church were reasonably wealthy local shopkeepers. They vied with each other to make impressive donations to various Church funds; they were elected to serve on Church committees—and the rest of the congregation were inevitably their best customers! This does not mean to say that all those church-going shopkeepers were not *also* sincere Christians. Far from it. At the same time one can hardly overlook the fact that it was certainly more profitable for them to go to Church than to stay away from it. It is at least possible that the same idea also occurred to them! Moreover, we are entitled to wonder whether some of them who were closely connected with Church activities did so for indirect personal gain.

So we must recognise that there are, and always have been many alternative reasons for church-going other than to worship God in all sincerity and truth.

This unalterable fact places the Church and the Christian Ministry in a most unfortunate position, and in all fairness we must sympathise with Church leaders who face this problem. Naturally they wish to preach to the biggest possible congregation, even if they suspect that a large number of the congregation are not genuine worshippers. Secretly, some of the clergy may be temporarily satisfied with this state of affairs. Surely there isn't much point in preaching Christianity to the converted? It is the sinners, the hypocrites and cynics, the unbelievers and half-believers who are most in need of the Church's message. Even if they attend Church for the wrong reasons, once they are there, they can be helped to see the Light.

### Where are Young Worshippers?

In many churches to-day, we notice that the majority of the congregation consists of middle-aged and elderly women, with a sprinkling of men in the same age-groups. Again, we may wonder at the reasons for this. Are these old stalwarts the only remaining "die-hards", the last surviving genuine Christians in a nation of irreligious sceptics and materialists? Or are we to take an even gloomier view and believe that even many of the "remaining few" still go to church chiefly because they may cling to "old-fashioned" ideas, or because they may be lonely and perhaps have no TV set? If this is true, what will happen to the Christian Church as death whittles away at its ageing congregations? This indeed would be a frightening prospect, not only for the Church itself and all who serve it faithfully, but for our much-vaunted civilisation.

For many reasons, some obvious, and some which may be obscure to us, many of the younger generation are not particularly attracted towards religion. Few of them are regular church-goers. Years ago children had to go to Sunday School and to Church and didn't even question the practice. Once they were within the precincts of the School or Church, the children listened to religious teaching and irrespective of whether they understood it or not they *believed* all they were told. They were considerably influenced by religion, and even if they were often unable to reach the high spiritual and moral standards demanded, they *respected* it.

How very different is the situation to-day! We may blame the parents or modern distractions and spurious entertainments or the out-dated methods of religious teaching or whatever else we wish. The harsh fact remains that many young people to-day have little respect for the religion that was treasured by their parents. What these young people actually *feel* in their own hearts, only they know.

Perhaps their whole attitude towards religion may be a pose, a veneer.

Some young people do at least *consider* religion and discuss what it has to offer them. The trouble seems to be—so far as the orthodox Church is concerned—that these young people ask too many awkward questions! They can be seen and heard on a Sunday evening TV programme, for instance, discussing religion and morals with Christian ministers. A genuine sympathy must often be felt for the ministers of religion who are the victims of youth's cross-examination. Intelligent and searching questions have threatened to "tie them up in knots" on frequent occasions, and some of the answers have been far from convincing.

### Materialism is Futile

These young people who seem to give serious thought to life, challenge, question, and often doubt some of the religious teachings of their childhood. For instance, as one young man was heard to say: "I no longer can believe the words of that old hymn I used to sing as a child, 'There's a home for little children above the bright blue sky', or that God is an awe-inspiring revengeful old man up in heaven as I was taught at Sunday School." Nevertheless many such young people realise how unsatisfactory and futile are the grossly materialistic outlook and philosophy of this age. They seek to find satisfactory answers to their questions and doubts, yearn for true spiritual knowledge and a faith which will satisfy their instinctive longing for some form of worship and religion.

Fifty years ago we used to believe (or profess to believe) the religious dogmas and legends. We accepted all of them, with blind faith, and if religion didn't seem to work for us when we needed it most, we concluded that *we* must have failed somewhere. This may well have been the truth of the matter, of course, and we clung to our faith.

Nowadays, however, most young people will not bother about regular church attendance unless they are first of all convinced, with some intelligence at least, that Christianity is based upon true facts and that ministers of religion can substantiate their claims that church-going is in any way important or desirable.

It is no use regular church-goers shaking their heads in self-righteousness and being so intolerant—as they often are—concerning the views expressed by and the attitude adopted by young people to-day towards church-going. There are many other people besides the younger generation who hold similar views and who do not attend any orthodox Church. Yet the majority of these people lead decent lives and live up to high, ethical standards.

One of the chief problems concerning the Christian religion seems to be that so many people find it difficult to believe many of the Bible stories. They regard some of those stories as pure legend; others they have grave doubts about. Are these people sinners because they doubt? Is it impossible for these numerous doubters to be called Christians simply because they are unable to accept some of the things recorded in the Bible or fail to understand the conflicting statements in the Scriptures? These are the sort of questions raised by the Doubting Thomases who remain outside the Church, and their number has grown rapidly in recent years, for this is the materialist era of sceptics and rebels.

There are no doubt many of the clergy who are seriously worried about the failure of the Church to attract more support than it gets. Yet recently some of the clergy maintained that they were full of confidence that the Church was able to hold its own against all worldly indifference, apathy or adverse criticism.

If the Church is *really* satisfied with the present situation there are many laymen who are not.

Alternatively, if we accept the fact that the power and prestige of the orthodox Church are continuing to decline, we must ask ourselves another important question: *Are the ideals of Christianity itself being widely rejected?* If we thought they were, we should be deeply concerned, for Christianity represents the very foundation of civilised Western society.

Certainly, in recent years, not only Church attendance, but Christian ideals have been sadly neglected or blatantly ignored. One recent Church Moral Welfare Council report condemns wild sex and drink parties held by teenagers in one area. The chairman is reported to have said, "Teenage morals are steadily deteriorating. . . ."

A woman journalist on the same committee wrote an article entitled *Challenge to Parents.* "You are only young once? You have got to have your bit of fun? Is it a bit of fun when you hear a 13-year-old say to a friend: 'We had to send him home in a taxi, he was so drunk'?" "Is it a bit of fun that a large number of 14-year-old girls in this town are pregnant? Or to find youngsters passing round obscene postcards?"

These forthright questions can be answered without any hesitation. A bit of fun? It is downright scandalous and frightening, especially as this unnamed town is not an isolated case. It is only one random example of a lamentable trend.

Do we need religion? It seems that we need it *now* more than ever before! The present situation *is* a challenge to all thinking men and women; a challenge to parents that cannot be ignored. Children reared in a Christian home are less likely to degenerate into the kind of teenagers described above. The orthodox Church has its faults, but it is battling against terrific odds in this day and age. It could be the final "showdown" between Good and Evil. It seems to be an all-out war, with religion and all its forces on one side, and moral

degeneration, violence and apathy on the other. There is nothing wrong
with Christianity. In fact, it seems to be our only hope of survival as
a civilised society. Why, then, does religion not make a greater impact
upon modern life?

### That Book—and that Bomb

Some people criticise the orthodox Church as being too stodgy
and old-fashioned in its *presentation* of Christianity. Another complaint is that generally speaking, the clergy, by virtue of their advanced
education and highly respected social position seem to be far removed
from the "man-in-the-street". Others complain that in matters of
vital importance to mankind, the Church often "sits on the fence"
instead of giving a firm lead. As one individual remarked the other
day: "Here we have high Dignitaries of the Church quarrelling among
themselves, like a lot of spoilt children, as to whether it is right or
wrong to publish a certain book which was the subject of a recent
High Court Case. But the problem of such vital concern to all
humanity of the threat of complete annihilation of civilisation by
nuclear weapons, the Church generally shies away from, or remains
strangely silent or refuses to discuss altogether."

Some of the criticism against the Church which we have mentioned
is not altogether justified, and often comes from those who may be
out of touch with it. For instance, not all clergy stand remote from
the man-in-the-street. There are many ministers, particularly in poor
parishes, who mix freely with the people, try to help them with their
many and various problems and give, ungrudgingly and unselfishly
both time and effort in serving their parishioners in whatever way
presents itself. These clergy really do try and *live* their religion,
working and sacrificing often where the tasks are exceptionally heavy
and the pay usually bad.

In regard to the criticism about the Church "sitting on the fence"
concerning matters of "vital importance to mankind", there are some
clergymen who refuse to sit on the proverbial fence. They speak out
boldly and fearlessly—often to their own detriment—for the welfare
of all humanity and against the things which they consider do not
conform to the ethics of true Christianity.

Obviously the examples we have given do not represent the attitude
or the outlook of the Church as a whole; nevertheless it is gratifying
to know that there are many clergymen against whom much of the
criticism of the Church can neither be substantiated nor justified.

This brings us to the matter of lack of unity within the Church
itself. Whilst it is not to be expected to find complete unity over many
insignificant matters, nevertheless surely the Church should speak
with one authoritative voice concerning such a world-wide dangerous
major issue as nuclear weapons?

### The Need for a United Front

For years, there has been a need not only of unity among the individual religious sects in particular but of unity among the divided Christian Churches generally. But more than ever before in these critical and perilous days, this need has now become more real and extremely urgent. Surely, when the world continues to stagger and stumble from one dangerous crisis to another, with the constant threat of the misuse of nuclear power hanging over all our heads, we cannot afford to allow bitter prejudice to divide the Christian Churches. Without relinquishing their own particular doctrines, the Christian Churches could work together and help to bring to an end present-day world-wide mistrust and tension and bring about a better and more tolerant understanding between all nations.

We need a Religious Mobilisation—a return to religion, greater unity between Churches of all denominations, with church-goers and good-living non-church-goers working together in close harmony for the common good—*if we are to combat effectively the sinister influences of our time and the evil forces that bedevil our modern world.*

# THE VALUE OF SELF-HELP

A LTHOUGH some modern ideas and innovations do not impress us favourably there is one modern trend with which, in the main, we are favourably impressed: the "Do-it-yourself" habit. It may have some disadvantages for a small section of tradespeople, but most of them have long ago readjusted their businesses to meet the common trend. They may receive fewer orders to make, mend and fix things for their customers, but they still supply the raw materials, and even "Do-it-yourself" kits. Some of this new generation of tradespeople even go so far as to offer free and friendly advice on the best way to tackle the job in hand. It is, perhaps, inevitable, that on occasions a "Do-it-yourself" amateur makes an awful mess of the job and has to call upon the local tradesman to come and put things right!

There was, for example, the man who received free advice from a local plumber on how to re-arrange the water supply in the bathroom of his house. He went home and did the work without much trouble and then retired to bed feeling very pleased with himself. During the night he was awakened by an unusual sound. He got out of bed to investigate and stepped right into a pool of cold water that had flowed under his bedroom door from the flooded bathroom.

Another man, bitten by the "Do-it-yourself" bug, spent ten minutes or so watching a plasterer working on the wall of a newly-built house. All the plasterer seemed to do was to hold in his left hand a little board laden with plaster, and then slap the plaster off the board and on to the wall with a trowel. This operation looked so easy that our amateur just couldn't wait to re-plaster a bad wall and part of the ceiling of his kitchen. He knocked out the old, cracked parts as best he could, made a mortar-board, mixed his plaster and set to work on the ceiling. Somehow he couldn't get the knack of scooping that wet plaster off the board. Sometimes the plaster shot over the edge of the little board and on to the floor; sometimes it slid off the trowel before he could slap it on the ceiling. Occasionally a patch of wet plaster dropped from the ceiling while he was trying to pick up the next trowelful. Once or twice all the mixed plaster slid off the board and flopped to the floor while he was trowelling the ceiling. Then his wife appeared—as very often wives do at awkward moments —and complained about the terrible mess in her kitchen. While he was explaining his problems to her, the rest of the mixed plaster set as hard as a rock on the board.

## The Value of the "Other Man"

The unfortunate victims of "Do-it-yourself" are legion. The mishaps they so often encounter provide us with considerable amusement and remind us of the old comedy song "When Father Papered the Parlour". Yet those of us who are observant, and who make a study of humanity, can learn many valuable lessons from these "Do-it-yourself" ventures.

For example, the man who tried and failed to do his plumbing job properly soon discovered where he went wrong, and he isn't likely to make a similar mistake again. The man who tried his hand at plastering for the first time, now realises why good plasterers are able to earn high wages. He now has a healthy respect for plasterers, no matter how messy their overalls may look. The other man's job often looks so easy that any child could do it—*until we try it ourselves*!

There is the "know-how" in every trade born of experience and practice which lead to skill and efficiency. The more adventures we have in our "Do-it-yourself" efforts, the greater is our appreciation and understanding of the *true value* of the "other man" in our society. The labourer is lost without the craftsman; the craftsman would not be able to earn a living but for the advertising men, the sales-staff and the executives, all of whom help to provide enough work for him and for others.

Every person in every profession and trade has to learn his job and "pull his weight" to keep the wheels of industry turning. The curious and old-fashioned ideas of some people concerning the "superiority" or "inferiority" of certain other workers, are fundamentally unsound. We are all dependent on each other and we all need each other for our very existence.

A man engaged in dirty, manual work may sometimes envy the "white collar" fraternity, and the professional man may look out from his office window and envy the fine physique and the sun-tanned bodies of a group of building workers. But none of us can have everything, and where would any one section of workers be without the others? The whole of humanity must live and work as a great team of interdependent individuals, and the sooner this is realised, the better it will be for all of us. Instead of complaining about all that we lack, we should be thankful for all that we *have*. Instead of criticising or despising others, we should feel grateful that many of them help us to obtain what *we* need.

These thoughts come crowding in upon us as we contemplate that other man's job and our relationship with him, following our "Do-it-yourself" experiences.

## Limitations of the Average Man

One of the great advantages of the "Do-it-yourself" enthusiasts is that they learn self-reliance, patience and persistence. Many of us, who may be highly intelligent and skilled in our own specialised daily work, may be almost helpless when called upon to do a comparatively simple job in the home or elsewhere.

It is rather comical that many a man who is capable of directing important business affairs, for example, is unable to renew a tap-washer or trace and repair a broken fuse in the house electrical system. Frustrated wives often have to learn to do these and similar jobs themselves. Not that this is detrimental to the wives concerned. A few of these "Do-it-yourself" home experiments can not only relieve the monotony of ordinary household tasks, but can spare these women the humiliation of being married to a "ham-fisted" husband or the annoyance of having to wait until the "handyman" husband returns home.

Nothing is lost by learning to do something different, useful and expense-saving. In fact there is much that can be gained. Early experiences of "Do-it-yourself" may turn out to be disappointing, but practice develops patience, persistence and skill—all of which are well worth cultivating. Of course, caution must be observed, especially when handling electric wiring and other jobs that could be dangerous, but this is simply a matter of common sense. The general principle of "Do-it-yourself," however, remains sound, and it makes life infinitely more interesting and exciting.

Men and women are creative by instinct. Sometimes, for various reasons, it is necessary to employ somebody else to do a job that requires special knowledge and skill—such as television maintenance or piano-tuning. There is, however, nothing more deeply satisfying than to create something by our own efforts. What it is we create doesn't matter very much. What is important to us is the fact that we have done it ourselves. We then regard our creation with the healthy pride of achievement.

Anybody can go to a shop and buy an article, or pay somebody else to make or repair something, but the personal satisfaction is very limited. The woman who knits a garment, or cuts out and makes a dress satis-factorily, gets far more personal satisfaction than by merely buying those garments from a shop. Even when there are slight faults in the self-made article, these do not rob the "creator" of the joy of her creation. She will do better next time, having learned from her previous experience.

The man who can service his own car and do running repairs, always has the advantage over the motorist who can only drive. Not only does the former person reduce his motoring costs considerably, but he is less likely to be stranded for long if his car breaks down through some minor fault. The man who tends his own garden and perhaps even builds his own greenhouse, receives far more satisfaction during his leisure hours than the individual who employs a gardener. In fact, in the latter case, the gardener probably derives more pleasure out of the garden than the man who owns it!

L.C.—6

We have so far illustrated that the "Do-it-yourself" man or woman acquires fresh skills, learns patience, develops the habit of persistence, accepts disappointment philosophically, and gets more fun out of life. He or she is also able to respect the accomplishments of others more easily and to recognise their true value to the community. The "Do-it-yourself" person soon realises how much we depend upon each other for our livelihood and existence, and that the menial worker fills a very important place in our society. He should not be regarded—or regard himself—as "inferior" to his fellows.

Among other points, the "Do-it-yourself" individual who learns from his mistakes, saves money in the long run. Above all he experiences the thrill of *creating* much of what he needs. He knows the pride of achievement, and the satisfaction of a greater degree of self-reliance and independence.

### Acquire Self-mastery

Up to this point we have examined the advantages of "Do-it-yourself" chiefly in respect of one's increased usefulness as a "handy-man". In passing, we have merely touched upon the psychological aspects of the "Do-it-yourself" habit: satisfying the creative instinct; realising the value of others and their accomplishments. But we can go much deeper than this.

The "Do-it-yourself" principle can be helpful in the mental and psychological spheres as well as in the material sense. Doctors can treat mental stress and emotional disturbances; psychiatrists can probe successfully into the patient's past history to reveal the causes of many psychological disturbances and offer specialised treatment; ministers of religion can provide spiritual guidance, comfort and advice, but we must also learn how to acquire *self-mastery*. For the control and mastery of the forces, emotions, instincts and reactions of life are some of the greater essentials to fuller and more successful living. There is so much we can and must do for ourselves, before we can achieve peace of mind and spiritual progress.

Far too many people these days expect to be nursed, protected and pampered throughout their lives. They imagine that a few bottles of medicine or a few boxes of pills should cure practically every ailment. They will rarely make any real personal effort themselves. When any trouble or defeat comes their way they usually blame somebody else, or "bad luck", circumstances, conditions, hostile environment or some other outside influence. These people never dream of doing some serious heart-searching and self-analysis to try and get to the root of their problems and maybe to discover some of their own faults. "Do-it-yourself," in this sense, simply doesn't occur to them. Yet it could be of tremendous help to them, and bring about many worth-while results.

Examples of the many and varied benefits which can be obtained by self-help, abound in the pages of *Psychology* every month. Let's refresh our memories by studying a few typical instances where the "Do-it yourself" principle should be adopted.

Many thousands of people suffer from self-consciousness and a sense of inferiority. As this weakness shows itself in almost every human activity, the sufferers are very often in a state of panic and misery. Consequently they are usually full of self-pity. They withdraw from human society as much as possible, and life, for them, can become one long nightmare. Nobody knows what these unhappy people endure—except those who have experienced it. Yet, there are many cheerful, self-assured men and women to-day who suffered all the mental tortures of chronic self-consciousness and inferiority in the past. How did they manage to escape from their dreadful plight, to the freedom of full and happy lives? Chiefly by helping themselves. If self-conscious people continue to hide in their self-erected and lonely "prisons" waiting for somebody to come and release them, they will wait until the end of their days. Except by offering good advice, nobody *can* help but themselves. They just have to make up their minds to mix with people, take a genuine interest in others and face unflinchingly their fears of this sense of self-consciousness and inferiority either in their inner consciousness or outer demeanour and learn how to overcome them. How can they do this? They must learn to think and act positively. They must use auto-suggestion —constantly reiterate affirmations that they are growing more confident every day, in every way. They must visualise themselves as being the confident persons they aspire to be and impersonate the part. They must stop wallowing in self-pity, which so often nurses and encourages thoughts of self-consciousness and inferiority. Difficult? Of course it's difficult! Nothing worth while is easy! But if these self-conscious people really do want to overcome their handicap they must do it themselves by using intelligently directed thought, auto-suggestion, visualisation and by persistent, unremitting effort.

### A Self-help Philosophy

Many other persons complain of loneliness. They expect other people to visit them often, to cheer them up. There are kind friends who may do this, but in some instances it is doubtful whether these good-intentioned friends are really helping the sufferer or merely pandering to his or her self-pity and martyrdom. Lonely persons who aren't senile or invalid, should get out and about to meet others and do little services for them. They should join suitable organisations and take more interest in life generally. Usually, these lonely people sit at home, get despondent and when neighbours *do* visit them, all they get for their trouble is a long tale of woe. Naturally, these luckless visitors soon tire of calling, and the lonely souls are fated to remain alone, oblivious of the fact that they could do a lot to help themselves.

Often we hear people complaining about their job and the unpleasant conditions it entails. Sometimes these people go on grumbling for years, but what do they *do* about it all? Nothing! They have not the courage to change their employment or to work or study to qualify for better jobs, or do their part towards improving the existing conditions. "Do-it-yourself" is a good motto when we recognise faults which should be corrected. Far too many people to-day are content to leave everything to the energetic and conscientious minority to perform. Of course, the "leave-it-to-others" brigade are ready enough to accept their share of any benefits which may be won by the efforts of others.

Enough examples have been given in this short Chat to indicate the moral and material values of the "Do-it-yourself" principle. This wholesome self-help philosophy, with its conscientious endeavour and persistent effort, not only brings an unfailing sense of satisfaction but it also builds confidence, character, personality and mental alertness.

# MAKING THE MOST OF LIFE

*What Man can dream of, that can he also accomplish. For dreams*
*are the architect's plan of Man's life work. The mind that has*
*envisaged the structure can also supply the material and the reality.*

*There is practically nothing that Man cannot accomplish or achieve*
*if he sets his heart upon it. But he must be in earnest. He must get*
*on with the job. He must not sigh in vain for immediate accomplish-*
*ment and spend the hours when he should be at work in longing for*
*journey's end.*

*Man can find much happiness—and fulfilment too—in the day-to-day*
*task of making his dream come true.*

*Disillusion, disappointment and despair attack only those who lay*
*down their tools before the whistle blows.*

\*     \*     \*

THIS is a grumbling age, an age of dissatisfaction, of grousing, of
sighing for the ideal existence and of failure to face reality. It is
an age of fault-finding, of carping, destructive criticism, an age when
everything is out of tune, an age befogged by the despairing clouds of
pessimism. And that alone accounts for a very large share of our
unhappiness and maladjustments. It would be true to say that we do
not grouse because we are unhappy; *we are miserable because we
grumble*! Half the population of the globe look back nostalgically
to the fictitious peace and security of an age that has gone—never to
return. Most of the other half look forward wistfully to an age that
is yet to come. Few, lamentably few, take joy in the present, accepting
with courage the difficulties that every age has inflicted upon humanity,
yet treasuring the advantages, the simple joys of ordinary existence
that are still available to Man.

Whatever the trials of existence, personal or social, there is still
laughter in the world, there is still the heart-warming companionship
of friends, there is still Nature in all her glory, there are still the balm
of sleep and the inspiration of solitude. However low-lying the clouds
may be, there is still a ray of sunshine to lighten the darkness. Far
be it from us to pronounce that "All's well with the world", but we
can say that all can be well—for us—if we become determined to live
the richer life.

And so, paradoxical though it may seem, *Psychology* propounds
the virtue of contentment! *Psychology* asserts that we should count
our blessings and be happy in our present state.

"What!" some readers may exclaim, "the Magazine that has
consistently preached that men and women should strive to better

themselves, to climb the steep slopes of splendid endeavour, to transform their environment and their lives—*Psychology* to tell us now that we are to be content with things as they are!"

But there is no real contradiction here. We are not arguing against wholesome ambition. We are not preaching a gospel of inaction. We have no eulogy for indolence. But what is being suggested is a form of *intelligent* contentment. Not the variety that results in a cowardly resignation to the will of Fate, a pitiful surrender to the caprice of Destiny, an easy acceptance of the poisonous doctrine of Fatalism. We are not urging that all of us should be content with our lot and never strive to change it. But what we do suggest is that we would do well to be content—and be as happy as possible—in our present circumstances, to find as much happiness as we can under present conditions, until our endeavours have succeeded in placing us in a higher niche of successful living. We are advocating the contentment that comes from an intelligent summing up of one's potential—in health, in ability, in *opportunity*—PLUS a determination to make the most of things until our endeavours have borne fruit.

To put it in a nutshell, we will assume that a person is determined to double his salary. Wouldn't it be foolish for him to be miserable while in the process of so doing?

There are but few people so placed that they cannot extract some enjoyment from existence. Let them make the most of life, savour its joy and happiness to the full whilst yet aspiring to the higher goal.

### The Divine Restlessness

*Psychology* has always encouraged the divine discontent, that inner restlessness and dissatisfaction that spurs men and women on to sustained endeavour. This is the very mainspring of personal life; it is the driving force of evolution. But the discontent of to-day is not divine—it is a childish longing for the moon, an immature fascination with every novelty, a spineless "spoilt-child" attitude to reality that expends more energy in grousing at circumstance than would be necessary to surmount the evils grumbled at.

The discontent of to-day is not the inner restlessness that urges the explorer to discover new lands; it is the petty irritable grousing of the invalid; it proclaims the sick mind, it is a symptom of dissatisfaction not with circumstance, but with the self. The discontent we need warning against, is not the spur to endeavour, but the sign-post to despair.

We should mark well the difference!

Let us personalise things to make it quite clear why we advocate that we should be both contented with our lot and yet discontented with our fortune.

Take the case of Mr. A. He is a typical example of the discontented man—the frustrated man—the unhappy man. The circumstances of his life are easy to enumerate. He is a professional man, in fairly good circumstances. He own his own home, possesses a car, has a family and is not unduly worried by matters of health, finance or social position. Yet his life is befogged by clouds of grumbling. His conversation proclaims his dissatisfaction with world affairs, with national affairs, with the morals of the country and the financial state of the realm; with the decadence of modern youth and with the futility of life in general. He looks out upon the world and sees nothing in which to find joy.

Is he happy? Of course not! He looks with a jaundiced eye upon everything and sours existence because of his inner disharmony. Yet, surely he has a number of things in which he could find some joy and happiness.

Granted that the world outlook is as black as he imagines it to be; even so, calamity has not yet overtaken humanity.

He could still enjoy the beauties of Nature—the purple and golden dawn, crimson sunsets, the majestic glory of rugged mountains, the blue-green expanse of endless, unfathomed seas, sweet songs of the birds, exquisite flowers of never-ending variety of form, colour and fragrance. He could find pleasure in his personal relationships and happiness in his family and home.

But his discontent is a blindness that cuts off any contact with the beautiful; it is a drug-induced lethargy that makes him unresponsive to life. It is a discontent that is akin to damnation.

### Accepting Reality

Mr. B is the other type. He is not very well off, he has no security in his work, was disabled in the war and his health is not all it might be.

Yet he is cheerful and of good heart.

He has not the money nor the social position of Mr. A, but he is determined to secure them, despite the handicap of a war wound and the disadvantages of lack of social opportunities.

Is he content? "Things might be much worse," he replies with a grin.

Is he happy? "I've no time to be unhappy," he answers.

He is content in so far as he accepts all his present difficulties, yet extracts the maximum enjoyment out of life despite of them. He is urged on by an inner unrest to better his position. To that extent he is discontented with life as it is, but is fully determined to scale the peaks of achievement.

Need we labour the point? Need more be said of the sensible, constructive creative attitude to life?

Mr. B is a man who has bravely accepted reality, who knows that he can, by endeavour, transform his lot, but who is not willing to cease living just because conditions, at the moment, are not ideal. He has the balanced personality which accepts facts and uses them to build the future.  If, for instance, he has planned to go out on a picnic and a wet day makes it impossible, he cheerfully accepts this minor set-back and settles down at home to enjoy a good book or to catch up with his "odd jobs".  It is a trite but true saying that it is no use crying over spilt milk.  Far better to accept the accident, live on water that day and make sure we take more care to-morrow.

This is a philosophy that our age seems to find singularly difficult to practise.  People tend to sulk and be miserable if things don't quite turn out right; to be upset by petty disappointments and to transform minor irritations into major calamities.

Far better to cultivate the ability to smile ruefully when things go wrong, to make new plans to conform with the changed circumstances and refuse to allow petty upsets to disturb our mental equilibrium.

There's the man whose day has been ruined because he broke his shoe-lace at breakfast-time; the woman reduced to abject misery because the morning milk boiled over.  Nor do we need to seek far for examples of men and women whose days are made wretched by similar irritations.

It is not a healthy state of mind and needs to be mastered.  It impairs efficiency, spoils the joy of living and beclouds the glory of life with the fog of petty annoyances.

Let us cultivate a sense of proportion; learn to accept the disappointments; learn to laugh despite them.

### Day-to-day Moods

We should never forget that the world reflects our inner state! Readers already know that "As a man thinketh—so is he."  It is equally true that as a man feeleth, so he finds the world around him.

If he is glum, moody, irritable, pessimistic, he will find plenty in the world around him, in his personal relationships, to disconcert him and to justify his mood.  If he is cheerful, active, optimistic, he finds the world reflects his positiveness and amid all the trials and troubles of the day has much to afford him joy, hope and inspiration.

Just let us keep an eye on ourselves to see how true this is.

There may be days when we are burdened with a load of unhappiness; our hearts are heavy, we are weighed down by personal problems and afflicted with more than our share of troubles.  Our mood is one of black pessimism and we set out upon our daily tasks with a jaundiced eye and an oppressed heart.  And we find that everything goes wrong; our fellow-workers seem difficult; our day appears to be full of petty upsets.  We return home to find but little cheer; we may seek escape in the cinema or at the club but derive little to console us. We remain sad and dispirited until sleep draws a merciful veil over our wretchedness.

And yet, a day or two after, we get up in the morning feeling good in ourselves. Our problems remain, but they do not seem so formidable. We set out to work with a smile upon our lips and a little song in our hearts. And strangely, the world around us seems transformed. Our associates at work appear to be more helpful and cheerful. We get through our tasks with ease and are buoyed up with a sense of achievement. We return home to find laughter and happiness in the family circle.

Our circumstances have not changed; but *we have*! We should always remember our moods affect our outlook on life. The destructive, grumbling pessimistic moods put blinkers on us. They distort reality. It is only when we face life with good cheer, that we see our problems clearly and have the heart and courage to get on with the job of living successfully.

When we look upon the world of to-day, we find much of its misery is self-induced and reflects the inner disharmony of individuals. This may appertain to our own personal lives and cause much of the unhappiness and frustration that we bear as a result of our attitude to life. We become grumblers when we should be cheerful "triers".

This is not the easy philosophy that "All's well with the world". We must not minimise our social, international or our own personal problems. They actually do exist. And they can frighten us at times. There are tremendous difficulties still to be surmounted.

Yet, in spite of all these problems, we should not take life *too* seriously. We should not exhaust ourselves in the unfruitful task of trying to change life but instead we should aim to accept it. Let us think of life as a great adventure. Even our most appalling defeats can add to the interest and colour of an adventurous life. The man and woman who never risk anything will never know the anguish of defeat, but they will also never know the joy of victory, the challenging tumult of struggle, the strengthening discipline of reverses accepted as mere incidents in life's unfolding drama and used as stepping-stones to ultimate triumph.

# WHAT'S *YOUR* LINE?

*Develop your talents to the full—*
*and then work with zest!*

\*   \*   \*

TELEVISION has popularised the feature entitled "What's My Line?" where a group of people guess the occupation of a stranger from the very minimum of clues. The feature is for amusement only, although, in passing, I might mention that it provides good examples of extra-sensory perception. The "guess-work" is so good at times that it is reasonable to suppose it has a basis in some form of telepathy.

But we are not so much concerned here with the entertainment as such but with its title. For the title offers a valuable clue to the fuller life.

What's *Your* Line?

A very pertinent question. For if you knew your "line", if you were fully aware of your own potentialities, you probably would be well on the way to more successful living.

What's *your* line? The line that you should follow in your occupation, in your social life, in the family circle, the "line" that will allow you to make the most of yourself? How can you make the most of your abilities, of your temperament, of all the gifts you have rolled up in that entity which is known as your personality? How best can you bring those gifts to rich fruition, making the most of yourself, and a success of life?

What's *your* line? It is a question well worth pondering. Not all of us are blessed with the same characteristics, temperament or abilities, but all of us have some quality, some talent that can enrich our communities and re-invigorate our own personal lives. Do you know yourself well enough to assess these qualities you possess and make the most of them? That is the problem that the question poses. What's your line? Answer that and you will be ready for the richer life.

What's *your* line? Should your role be one of success in politics, in the arts, in science, or in business or profession; or do your inclinations suggest that you would find happiness in the *cool, sequestered vale of life,* find fulfilment in a smaller arena, in family life, in being of service to the local community? Only you can answer the question. But you may be sure of this: whatever your predominant desire, whether for wealth, fame, fortune or success in some particular activity—*this you can achieve* if you are serious about it, if you are prepared to bring into play all the resources of mind, all the creative genius of your Subconscious Mind.

The failures of life usually are not those who lack ability, but those who lack application. Those who have striven hard, yet failed more often than not, have failed because they did not bring into play all the resources they possessed, did not assess their personal qualities accurately nor make use of the *creative* powers of the mind.

The greater part of unhappy human beings are unhappy because they have made no move to live successfully. They sit aside wishing and waiting for life to come up to them. They sigh and are full of self-pity, whilst all the time life passes by on the highway, and yet all they need is to be up and doing and become part of it.

### Start Now

What's *your* line? Each one of us should try and answer that question to-day; try to make up our minds just what we wish to be, and set out upon the task, in however humble a fashion right now.

Let us give an example.

Suppose a young man wishes to become successful in the business sphere, but as yet he is only a humble clerk, earning the minimum salary, and as far as he can see, with very little prospect of advancement in either salary or status.

What can he do about it? He can start at once to fit himself for the greater responsibilities when they come along. He can commence, here and now, to be really efficient at his job, to be more conversant with it than even his superiors, to know from A to Z the business in which he is engaged. He can begin to train himself in what we could term "business habits", to teach himself to think logically, to act wisely, to train his personality, in fact, so that it approximates the personality of a successful business man.

"But the goal is so far off," the young man might say. Possibly, possibly not. It is amazing what changes take place in a person's environment when he takes himself in hand.

The trouble with the majority of us is that we see too vividly the discrepancy between what we are and what we wish to become, and are daunted at the change that is necessary in ourselves and in our fortune. We forget that small changes—small changes over a period—can often transform the situation.

As another illustration, suppose a man sets out to walk five miles. If he strides out, keeps on striding, enjoying the scenery and taking pleasure in the walk—the five miles are soon done. But if he were to calculate the effort necessary to lift one foot off the ground, place it forward, then bring up the other foot and place that forward, and calculate that he would need to do that about six thousand times before he had accomplished his objective—don't you think that the task would daunt him?

Again, suppose a man sets out to paint a room. He makes a few strokes with the brush and then compares the small portion completed with the vast expanse yet to be done. Obviously he would become dispirited and discouraged.

There is only one way to tackle such a job—*KEEP AT IT.* The results that come from the right application to a given task would surprise most of us, and we would find that it does not take as long as we had at first imagined.

Let us apply this lesson to the case of the young man we have previously discussed. He is discouraged by the tremendous difference between his present status and the ideal at which he aims. But the discrepancy is great only to the pessimistic eye. Were he to follow the rough plan we have outlined, set about the task of making himself ready for the greater responsibilities he wishes to assume, the discrepancy that daunts him would dwindle rapidly.

Most of our dreams can be realised quicker than we imagine if we stop wishing and waiting and start to work.

### Human Types

"All this is very elementary," some may say, "and I don't see a very close connection with the question, 'What's my line?'"

Elementary truths are usually those that are ignored and the connection of the foregoing with the question at the head of this Chat is closer than many people think.

"What's *your* line?" Has each one of us ever bothered to find out? Are the special talents inherent in each individual suitable to make a success in, say, business or profession, in social or domestic affairs? For whilst the line of *least resistance* is something often frowned upon by some philosophers, as indicating something of a lack of moral fibre, Practical Psychology extols its wisdom in certain instances.

We have already said that what we wish strongly enough to become —that we can accomplish. Demosthenes himself has proved that a person with a stutter can become the world's greatest orator. And the individual who dislikes figures can become a brilliant mathematician. But the point which we should remember is that—if we strive to accomplish something of this nature—something out of accord with our natural (conscious) gifts—then we will have a much more difficult task than if we were to seek success in a field more congenial to our natural abilities.

Men and women who are passionately fond of music will find success in that field more easily than if they were to seek achievement in, say, the business world. People who enjoy company, who are excellent mixers, will find success more readily in a field offering scope to their bent, than in a field where solitude is the main keystone of achievement.

What's *your* line? Each one of us would do well to find the field of endeavour best suited to our natural aptitude.

When we discover this, we find the easier path—the line of least resistance—to achievement and success.

At the same time we should not forget that the mind can work miracles. It can fit us for success in a field that seems an impossible one; the mind can *create* the qualities necessary for achievement.

First of all, we should decide definitely what we want to accomplish. Secondly, we should make the maximum use of our natural abilities to achieve that end, choosing the easier path if such a choice is advisable, but secure in the knowledge that we can accomplish what we set out to do, if we make use of the magic of the mind.

### Self-Analysis

Modern thought tends to depreciate self-analysis, to call it morbid and to dwell upon its ill effects. It is unwise, it is suggested, to be for ever examining oneself, to be perpetually turning the gaze inward. Rather we should forget ourselves and look outward, so modern philosophy asserts.

Psychology agrees with this in part, but in part only. Psychology asserts that ignorance of ourselves is very often responsible for failure and folly, frustration and lack of fulfilment.

We should have a periodic examination of ourselves—*not morbidly because we can find nothing better to do*, but dispassionately as a scientist would examine life under his microscope. It pays to get to know ourselves—for the purpose of improving ourselves, correcting our weaknesses and buttressing our strength.

"Know thyself," but we should not forget to put the knowledge to some good use. The evils of self-examination do not arise out of the examination itself but out of a failure to take action afterwards.

The person who is continually looking inward upon his weaknesses, brooding over them, would be better off looking elsewhere than into his own personality.

Such a person is like someone with a festering sore, prodding it, doing anything except taking the obvious step of having it treated.

We should look at ourselves—as previously suggested—as a doctor would look at our bodies, and be ready to take appropriate steps when the examination is over. That is the secret of healthy self-analysis.

We have already indicated earlier in our Chat that we would do well to find out our natural bent. This is self-examination on the plane of our Conscious Mind, the seat of our intellectual assets. And, for those who are determined to find out the best—and the worst— about themselves, this examination is not very difficult.

But self-examination does not end there. It has scratched only the surface of that being in each individual called "YOU". It has not dealt with the instincts, with our inherited characteristics, with the more deeply-rooted traits of character and temperament. These have their roots in the Unconscious Mind.

A simple way of illustrating the different phases of the Mind is to compare them with a business organisation manufacturing a certain commodity.

On the top floor are the clerks, salesmen, accountants and so on. Their activities are concerned with disposing of the product and keeping the books and records. On the floor beneath we find the production unit, the people who actually *make* the product. They provide the matter, the *energy* that keeps the people on the top floor busy. So it is with the Mind.

The Conscious harbours the faculties we use in our ordinary lives, but the energy of our being comes from the primeval instincts which have their roots in the Unconscious.

An examination of the Unconscious is not as straightforward a matter as that of the Conscious Mind. We're dealing with forces which we find difficult to name or to define. A study of the Unconscious deserves a special article, and a subsequent Chat will deal with this topic. From time to time there have been in *Psychology* other articles which have dealt with this matter, so regular readers will have some knowledge of the method of self-examination on this plane.

Nevertheless, let us again stress the fact that the Unconscious Mind is the Power-House of our being. It provides the energy so that our conscious faculties can operate. It follows that any conflict below the level of Consciousness will lead to a reduction in the flow of this energy, and will make us listless, tired and depressed. It is in this part of the Mind that the "nervous breakdown" is born.

Those men and women who are normally happy, with the normal quantum of zest and desire to live, can leave the Unconscious Mind to perform its functions adequately without any help from their Conscious Mind.

But those people who are irritable, easily tired, and often depressed will find the root of their trouble in the Unconscious Mind.

Let us take the case of a young married woman who was in an acute state of depression, fed-up with life and irritable, so that her condition had brought on a crisis in her relations with her husband. He became so tired of her "nagging", fault-finding and moods of depression that a break was threatened in their marriage.

Young Mrs. X had been to her doctor, who diagnosed no physical ill to account for her state. He prescribed a tonic, a rest, a short holiday and a change of scenery. She went away for a break—in hope—but returned in despair. She consulted a psychiatrist to see if he could provide a remedy.

Without detailing her case in full, examination soon provided the clue to her unrest. *It was simply that she had not enough to do.* The task of looking after her husband in a home which was provided with all the labour-saving devices imaginable was one that did not use half of her energies.

Mrs. X had no friends, only casual acquaintances. She had no children; she envied her husband his "interesting" way of life, without putting the envy into words. She was unfulfilled. Life had no purpose. The energy that Nature intended for running a home, looking after the family, leading a useful social life, was turned inwards unused and thus it soured her whole life.

This case has been simplified as much as possible, in order to emphasise that what was wrong with Mrs. X was partly the frustration of her maternal instinct and partly the fact that her energies were running to waste. But the point to note is this. We must recognise that once these unconscious conflicts are brought out into the open, the cure usually is effected. We have to understand in order to be free. It is when these conflicts and upsets take place unconsciously that they have power to harm us; bring them to the light of day and they are resolved.

The treatment given in the case of Mrs. X may be compared with a surgical operation. Analysis probed and reached the centre of the trouble and removed it.


### Mental Images

There is another psychological method that may be used. It is that of releasing the creative, curative forces of Mind so that the trouble is removed. We have already referred to the two upper structures of the Mind, the sales office where the clerks, accountants, and salesmen work (the Conscious Mind) and the power and production side (the Unconscious Mind).

The third portion is the Subconscious. This is the Managing Director's domain. It is here that the policy is laid down, that the over-all plan is formed. And there we must desert our analogy. For the Subconscious Mind is also a vital, creative force.

As we have seen, psychological maladjustments take place in the Unconscious Mind. One way of settling these mental "disputes" is to send someone down to this phase of Mind, as it were, from the Conscious Mind to see what is wrong. The other means is to ask the Managing Director, the Subconscious Mind, to exert his healing, creative influence. We can do this by implanting upon the Subconscious Mind the *idea* of being well, successful and happy. Then we should form a vivid mental picture of ourselves *as we wish to be*—free of frustrations, upsets and disappointments, the happy confident individual that we aspire to be.

We should keep this image with us all the time. We should not allow trivial upsets of the day to mar the picture. Let us think of it during our free moments throughout the day. If possible, it is advisable to lie down, to close our eyes, entirely relax the body and clear every thought out of the Mind except the one specific thought. Then just before we fall asleep at night we should hold the picture steadily in front of our Mind and recall it consciousness on waking in the morning.

What we are doing is to give instructions to the Subconscious Mind to make us become like the picture.

The law of the Subconscious Mind is suggestion and it is according to this that it acts. The Subconscious Mind does not think, reason, balance, judge or reject. *It simply accepts the suggestions handed down to it, irrespective of whether they are good or evil, constructive or destructive.* Therefore we should crowd our Subconscious with positive suggestions, mighty affirmations and dominant impulses.

The Conscious Mind *thinks*; the Unconscious Mind *feels*; the Subconscious Mind *creates*. And the creative resources of the Subconscious are released whenever a vivid enough impression is made upon it.

So let us visualise what we want to become; draw up that image of the happy and fulfilled personality we wish to achieve and live with the image day after day.

Then let us start at once to realise that splendid vision; impersonate the part, seriously, earnestly and confidently, and gradually we will become identified with it.

Let us avoid negatives; refuse to repress—let all our thoughts, words and actions be positive and constructive. And finally, "Whatsoever things are true, honest, just, pure, lovely, of good report—think on these things."

# DESIRE VERSUS DUTY

EVERYBODY has experienced at some time or another, upon waking up, that "Monday morning" feeling. The bed is warm and comfortable. Through the window the outside world looks cold, gloomy and uninviting. It is time to get up and prepare for work. *Work*—becomes a depressing thought, especially after a pleasant, carefree week-end.

What is the reason for this fit of depression? Probably a number of factors are jointly responsible. The dreary months of winter have perhaps undermined our health and spirits to some extent. Possibly there are some tricky problems waiting to be settled at business, or family responsibilities are weighing heavily upon us.

Let us try to analyse the situation. In simple terms, our temporary depression is caused by a mental-emotional conflict between desire and duty. Duty calls us to be up and doing, while desire tempts us to remain in that cosy bed until we feel like getting up.

What is the result of this inner conflict? In the example we have mentioned our sense of duty gains the victory. The civilised environment in which we live brings extreme pressure to bear upon us. Much as we may desire to lie in bed for as long as it suits us, there is a nagging realisation that we dare not indulge in such luxury. We must have money to provide the *necessities* of modern life—not to mention the little luxuries we now regard as necessities. To earn money we must work, and in order to work we must get up. So with considerable reluctance, up we get. Duty wins an initial victory.

Duty has defeated desire through the force of circumstances. But what has happened to our very human and understandable desire? This is an important question, and when we attempt to answer it we discover that our desire hasn't vanished. It has merely been pushed down out of sight for a while. There it is, bubbling to express itself again at the slightest opportunity.

There is a very good reason for this. Desire is creative. This world and the whole universe exist because of the *desire* of the Creator. Civilisation, as we know it, has developed through the ages from primitive existence because Man *desired* to develop in this direction. And our present desires will determine the future of mankind.

Now we are really getting near to the crux of the matter. How could we live at all without desire? The human body requires air, water and food, to maintain its existence. Therefore we *desire* to breathe, drink and eat. These are instinctive desires for our self-preservation, which is itself a fundamental desire. When we desire food, we don't just sit and think about food, we find some way of getting it, to gratify our hunger. Normally, this is a fairly simple procedure. We buy our food from the shops and prepare the meal.

Suppose, however, we were shipwrecked and washed up on an uninhabited island? Our desire for food and drink would in no way be diminished. Our natural desire to live would drive us to *think*— where can I find something to eat? Our wits would become sharpened as our thirst and hunger grew keener. Our ingenuity would be tested to the utmost. Somewhere, somehow, we would find something to eat and drink.

So it is, that desire encourages the acquisition of knowledge and wisdom. It is the creative force behind evolution.

### Jangling Disharmonies and Conflicts

What can we discover about Duty? Observation of the simple example of that "Monday morning" feeling indicates that there is often a conflict between desire and duty, and this can lead to considerable mental and emotional distress.

Take the case of a good woman, who is married to a rogue of a husband. She may well desire to leave him and escape all the anxiety and misery his behaviour loads upon her. Then she remembers her marriage vows by which she promised to remain faithful to him "for better or worse". She may also have children to consider. Here is a dreadful conflict between desire and duty. It is even difficult to decide what her duty *is* in such circumstances. Duty to whom and what?

According to the marriage vows, it appears that she has a duty to remain tied to her despicable husband. On the other hand, is she doing her duty to her children by risking their moral contamination under the influence of such a father? Then what about her duty to *herself*? Is she being fair to herself by remaining faithful and tied to an objectionable marriage partner? In this fairly common dilemma religious principles and beliefs must be taken into account.

Sometimes we are confronted with a conflict between desire and duty quite unexpectedly. A case comes to my mind concerning a salesman employed by a well-known company. Mr. R was a conscientious and perfectly honest young man, and he was particularly friendly with a senior salesman on the staff to whom he was indebted for his training. There came a day when the senior salesman died suddenly, and young Mr. R was particularly upset by this tragedy.

A few days after the funeral Mr. R received an urgent request from the late senior salesman's widow inviting him to call at her home. When he arrived, she explained, with obvious embarrassment, that a quantity of the firm's goods was stowed away in an upstairs cupboard.

The senior salesman had not stolen this property. He had bought it himself, temporarily, and made out fictitious sales slips in order to win a coveted prize from his firm in a special sales competition among the sales staff. His widow now begged Mr. R to re-sell the goods for her, as she badly needed the money.

What a predicament for Mr. R. He felt that his duty to his employers was to report what had been going on. If he did this, however, he would be exposing his old friend as a cheat, and undermining the respect of his colleagues for the senior salesman who had competed *unfairly* against them in the sales competition.

The widow was in need of the money tied up in unwanted stock, and sentiment prompted Mr. R to help her out by disposing of it to his own customers. Yet if he did this good turn he would be seriously depleting his own turnover for a period and so risking the displeasure of his employers.

In this case, duty and desire fought to pull the unfortunate Mr. R in several directions at once. He *desired* to spare the good name of his former friend and colleague and to help his widow. Yet he was reluctant to jeopardise his own sales record by trying to dispose of stock that had already been "sold" so far as his Company was concerned.

Early consideration of this problem led Mr. R to believe that his predominent *desire* was on the side of his deceased friend and the widow, whilst his duty to himself, his firm and his other colleagues lay on the other side of the balance.

Further consideration convinced Mr. R that even his *desire* was divided, for he was conscientious enough to desire to do his duty to his employer and himself, as well as to shield his old friend and help the widow. He could not do *both*, that was quite clear.

In the end friendship and sentiment won him over. He resold the "white elephant" stock, and survived the "rocket" he got from his company because his apparent sales had slumped so very badly that particular month.

## Conscience and Judgment

This eternal problem of desire versus duty, and the conflicting loyalties it so often involves, is a nightmare to many of us at times throughout our lives.

In many cases no fixed rule of conduct can be laid down. It is an individual, personal matter of conscience and judgment.

In the case of Mr. R, many of us might regard him as a fool for jeopardising himself to protect his friend's good name, and to aid the embarrassed widow. Others may admire Mr. R for his "noble" act of friendship. Some may accuse Mr. R of being as deceitful as his former friend, by "covering up" his dishonest actions.

Who is qualified to judge Mr. R's final decision? He did what he considered to be right by his own moral standards.

"All duties are matters of conscience," says a philosopher, "with this restriction, that a superior obligation suspends the force of an inferior one."

If we accept this as being true, we are left with the responsibility of using our own judgment as to *where* our duty lies in any given circumstance. Yet whilst the responsibility is ours alone, we cannot expect to be right every time. But if we do what we honestly *believe* to be our duty, then at least our conscience will be clear, even if we do find, later on, that we have made a mistake. If we act *against* our conception of duty, then we can expect a guilty conscience to give us some sleepless nights. The choice is ours alone.

There are occasions when the direction of our duty is clear-cut and unmistakable. When our desire lies in the same direction it is easy for us to decide what to do. Even if desire pulls us the opposite way, our conscience tells us where duty lies. Decision becomes more difficult when duty is divided and loyalties are strained. Then we stand alone, to tackle the difficult problem of judging *which* duty should take priority.

Perhaps the greatest danger we are likely to face in this matter of duty is when we allow sentiment to dictate our loyalties. If we are too soft-hearted and sentimental, it is easy for us to feel a sense of duty towards an unworthy person or cause. This *misguided* sense of duty can soon involve us in a lot of trouble.

A religious man will consider that his first duty is to God. A soldier might feel that his first duty is to his commanding officer and the Crown. A wife may feel that her first duty is to her husband— or she may *transfer* her loyalty to her children in certain circumstances. A business man will probably realise that he has a duty to his customers, to his shareholders and to his workpeople. All manner of conflicting loyalties and shades of duty can arise.

## Be True to Ourselves

Is there any way in which we can reconcile these often opposing loyalties, and at the same time guard against the encroachment of pure sentiment? Yes, there is such a way. We can realise that our highest duty is to *ourselves*. Even the religious person will not dispute this, if he realises that by being true to ourselves we are in fact being true to the *God within us*.

Shakespeare put it concisely enough:

> "*To thine own self be true,*
> *And it must follow, as the night the day,*
> *Thou canst not then be false to any man.*"

If we try to live by these words of wisdom, we shall be able to decide where our first duty lies, and our conscience will remain clear.

It only remains now for us to try and settle any possible dispute between duty and *desire*. Certainly our desires are not to be ignored or constantly subjugated and crushed, otherwise we shall stifle all ambition. Desire brings achievement, the glory of conquest, activity that builds, the ambition to do and dare. Desire is a creative force not to be denied. Desire keeps life itself in motion. What, then, can we do when desire reveals itself as the enemy of duty?

There may be a wide divergency of opinion concerning the answer to this most difficult question. Yet having reasoned about the problem so far, we come to the following conclusion. We are the product of our predominant desires. Our thoughts, emotions, volitions and behaviour are largely coloured and determined by our desires.

So this means that we must discipline desires and control them. Properly controlled and directed desires have been the spur to all golden endeavour—racial betterment, service, discovery, fame, adventure, achievement—these have been the impelling motives in all progress, individual and racial.

Likewise, unrestricted and uncontrolled desires have led men and nations to their doom.

This giant desire can lift us to the heights or lure us to the depths. The same mighty force which can raise us to lofty summits can drag us to destruction if not properly controlled and rightly directed.

We should be true to ourselves (the God within us); our desires should harmonise with our sense of duty—otherwise we must change our desires. We must concentrate on these changed desires until they become stronger than any former predominant desires.

We should be guided by our reason and conscience in deciding just where our duty lies. We should do what we honestly believe we ought to do. The word "ought" is the key in deciding between desire and duty. *And the individual who keeps this word foremost in his mind, and visible and revered in his heart, is indeed the individual who is supreme in the citadel of his own conscience and rich with the knowledge that he is true to himself.*

# AMBITION—VIRTUE OR VICE?

WE are living in a period of prosperity. Trade and industry are booming, wages are the highest ever, our roads are choked with an ever-increasing number of motor cars, housewives enjoy the use of ingenious labour-saving devices, the general standard of living is climbing steadily, and we have more and more leisure—and entertainment to fill it. In short, Man's worldly ambitions are being realised with bewildering rapidity.

Is ambition a virtue or a vice? Does it increase our happiness? Are Man's ambitions approaching complete fulfilment? Where are our ambitions leading us? These are some of the questions for discussion in this Chat.

To some extent ambition is inborn in us all. Any normally intelligent child attempts to grasp what is temporarily out of his reach. He tries to perform more and more difficult feats. No matter what he has, he wants something more attractive, while Mother smiles indulgently. Later the child's education is directed towards encouraging and developing his natural ambitions. He is crammed with knowledge so that he may eventually enter the business or professional world well equipped to advance his ambitions still further.

When our young people are launched into the mart of competitive industry or profession, they soon discover that ambition is praised and encouraged by go-ahead employers. The employers themselves are ambitious—to advance business, to expand their interests, to increase their profits and their prestige.

Clearly, ambition is widely regarded as a valuable asset, even a virtue. Surely there could be little or no progress in any direction without the fire of ambition? Ambition drives us on to ever greater heights of achievement. We are *men and women*—not household cats, content to eat, sleep and die of old age without achieving anything.

## Difference of Opinion

What have the world's greatest thinkers said about ambition? Carlyle observed that "No man is born without ambitious worldly desires." Cicero noticed "that men of the greatest and most shining parts are most actuated by ambition". T. D. English saw ambition as "the germ from which all growth of nobleness proceeds".

Yet it is shattering and humiliating to find that the overwhelming majority of great philosophers, ancient and modern, regard ambition as a curse rather than a blessing.

Here are a few of the descriptions given to ambition by these philosophers: Sin—vice—a mounted devil in the heart—unquenchable fire—proud-crested fiend, the world's worse foe—a cheat—idol—lust —a rebel—devouring bird—deadly tyrant—inexorable master—avarice on stilts—torment.

Perhaps Thomas Brooks caps all the above descriptions in these words:

"Ambition is a gilded misery, a secret poison, a hidden plague, the engineer of deceit, the mother of hypocrisy, the parent of envy, the original of vices, the moth of holiness, the blinder of hearts, turning medicines into maladies, and remedies into diseases."

Faced with these contemptuous descriptions of ambition, delivered to us by undoubtedly brilliant minds, we must surely hesitate to accept fully the popular belief that ambition is a virtue. Evidently there is a difference of opinion, even among the wisest of men, but can the majority of them be wrong?

Try to imagine a world *without* ambition. Were it not for Man's ambitious enterprise we should still be living in the Stone Age. In fact it is probable that even our Stone Age ancestors would not have survived at all without ambition. Animal instinct would have compelled them to eat and to reproduce themselves for a few generations, but without ambition to drive them on they would surely have deteriorated and died out. They would have had no incentive to combat their enemies—the wild animals and the elements. The hostile forces of Nature itself—heat, cold, tornado, rain, flood, fire, earthquake, pestilence—would have wiped them out in the end. The instinctive desire for self-preservation is itself an ambition!

## Ambition is Implanted

Therefore, we can agree that Man, since the beginning of his existence, has experienced the compelling drive of ambition. If ambition is the wicked passion that so many of the world's great thinkers would have us believe, we can hardly feel guilty about it; ambition is an inescapable part of our make-up, implanted within us by the Creator. How else could evolution be maintained?

Ambition is like hunger. It is ruled by its own appetite, and that appetite varies considerably in every individual. We have heard of figure-conscious office girls who manage to exist all day on a cup of tea and a bun. Others may require their mid-morning biscuits and a substantial midday meal, as well as tea and supper later on. In the same way, some of us are content with the minimum of money, possessions and power, while others have an insatiable passion for achievement, progress, prestige and the luxurious living that riches can buy. Probably most of us hover somewhere between these two extremes.

## Motive and Direction

These thoughts provide us with a pointer to answer our first question. Is ambition a virtue or a vice? It depends upon the force and extent of our ambitions, and in what direction they are driving us.

Napoleon was an ambitious man, and he ended his days in lonely exile. Hitler was insanely ambitious. His ambitions resulted in wholesale murder, world-wide suffering and bereavement—and in his own disgrace and suicide. When we consider extreme examples such as these, we must agree with philosophers who declare in the strongest terms that ambition is one of the greatest curses of mankind.

Yet, *in moderation and healthy direction*, ambition is a very desirable quality. In the business world there are countless examples of ambitious young men who have mastered their trade and built up their own businesses. Now they are providing employment for—perhaps thousands of people; they are producing useful goods; they are increasing not only their own prestige, but the prestige of the nation; they are satisfying their customers. Can ambition be a sin, or even an undesirable feature of these cases? Certainly not!

We can go further and consider the ambition of surgeons, doctors, matrons and nurses to heal the sick; the ambition of religious leaders to uplift our morals, strengthen our faith in God, and to encourage spirituality generally; the ambition of teachers to mould young minds into healthy and knowledgeable channels; the ambition of parents to give their children a better chance in life than they had. How can *anybody* deny that in these and similar examples, ambition is a rich blessing? Aren't the worlds of challenging service, of culture, mental improvement, invention and creative accomplishment dependent upon ambition?

So, as we examine the advantages and disadvantages of ambition, we must conclude that it is quite wrong to generalise. Ambition can be a noble and creative force or it can drag us and others down to the uttermost depths of degradation. Ambition itself is neither good nor evil. It is a peculiar driving power, inherent within us, *which can be used* for good or ill. The result of its influence depends not only upon the extent of its demands within each individual, but upon the motive and direction of our ambition.

When we try to decide whether or not ambition increases our happiness, we are up against another very difficult problem. If an individual is always wanting something just beyond his grasp or aspires to be what he is not logically qualified to be, and frets and worries over these unattainable ambitions and thwarted desires, then he will become nerve-wrecked and disillusioned, restless and unhappy.

Then there is the ambitious person who is avaricious. The more he gets the more he wants. He spends his entire energies on mere accumulation. He finds himself, as it were, on a treadmill. He climbs and climbs but finds the summit of his desires more and more elusive. Ambition can so easily degenerate into sheer avarice; then happiness becomes but a fleeting shadow, and misery lies ahead. This is the real danger foreseen by all the great philosophers who regard ambition as a curse.

The man with very little worldly ambition seems to be *content* with almost the bare necessities of life. He appears to be happy *without* ambition. Yet how many of us could be satisfied with the minimum required to keep us alive? Possibly there are still a few genuine tramps left who have no responsibilities whatever and refuse to accept any. These queer characters are probably happy enough in their own way, but most of us would not relish such idleness. Even if our personal ambition is strictly limited, we are being prodded on all sides to improve our position in life.

Keeping up with the Joneses is a highly popular form of ambition in these days. This is another trap into which many ambitious people fall. The youth graduates from walking to a bicycle, then wants a motor-cycle, then a car, then a bigger and better car. When he marries he wants a television set. His wife wants a vacuum cleaner, a washing machine, a clothes drier—and possibly holidays abroad. It is so easy to obtain all these things—on hire-purchase terms. The *insatiable ambitions* of many families have lumbered them up with hire-purchase commitments beyond all reason. These debts hang heavily upon the people concerned, causing anxiety, nerve strain and general depression. When ambition prompts us to live beyond our means it can never bring happiness.

### Patience and Control

We are not arguing against wholesome ambition. We are not advocating inaction or eulogising indolence. But we do suggest that ambition should be rightly organised, intelligently directed and kept within bounds, otherwise it can rob us of peace of mind and blight our happiness. *Moderation* is the keynote; we should control our patience and allow our ambitions to advance one small step at a time. As Longfellow said: "Most people would succeed in small things if they were not troubled with great ambitions". The over-ambitious person makes the big mistake of wanting too much, too soon. He is certain to be disappointed, or to crash heavily and unexpectedly after straining himself to reach the summit of success in one leap.

Examples from real life are to be found every day. Quite recently there was the case of an astute business man who worked diligently, and from small beginnings built up a highly profitable business *within three years*. His friends were stunned with shock when his body was found in the river. It is very difficult to be keenly ambitious *and* happy. So many other desirable things have to be sacrificed on the altar of ambition.

Every individual has to decide for himself whether the ultimate goal of his ambitions is likely to be worth the personal sacrifices he is making in order to achieve it. In this we stand alone, for only *we* know the cost of our ambitious ventures and whether we are fully prepared to pay for them.

There is no doubt whatever that the happiest ambitious people are those who are genuinely concerned for the good of others rather than for purely selfish interests. It is significant that the ambitious person whose guiding principle is Service before profit, usually builds up his own prestige and material security almost automatically, at the same time. This applies both in business and professional life. The smart business man isn't the mean, cheese-paring money-grabber, but the man whose chief ambitions are to satisfy his customers and to encourage his workers to protect his interests, by giving them fair treatment and adequate rewards.

Similarly, the smart professional man isn't a fee-snatching vulture, but a good-intentioned, friendly adviser to those who require his services.

### Vital Question of To-day

Are we reaching the limit of our worldly ambitions? Compared with even fifty years ago, we are living in El Dorado. Yesterday's luxuries are to-day's accepted necessities. Labourers, domestic workers, shop assistants and clerks are no longer impoverished slaves of little consequence. They have won their rightful places, as respected members of society; important members of the various teams of workers who help to keep the wheels of industry turning. Foreign travel is now within the reach of millions, whose parents could only share, in their imagination, the adventures of their favourite author of travel books. Surely we now have almost everything the heart can desire?

No, generally speaking, Man's worldly ambitions are insatiable. They drive him ever *onward*—though not necessarily upward in the spiritual sense. Even the whole world, with all its untapped resources, isn't enough to satisfy modern Man; he wants the moon and the mysterious planets of outer space.

Where will it all end? This is *the* question of the century, and who dares to predict an answer? All we can say is that just as the highest trees are most vulnerable when lightning strikes, so Man is in greater danger, the higher his worldly ambitions soar.

The phrase *worldly ambitions* has been used by design, for here is the crux of the matter under discussion. We do not see anything wrong with worldly ambitions if they are not permitted to undermine our spiritual obligations. The world was made for Man. It is his temporal home, and without doubt the Creator intended him to explore it and to make use of his discoveries. Unless these wonderful discoveries enable Man to gain a nobler conception of himself and the higher purpose of his existence, however, they are but worthless trinkets. They are of no more value than a chest of gold ingots at the bottom of the sea.

"Man was marked a friend in his creation to himself, and may, with fit ambition, conceive the greatest blessings, and the highest honours appointed for him, if he can achieve them the right and noble way."

Let us remember these words, for they can help us to keep our ambitions wholesome and healthy and our motives exalted and inspired, so that our lives may be filled with spiritual tranquillity and inner peace.

# HABITS, THOUGHTS AND ACTIONS

*"All is habit in mankind, even virtue itself."*

\*   \*   \*

HABIT predominantly conditions the behaviour of men and women. Their daily acts are performed in faithful subservience to habitual grooves.

Character building and a large part of the secret of success are very often hidden in what we call "habit". In the main, all that we amount to comes from the habits we have formed.

The difference in the formation of habits is often due to the difference in the achievements of individuals. The lives of thousands have been retarded and often ruined by negative and harmful habits.

There is no mysterious or secret formula whereby men and women may transform their lives, and achieve life's good things. The only way is the slow and laborious but worth-while method of substituting good, positive habits for those that are wrong and negative.

There are many individuals who complain that success in life does not come to them, that they do not have the "luck" that others seem to have. But it is impossible for them to make the progress they desire as long as they are shackled by habits that retard. So very often what these people call fate is a web of their own weaving—the thoughts and acts that have become habitual.

## The Influence of Habit

Human destiny hinges upon the influence of habit; life can mean either development or retardment in accordance with whether each little habit has been perfectly or carelessly formed. The character of our lives depends upon the nature and the strength of our habits. We become the product of our habits, for after they have been practised long enough they become automatic and imperious. "Habit with its iron sinews clasps and leads us day by day."

Life itself is a series of habits. We can accomplish very little but for the aid of habits, for they make a large part of our activities automatic.

In driving a car we do not have to think when changing gears; in playing the piano we do not plan each movement of the different muscles used. These things are matters of "habit", for they have been practised until they have become automatic. Whatever is learned thoroughly becomes automatic.

Positive, creative individuals become so by regular repetition of positive, creative thoughts and acts until such processes become habitual.

Men and women may acquire forceful or weak personalities according to their habits of thought and action. If they have the self-confident, decisive mental attitude, they will become strong, creative characters; if they harbour hesitating, doubtful, self-depreciating thoughts, they will become negative and ineffectual personalities. It is all a matter of habitual thinking and acting.

## Building Character

Habit may be looked upon as the silent partner to help us to do whatever we want to do. Habit can be of tremendous advantage in enhancing our own interests and welfare, or it can stand in our way and hold us back according to how we encourage it. What we think and what we do eventually become part of us. This is the way the character is built. A slovenly habit brings about a slovenly character. Good, positive habits ensure good positive characters.

The habit of being courteous, accommodating, kind, methodical, of keeping appointments promptly, completing each daily task, of never being idle, these are some of the assets of life that cannot be over-estimated.

The habit of giving of our best gives us a sense of self-possession.

The men and women who complete each daily task acquire a feeling of serenity; they are conscious of not having done any shoddy work, of having steered clear of all shams; and they enjoy the satisfaction of knowing that they have a clean record.

Those who are masters of their crafts, and are conscious of possessing the ability to do efficiently whatever is undertaken, acquire an inner satisfaction which the slipshod, half-hearted worker never knows.

Happiness, achievement and success come to the individual who feels within him the power to do whatever he undertakes as well and efficiently as it can possibly be done. This buoyant sense of power stirs the faculties to their fullest development. It unfolds the moral, mental and physical forces. And this very growth, the consciousness of an expanding mentality and of a broadening horizon, gives an added satisfaction almost beyond the power of words to describe.

## Changing Habits

Habits can be discarded and changed in the reverse order of their making, but it is a much slower process. It may require many months of self-discipline, but the rewards are rich and so the efforts are well worth while.

The "conquest" habit is a great stamina producer and character builder. The young man who is looked upon as being successfully organised and imbued with the spirit of achievement inevitably thinks and acts like a successful individual. His future is more or less assured, for people are looking for and wanting that sort of attitude.

It is easy to pick out the men and women with this "conquest" habit. They are not full of alibis, neither do they dodge, falter nor waver. They know what they want and go after it with vigour and determination. They fix a goal and make everything contribute towards that splendid objective. They put imagination, vision and creative enthusiasm into their daily tasks.

There are many smaller habits that go to make up this "conquest" habit, such as seeking ways of doing work better, more efficiently and more quickly, of grappling with difficult problems immediately they arise, and the "do-it-to-day" attitude.

The habit of idling, dawdling and inertia—the putting-off attitude—paralyses the initiative, kills self-confidence and counterbalances many other success qualities.

Many men and women do not realise that they are being moulded and fashioned into certain conditions of character by their ordinary daily habits. What they do to-day is influenced by the habits of thought, and by the action of yesterday.

In the passing of time—even within a month—habit leaves its mark somewhere on the characters of men and women. Some may develop a habit which plants the seed that can wreck them morally and physically. On the other hand, a habit can start them along the road to more successful living. It all depends upon the individual himself in making the choice.


### Success Qualities

Another good habit to form is that of "promptness"—in keeping promises concerning time. When a person can be trusted to be always on time, people unconsciously feel that he will also be trustworthy in other directions.

The habit of promptness plays an important part in the building-up of a career. Such a habit greatly helps to develop decisiveness. Those who are always dilly-dallying usually are weak in making decisions; and that very often can be detrimental to achievement and success.

In industry much emphasis is placed upon the habit of promptness, for this is often allied to other qualities that make for success. The slipshod, slovenly person is usually not noted for his promptness. Promptness goes hand in hand with system, order, accuracy, thoroughness, persistence and keen appreciation of the value of time.

The positive character is usually prompt in keeping appointments, whilst the negative one is indifferent to keeping to time.

The prompt individual is more likely to be one who has decided what he wants more than the one who is habitually late. And so it is that the qualities which make for efficiency, achievement and success are closely allied to promptness, initiative, accuracy, system and order.

There are many men and women who often wonder why employers attach so much importance to the matter of promptness. These people may think that being a few minutes late—time they can make up later—is of small account. But this lack of promptness may be an indication of other failure qualities—inefficient and detrimental qualities.

The characteristic of promptness rarely goes alone. The prompt man usually is systematic; he is not a procrastinator. He does not put off important matters. The man who is prompt has an alert mind and is progressive.

When a person can be depended upon to keep his appointments promptly, he can usually be depended upon in other directions.

Those who have a high regard for time, who look upon it as one of their most valuable assets, have many other splendid qualities. The determination to make every day count to the best advantage cannot be separated from the successful life.

It is a great thing to form the habit of putting high value upon time, of thinking of it as life's most precious capital.

By making the most of every passing minute we go far towards making the most of life itself.

# GOLDEN MINUTES

*"Not marble, nor the gilded monuments*
*Of Princes shall outlive this powerful rhyme;*
*But you in these contents shall shine more bright*
*Than unswept stone besmeared by sluttish Time."*

\* \* \*

THUS wrote Shakespeare, who, foremost among the immortals, could afford to defy the arch-enemy Time. For though empires wane and kingdoms perish, though new worlds arise from the ashes of the old, though Man himself may climb to heights yet undreamt of, yet the verse of the master artist echoes down through the ages. For Shakespeare, though subject like other men to the eclipse of Time, still remains a living force; his work has raised him from the valley of Time to the peaks of Eternity.

And no poet ever was so confident of the immortality of his verse. Throughout his works we have the undertone of insistence that his accomplishment would endure, that his name would last "not for an age—but for all time".

The fragment of the sonnet quoted above came to my mind very forcibly as I recalled a sermon I heard many years ago. The long-dormant echoes of that old sermon were brought to life in a very strange fashion.

I was studying some of the plans for commercial television and the phrase "buying time" kept cropping up in the matter I was reading. Then into consciousness came a fragment of that sermon of bygone years, and I was carried away to an almost forgotten summer whilst I listened to the drone of the preacher's voice. "You cannot buy to-morrow" was the theme of his discourse. And it suddenly dawned on me how wrong he was, how his philosophy gave a false emphasis to the message of the Master.

The theme of the sermon, as I remember it, was that when a man or woman came to the end of their days, then not all the gold or precious jewels in the world could purchase an extra lease of life. Physically that is a fact, but it is a fact that the Church in general loves to ram home to us—and for what purpose? There is nothing very startling in the revelation that death comes as the end, that the lot of all of us is to reach a certain span, and then naught can avail us to overcome the Last Enemy.

But the great religions of the world have little to do with Time. They stress not Man's mortality but his immortality; they emphasise not Man's short span upon the earth but his potential for eternal life.

It is not our purpose at the moment to do more than just pay a passing reference to the seemingly wrong bias given by organised religion to the simple message of the Great Galilean. Rather let us stress another aspect of the subject. And that is—to a certain degree we *can* buy Time; we can make Time our ally and not our enemy.

But not by wealth or power of position!

We can become the master of Time by filling the unforgiving minute; we can make Time our ally by living our lives in such a way that effort, courage, perseverance and enterprise can make us master of, and not a slave to, Time.

And to those who grasp the implications of this message, even death itself no longer retains its terror. For those who make Time their ally, who live their lives devoted to some great purpose, the end of life becomes like a restful sleep after a hard day's task, a blissful slumber that precedes a brighter dawn, another Great Adventure.

### The Last Enemy

The concern of Practical Psychology is so overwhelmingly with men and women learning to make the most of themselves, with attaining the richer life, that it may be that not enough attention has been paid to the subject of death. But that does not mean that Practical Psychology is afraid of or fights shy of the subject.

Now and then it must cross the minds of all men and women, but more so when the temples begin to glisten with the frosts of life's autumn, that the time will come when the "day's work" will be done, when we must give up the struggle and enter into the last sleep. But, except in the case of morbid imagination, the thought does not occur very frequently to the average person. Nevertheless, this may be the occasion for a word or two on the subject before returning to *Psychology's* main preoccupation—which is life.

To-day there would appear to be a very great difference between us and our grandparents in our attitude towards death. Whereas they were quite sincerely convinced that there was a hereafter, they dreaded the possible punishment that it might hold in store for misdemeanours in this terrestrial life. On the other hand, our modern age is by no means so confident of survival and its fears are based on that uncertainty of personal immortality. In other words, our grandparents feared death because it might mean a hereafter of punishment; we fear death, when we do fear it at all, because it may mean the end.

What has Practical Psychology to state on this subject? Unlike many religious organisations it refuses to be dogmatic, believing that the fully-realised man and woman will see and know the truth for themselves. It does not state categorically that there is a paradise beyond, for there is very little knowledge upon which to work. We cannot draw a map of that land "from whose bourne no traveller returns".

But the fundamental teaching of Practical Psychology is that we are emanations of the great Universal Mind; we are the physical embodiments of the great Creative Energy that floods the universe. The path to self-realisation is that of achieving oneness with the Universal Mind. And though the body perishes, that spark which animates Man is beyond the reach of any physical catastrophe. The essential, vital spark within us is from eternity to infinity.

However, it is not the purpose of this Chat to delve deeper into the matter. For every man and woman who study Practical Psychology will find their own way to achieve contact with the Infinite; to each individual will be vouchsafed some glimpse of the Truth Eternal.

All we need say is that Practical Psychology can give us the vision and the courage to be beyond the reach of the fear of death; that it can give us an assurance that the apparent defeat of Man by the Last Enemy is in reality the Final Victory.

### Killing Time

Let us now return to the main theme of Practical Psychology— which is how to get the best out of life. The only reason for our dwelling upon the subject of death was to substantiate the claim that it is not a bogy from which Practical Psychology runs away. For Practical Psychology can offer us the means of living abundantly and of facing death without undue fear.

The only death that need hold any apprehension for us is the living death we impose upon ourselves when we try to "kill time".

This is a phrase we hear far too often nowadays in one form or another. There seems to be a modern capacity for being bored.

We read with some trepidation of many teen-age boys and girls with nothing better to do than to dress up in fancy clothes and waste their time on the streets or in dance halls because they have to be amused —they've got to kill time. And some of our "youth experts" explain that it's all because they have no opportunity of employing their leisure creatively.

Whatever fun and excitement the lives of these boys and girls may hold, may heaven protect us from such a living death!

We are not trying to suggest an easy solution to the problem, but surely these young people would get more fun, more pleasure and some sense of achievement if they found more creative employment than trying to kill time.

But it is not only the young people who behave in this respect. We can find people of all ages who are thoroughly and absolutely bored unless there is a good programme on TV, unless they are going to a show, entertaining friends at home or have some such other undertaking in the offing. One could assume that there were no books to read, no new fields of knowledge to explore, no momentous discoveries to make about themselves, no purpose in life to which they can turn their energies. It would seem to these people that there is no glory in the setting of the sun, no colour and romance in a busy city street, no balm for the soul in a quiet stroll along a country lane, no hint of mystery in the song of the birds at twilight, no silent music in the mystery of night.

We are not decrying pleasurable spare-time activities. Far from it! They all have their place in life and are essential to well-being. But the purpose of leisure, of social intercourse, of our games and of the "evening out" should not be to kill time, but to refresh us physically and mentally to meet our daily tasks and help us in our aspirations towards more successful living.

The people who are always killing time are killing their own opportunities in life. The men and women who succeed are those who make time live by making it useful.

If we want a simple test to prove whether we are leading full lives, we should ask ourselves this question: Do we have plenty of time or do we fill our days in such a way that we can never really find enough time for all we wish to do?

Let us hope the answer will be that we find ourselves with so much to do that we have to ration our time.

## Peering into the Future

It has long been the goal of social progress to obtain a greater degree of leisure for the average man and woman. We have achieved much in this way in the last twenty-five years or so. Where previously the average worker worked fifty or sixty hours a week, the average is now nearer forty hours per week. And this is all to the good. With increasing mechanisation, it is quite likely in the near future that the average working week will consist of thirty hours, and before the close of our century, we should not be surprised if the average person works only six hours per day, three days a week, and for only about eight or nine months of the year.

This is not a far-fetched dream, but a reality that may be forced upon us by the harnessing of atomic power to constructive ends.

And a very good thing too! *Provided* that the leisure that will be so gained can be devoted to constructive use. For leisure that men and women fail to use can be an infinitely greater curse than the long hours of drudgery ever were. If, in the future we have envisaged, this spare time is not profitably filled, then it can mean ruination to the human race, for leisure without the means to employ it can rot the very soul of Man.

And it is here that a great responsibility lies upon those of us who have seen the light. It should be our duty as citizens to influence others towards the full life, to help those to whom leisure will mean only more and more time to kill, to show them the way to employ leisure creatively, to use the golden hours to find the richer life.

This is a prophecy which may well be Mankind's greatest problem in the near future.

And despite what some of the politicians may assert, the provision of recreational facilities, the higher standard of material life, the establishing of clubs and recreation grounds and the multiplying of mechanical means of amusement will not solve the problem.

For essentially it is a *personal* problem. It is a question merely of whether the individual will try to "kill time" or whether he will make time his ally, employing his leisure to the enrichment of his personal life, to the benefit of humanity, to the attainment of a high purpose.

Perhaps some of us may think that we have taken a peep too far into the future. I don't think so. For the problem is with us now and it is not in the social sense alone.

Before we come to the end of our Chat it may be beneficial to us to answer the following questions:

Do we ever find ourselves trying to "kill time"?

Do we become bored at work or during our leisure hours?

Do we find ourselves with nothing to do, no book to read, perhaps an evening's entertainment cancelled, that odd hour which throws us back on our own resources?

Do we make the maximum use of every minute of every hour?

No one can answer these questions for us—it's up to each of us to examine ourselves critically.

We shall find more happiness and achievement not in trying to move faster the inexorable hands of the clock, but by bending our energies—in work or play—so exclusively upon whatever we are doing that time will no longer seem to matter.

It is only by filling the unforgiving minute that we can find more happiness and contentment. It is only by using our time creatively that we can find achievement and success.

# WHAT PRICE SUCCESS?

THERE are numerous different theories as to what comprises success, for it is such a relative thing. Success to one individual would mean failure to another. Nowhere shall we find the curse of false estimates more evident. So many men and women mistake the transitory and effervescent for the abiding and permanent. The means to the end are persistently mistaken for the end itself; tinsel is taken for gold; the superficial obscures the real.

Success to some people means money, fame, power. But success is not to be found in the mere accumulation of money. The world is full of pitiable failures who have accumulated vast material wealth. Many of them are lonely, despondent and neurotic.

Money, if rightly used, is a means to success. As a medium of exchange it is important and its possession is not to be despised. The wise use of money may greatly facilitate the achievement of success, but it is a means to that end and not an end in itself.

Then there are others who believe that fame and power are the measure of success.

There are thousands of people who spend their entire lives to gain public recognition. They bask for a short time in the sunshine of public favour and then feel the sting of criticism, envy, suspicion and hatred. The "cheers" of to-day become the "boos" of to-morrow. They realise perhaps too late that fame is an elusive thing—here to-day and gone to-morrow.

Public opinion is indeed fickle and shallow. It raises its idols to the pinnacle of approval to-day and hurls them into oblivion to-morrow—smashed and deserted with each passing whim. The halo of fame turns quickly into a crown of thorns.

### No Set Standard

So it would seem that we cannot set up a single, uniform standard of success and expect everyone to agree to it. Just as tastes differ, so do modes of life; those which are highly pleasurable to some may be odious to others.

One thing, however, seems certain. And that is, that successful men and women need not necessarily be wealthy or famous or powerful.

The truly successful individual surely is one who leads a full-orbed, well-balanced, harmonious life; who is keenly interested in his job; whose vision is clear and whose tastes are simple; an individual with

a mind that is broad and alert; whose loyal friendship, kindly understanding and sympathetic service can be relied upon.

There may be only a small number of men and women who succeed
in this sense but their influence is spread afar.

### Many Strive—Few Succeed

We have dealt briefly with several of the numerous theories about
success.　There are, of course, also many degrees of success.　And
for every man or woman there is some degree of achievement to
which they can aspire.

Thousands strive for success of one kind or another.　But there
are precious few who attain it.

What is it that brings one person success, and what is it that brings
mediocrity and failure to another?　The chief reason seems to be that
some people succeed because they pay the price of success, and others,
although they may claim to be ambitious to succeed, are unwilling to
pay the price.

There are other reasons, of course, and they are many and varied.
Suppose we take a look at some of them.

One of the greatest enemies of success is *lack of purpose.*　So
many people follow the lines of least resistance, spend all their energies
in routine activities, and end up without the realisation of any splendid
goal or objective.　They drift through life, with no aspiring hope,
no goal in view, and with no superb ambition to do and dare.

Those who succeed have a goal.　They know what they want and
go after it, making every dream, every effort, every deed bend towards
its realisation.

Closely allied to rigidity of purpose is dogged persistency.　So
many give up just short of success.　They start out with great enthusiasm
but it generally oozes out before they reach their goal.　Men and
women may be well educated, honest, industrious, have good opportunities come their way, yet give up the struggle for success when the
goal is only a little way ahead.　Their failure to take the last few steps
made all the difference between failure and the yearned-for success.
More people fail from lack of staying power than from almost
anything else.

> *"Genius, that power which dazzles mortal eyes,*
> *Is oft but perseverance in disguise.*
> *Continuous effort, of itself, implies*
> *In spite of countless falls, the power to rise.*
>
> *'Twixt failure and success the point's so fine*
> *Men sometimes know not when they touch the line.*
> *Just when the pearl was awaiting one more plunge*
> *How many a struggler has thrown up the sponge!"*

### The Creed of Failures

The belief in luck is another enemy of the achievement of success. There are many people who believe that some are born lucky and some unlucky. Admitted, it is better to be born under wealthy circumstances than to be born in poverty-stricken surroundings. But that is not what these people mean. They believe that fortune smiles only on a selected few and frowns upon the great majority. This is a creed that can lead only to failure. It is often caused by envy. Yet it is a popular doctrine because there are always more people who fail than succeed.

Men and women of attainment banish such thoughts, because they know from experience that their own achievements have not come about by luck but by determination, self-sacrifice and persistent endeavour.

### No Success Without Work

*"The heights that great man gained and kept*
*Were not attained by sudden flight;*
*But they, while their companions slept,*
*Were toiling upwards through the night."*

Another contributory cause of failure is that so many people look upon work as a penalty or a curse. They work only because they must eat. Success is not for them, for it doesn't come to those who have no taste for work—the indolent or the slackers.

No one ever made a lasting success except by unremitting toil. The methods vary, as they must, but the actual basis of the successful life is hard work. This is not always apparent because we are apt to look at men and women when they have achieved success. But what we so often fail to see is the years of toil and effort behind it.

### Facing Facts

Another factor that is detrimental to success is the making of alibis.

Some people constantly are explaining and apologising for themselves—finding excuses for their failings. "If only things were different", they say. But it is not dreaming and wishing but acting and working that *make* things different. Dreaming and wishing are worth nothing at all unless backed by determination and effort.

Those who succeed don't dodge, don't camouflage but face facts as they are in reality.

### Basic Conditions

We have discussed only what may be considered the chief enemies in the attainment of success. There are, of course, many others.

Perhaps some may ask, "Is success worth the price it calls for? Is it worth while?" That we must all decide for ourselves.

I believe it is, for it brings out the very best that is in men and women; to overcome set-backs, break down barriers and defeat circumstances that stand in the way of their purpose. Hard? Of course it is! That's why so many never attempt to achieve success. They see the difficulties, consider the cost and are unwilling to pay the price. They answer the siren call of the rut and remain in the ranks of the failures for all time.

It is up to men and women to ask themselves whether they are willing to enjoy the comforts, the rewards and the glory that go with achievement, or to accept the uneasy and inadequate contentment that comes with mediocrity and failure.

Like everything else in life success has got to be paid for. There is no easy nor royal road to achievement. Those who win must expect to face constant discouragement and disappointment and surmount many difficulties and set-backs. For success is never achieved without struggle—intense, incessant, implacable struggle. It calls for rugged determination, self-sacrifice and vision. It means persistent effort and unremitting toil. These are the basic conditions of all-triumphant endeavour and surging success.

# MAKE UP YOUR OWN MIND

IN all conditions relating to human behaviour there is a certain element which has not received the recognition demanded by its importance in the lives of every one of us. And that element is *interference.*

There are few phases in our lives in which interference doesn't play an important part. For instance, a man decides to buy a pair of shoes. He has made up his mind that he wants brown shoes, the style to be decided upon on arriving at the shoe shop. It would seem entirely outside the bounds of all reason if, later on, he should walk out of the shop with a parcel containing a pair of black shoes, the style of which he utterly disliked. Yet that is what happened.

Perhaps the shop assistant who attended to him had a complex about people wearing black shoes. Or he may have been a high pressure salesman who talked the man into buying shoes he really didn't want. But whatever the reason, the shop assistant made up the man's mind for him. And with a sort of dazed look in his eyes, he made an excuse to himself that he could anyhow use a pair of black shoes.

But he still wanted brown shoes. Perhaps the next time he tries to buy them he will be more successful.

There are so many people who, in trying to arrive at a decision, ask the advice of everyone—with the result that they invariably do the wrong thing.

Instead of asking anyone what we should do, why don't we do as our own conscious or unconscious minds dictate, and make our decisions, or our mistakes, according to the reaction of our mental processes?

How often do we become determined, after cleaning up some unfortunate incident, that never again will we allow complications to enmesh us, and yet, a short time later, find ourselves bound up in a mass of detail, like one of those mountain roads with hundreds of diverging paths, lying in wait to beguile our straying feet?

For example, one might be feeling happy and carefree and then suddenly meet someone who might sweep away all reason and leave only a vibrating, pulsing whirl of emotions, such as in the case of a violent attack of infatuation.

People who are emotionally controlled are to be greatly admired. But controlled emotions, properly understood and constructively used, in conjunction with imagination can work wonders.

111

## Intense Desire

The creative artist, the great architect, organisers of vast industries who construct artistically with material things must first of all have the *emotional urge*.

This does not mean idle dreams or wandering discontents, but an intense desire springing from the very core of their being. They must also control to the full that tool of the mind—imagination —before they can bring into being their particular form of artistic expression.

These people, however, when they get this urge, very often find that conditions, circumstances, ideas and people immediately set up an interference. But those who succeed keep the vision clearly before them, somewhat in the same way as a person will keep the photo of his beloved on his dressing-table, and gradually the qualities he *imagines* in her will become part of his subconscious mind and cause him to clothe the person in the picture with virtues that do not belong to her.

The great difference between creative people and the average man or woman is that the former are able to concentrate fully on the things of which they dream. They become inflamed with some mighty purpose and concentrate all their energies towards its realisation.

In the main, this means that the urge allows of no ease, rest, contentment or happiness as the masses interpret these things. Yet it brings a *deeper* happiness and a spiritual uplift far greater than persons of the more placid type could possibly imagine or experience.

These creative people may face opposition and obstacles, may be starved or beaten, but the creative urge is stronger than mere physical pain. Adversity and persecution, discouragement and misfortune cannot swerve them from their fixed purpose, nor quench their indomitable determination to reach their goal.

Those who have had the courage to ignore interference have blazed new trails, broken precedents, brought about further advances along the road to progress and led the race to loftier summits.

Arkwright is an outstanding case. His models of the spinning frame, the product of years of toil, were smashed by his wife. His fellow-townsmen drove him from their city, his life became unsafe, with no voice raised on his behalf, yet he remained true to his splendid vision of economic reconstruction.

Columbus was mocked, ridiculed and persecuted, yet he steadfastly pursued his campaign of exploration. He faced a hostile and mutinous crew, yet he remained true to his purpose and his discovery remade the subsequent history of nations.

Why is it that high hopes, optimism and determination to reach a set goal are always subject to sneers, jeers and prophecies of disaster? Strange as it may appear, it would seem that the majority of people do not want men and women to devote themselves to great achievements.  The masses worship great achievements after they have taken place; they eulogise the dead, but when faced with living human beings who are struggling to succeed immediately become hostile.  The tendency of the mass-mind is to pull down not to help upwards.

## Detrimental to Welfare

Perhaps children are the most interfered with of all.  Children often with whimsical looks on their little faces, continually are stopped from doing what they want to do.  "You mustn't do that.  Don't make a noise."  There's a host of other "mustn'ts" and "don'ts" heard in almost every home.

The result is that we often breed a lot of inferiority complexes that have to be weeded out perhaps after years of inward suffering. Interference with children should be cut to a minimum.  Most of the "don't do that" or "you mustn't do this" should be avoided.  Children should be taught to make up their own minds as early as possible. Of course, they must be guided and facts presented to them as an adult sees them.  But, at the same time, they should be taught to make up their own minds.

Progress continues and the majority of great achievements have been made and won because interference was thrown out and kept out of the individual's life.  The undue interference, too, of wife, husband, children, money, luxury should be pushed overboard.

The workaday world is full of "I-told-you-so", "It-can't-be-done" men and women—people who stick out a foot to trip up the individual who does his work in an original way, or in a manner somewhat different from the masses.

So when we are told that someone is going to do something that may seem ridiculous to us, let us curb that discouraging remark that may rise to our lips, even although our advice may be well meant, and we believe that, from our viewpoint, the proposition should be discouraged. For our interference *may* rob the world of something new and wonderful.

## Other People's Opinions

We all know it is hard to do something we believe is right in spite of the interference of other people.  Yet there are times, maybe, when it is a good thing for each one of us to say: "Right or wrong—that's my idea and I'm going to stick to it", no matter how many well-meaning friends and acquaintances may advise otherwise.

But so many men and women are afraid of the opinions of others. They will not risk disapproval and they set a standard of conduct based on: "What will people say?"

The creative individual, on the other hand, allows nothing to intervene between his desires and actions. He ignores the standard set by other people. He doesn't care a rap what the world says or thinks. His activities are not dictated to him by others. He is not led away or pushed around. He lives his own life. He makes his own decisions, maps out his own programme and determines his own conduct. The progress he makes is under his own steam.

This does not mean that we should rush into things without facing facts. We should consider both kinds—the optimistic and the pessimistic. And usually we shall find that the encouraging facts far outweigh the others.

We can all take our choice in regard to which facts we will "face". The stimulating ones are just as real as the discouraging ones, and are always more substantial.

Those who succeed do so partly because they are the people who see the facts of opportunity when so many others see only the facts of misfortune.

Yes, by all means let us face the facts. But in doing so let us be sure *which* facts we are going to face.

Finally, let us break free from the shackles of interference  and find joy and fulfilment in true, creative accomplishment.

# MODERN COMPLEX LIFE

*Can mankind survive this power-mad age?*

\* \* \*

NO doubt we have all been impressed by the phenomenon we find in practically every town and village we visit—an appeal being made for funds towards the restoration of the local church.

Time and the death watch beetle are undermining the architectural splendour that has stood for centuries. Dry rot is bringing to ruin some of Man's finest work. Our churches in particular are becoming victims of the frailties of old age.

And the appeals being made are, on the whole, meeting with a very generous response. The public has a deep and abiding affection for the local or parish church. We contribute very generously in cash to preserve the fabric of our churches.

If only we could contribute in like measure to the spirit necessary to awaken the Church as an institution. As it is, it seems that we are preserving the outward show whilst neglecting the inner meaning. We preserve the building, but without something more, all we retain are bricks and mortar and wood. And whilst most of us are in favour of preserving our heritage from past ages, we may become deeply and acutely conscious of the fact that the Churches should have more to offer than just a structure to satisfy historical curiosity.

Our age is in need of spiritual guidance, in dire need of moral leadership. We are in danger of becoming a race of giant ants in an infinitely complicated ant-heap.

The brains of science cannot save us, nor can the well-intentioned philanthropy of political parties who are determined to feed, clothe and keep us from want. All these are good things. Let us have them by all means. But they are not enough to enable us to preserve our dignity as men and women; they are insufficient to enable us to find fulfilment.

Only a new and powerful spiritual leadership can awaken us to our danger; can teach us to make use of our freedom from want in order to ennoble life.

We need leadership—guidance to raise us up from over-pre-occupation with the material ends of life alone. We need to be quickened to appreciate beauty, to see nobility, to strive towards fulfilment. It is this spiritual leadership that the Church should give. Yet the Churches fail us.

Look at our daily newspapers. What do we find? Plenty to

interest the ordinary man and woman. The topics are many and varied. A searchlight thrown on the pettiness of Man. His sins, his crimes. There also we find pronouncement on modern problems by scientists, politicians and philosophers. But rarely is the voice of the Church raised either in the newspapers—or anywhere else for that matter—on any worth-while subjects. Sometimes a parson may be heard to complain of the mess made by confetti at some fashionable wedding. Occasionally, a minister holds forth upon the iniquity of men and women in the pursuit of pleasure.

But what does the Church say about the vital things of to-day— sex, for instance? Or the H-bomb? Nothing! It sits on the fence and remains silent.

And their sermons. Do they deal with modern complex life? They do not! For the majority of them are based upon creeds, theology and Biblical characters which have little or no bearing on the problems of to-day. Surely sermons taken from the daily problems of the different types of men and women would be more in keeping with the needs of the twentieth century? Why not build sermons around subjects which concern everyday living; matters that bother the Marys and the Toms of the community; that puzzle young lovers, the new mothers and worried parents; that concern the youths, the men and the breadwinners? Why not sermons about marriage and love, and romance as well as thrift, inflation and industry? These are some of the things that make up the lives of every man and woman in Britain to-day.

Despite some honourable exceptions, the Church as a whole is out of touch with the majority of people. It plays no vital part in the lives of ordinary men and women. Hence the churches are empty. Agnosticism is growing. This is indeed a tragedy, for life needs the inspiration and sense of cosmic relationship which religion affords.

We need the spiritual leadership of the Church, but the Churches seem to be bereft of leadership. The real message of Christianity is mankind's one hope of surviving in a power-mad age, the only hope of avoiding the twin pitfalls of complete slavery or utter annihilation.

Christianity is still the hope of the world—but it will remain only a hope until the Churches preach the Gospel according to the Master and not according to the ecclesiastical bodies.

### Man—the Individual

True Christianity is the only hope that Man may be ennobled by the advance of scientific discovery and not degraded or utterly destroyed by it. For it is only the message of the Man of Galilee that can enable Man to realise that he is superior to the mighty powers he has unleashed, that all material discoveries, all the miracles unfolded to him by science, are only the means to the end of fulfilling his dreams.

Once let the scientists rule the world and we lesser men will be the mere hewers of wood and drawers of water, mere cogs in the ponderous machinery of its dominating ideology, the slaves of the superior brain, powerless in the grip of our scientific overlords. Only "they" will hold the power; the ordinary man and woman will be merely tools, unable to fashion their own lives other than at the dictates of the masters.

If we rely on political means to rescue Man from slavery, we look in vain. The politician is concerned, not with Man as an individual, but with groupings of men and women within a state or nation. Political means, however well-intentioned, are no substitute for the free man. The enlightened politician will, no doubt, ensure that we are well fed, clothed, housed, and with all our material wants cared for. He can do no more. He cannot light within our hearts that flame of faith which is the glory and the only glory of human life.

We cannot look for salvation to any "ism", for these ideologies do not liberate but enslave. They have a limited objective, that of securing precedence for some particular creed. They are not concerned with the individual. It is only the philosophy of the Galilean that takes into account Man's individual needs, his yearnings, interests and aspirations, that looks kindly upon his blind and blundering search for truth, his hunger for beauty, his desperate longing for fulfilment.

And the message of the Master has been distorted by centuries of false dogma and misleading propaganda.

Perhaps the Churches will eventually take their rightful place as the spiritual leaders of mankind, will awaken to a sense of their responsibilities and proclaim the truth that men and women are desperate to hear.

A new crusade is called for. Not to rescue some holy land from the grip of a savage heathen, but a crusade to rescue ordinary humanity from its slavery to dogma, from its subservience to creed, to awaken the ordinary man and woman to a realisation of their high destiny, to an understanding of their powers, to light a torch of faith that will illumine our century, to keep high the flag of courage, to lead an army that shall proclaim the glory of the fulfilled man.

## The Mythical "Golden Age"

All along the centuries, the Churches have taken too literally the story of the fall of Man. According to this doctrine, our first father and mother—Adam and Eve—were placed in a Garden, a veritable Paradise on earth. No sin existed there, no want; all was perfect and Man should have been content. But Man insisted upon tasting the fruit of knowledge and this led to the "Fall". So our original parents were cast out of Eden, out into an imperfect world, there to earn their bread by the sweat of their brows.

There is no need to dwell too long upon this ancient story. It is sufficient to stress that many religions look back to some similar "Golden Age", when Man lived without labour, when there was no evil, when all was contentment.

We have even a pseudo-scientific theory of the "noble savage" who centuries past lived in some form of Eden without toil, with no desire for change, all contentment until some sin cast him out upon the harsher world, there to struggle for mere survival.

What seems to be wrong is the assumption that long, long ago, men were perfect, but have since become imperfect; that the "ideal" existence lies somewhere in the past, that this existence consists of having plenty to eat and drink and little or nothing to do.

If that alone be Paradise, then modern science can give it to us to-morrow.


## Adventure and Progress

Let us face the real facts. Man did not "fall"; he has risen. He has developed from being a close relative of the animal into the ordinary people we see around us every day. From leading a life that was nasty, brutish and short, he developed sufficient intelligence to build the Pyramids; he founded a few states in the Greek Islands and developed a mode of life that amazes us even to-day. From a hunting, and hunted creature, living in the primeval forest, he sounded the undying music of Beethoven and penned the immortal lines of Shakespeare. From a life completely at the mercy of the elements, he adventured into the infinity of the universe and sought for truth even in the infinity of the atom.

The story of Man would seem to be not that of a fall occasioned by original sin, but the story of a breath-taking adventure into civilisation and independence. Man has marched forward. Admittedly, he has often taken the wrong road. True, his developing mind has sometimes been used destructively. But the better way of life he is now seeking lies not in some mythical past, but in the immediate future.

That illustrates the difference between the approach of orthodox religion to the problem of Man and that which we have enumerated. The former assumes Man to have been perfect, and to have degenerated. The latter knows Man to be imperfect, but believes that he eventually will reach perfection through the divine power within him.

Can we appreciate what difference this can make in our approach to the problem of to-day? Man is not a fallen angel but an embryo god. The "Paradise" he seeks is not of some eastern garden where the fruits of the earth drop into his lap without any effort on his part, where toil is unnecessary and contentment reigns supreme. No, the ideal of our liberated Man is that of struggle towards perfection, that of realising a continually unfolding dream, of pursuing a noble aim that is as high as the heavens, of fulfilling all the innate goodness and beauty within him.

## Mind Supreme

Man has developed to an amazing degree his capacity for invention. So much so that he frequently worships his invention rather than uses it to achieve his larger objective.

Ask a modern engineer for a machine that will perform some intricate and difficult task for which, at present, no machine exists. He does not throw up his hands in despair; nor does he lie down waiting hopefully for inspiration. He sits down and considers the problem and gradually builds up a machine that will perform the task required of it.

Ask the physicist for a metal that has some specific properties not found in any metal that we know to-day. The metal, supposedly, must be as hard as steel but as light as aluminium. It must be resistant to certain acids, yet must have the appearance of pure gold. No matter how difficult we make his task, he will—with his background of scientific knowledge—study the problem and eventually produce the metal.

Ask the scientist for a bigger and better atom bomb. It may take time, but he will produce it.

In other words, when Man is dealing in the realm of the material, he knows that his mind can "comprehend the wondrous architecture of the world". He has no doubts, no fears. He studies the problem, and provides the solution.

Man's mind, however, so far has been used chiefly in order to win the means to a fuller materialistic life, in the conquest of matter, and to understand the mechanics of Nature, all of which are, of course, indispensable to his self-preservation and survival.

But seldom has the mind been used to comprehend the spiritual side of life, to contact the great Creative Force that brought the universe into being, that sustains the myriad forms of life upon our planet, that permeates even the furthermost star, that moves in infinity and yet can act upon the finite plane.

The human mind is part of this Creative Directing Intelligence and Man can contact this divine reality within and learn to use this tremendous force. Once he comes into realisation of his "at-one-ment" with this great Creative Sustaining Principle of the universe, life will take on new meaning. For it is the divine alchemy that shines like a bright flame to guide him through the dark vales of life, to fire his will when hope burns low and despair mocks his efforts, that can banish defeat even at the eleventh hour and crown his efforts with victory.

L.C.—9

# A TRUE COMPARISON

NOTHING takes the joy out of life like picking a wrong standard for comparison and trying to measure up to someone who is out of our class. The light-weight boxer never worries because he cannot compete with a heavy-weight; he is content to fight someone in his own class.

The majority of men and women are, in the main, accountable to themselves alone, and as a result their happiness is very much more in their own keeping than is usually imagined.

Many expressions such as, "I am not as strong as so-and-so", "I cannot work half as hard as he can", or "I cannot do this, that or the other as well as the other person", denote habits of comparison that lead to entirely erroneous conclusions and bring unhappiness to those who do not know what they have a right to expect of themselves.

The man with the under-developed muscles may have a highly-developed mentality. But both kinds of development, as well as all grades and mixtures of both kinds, are needed to perform the world's work.

If we measure our own abilities or successes by those of our neighbours, we may be quite wrong in concluding that, because they are cleverer or richer than we are, they are more efficient or get more out of life than we do.

We may perhaps draw a comparison with the incident of the widow's mite. The princely sums given by the rich men were as nothing compared with the humble offering of the poor woman who gave her all. They had given only a tithe of their vast wealth, while the widow had parted with all she had.

So the seeming greater success of our neighbours may be very much less than what they could accomplish with their natural capacity and opportunities, while our comparative inefficiency may really be a far greater achievement when judged by a standard that compares what each person does, only with what each person is able to do.

## Individual Differences

There is an old saying, "In the country of the blind, the one-eyed man is king". But the subjects in that country would not compare themselves with the one-eyed men or the two-eyed men, but with their equals, who have no eyes.

The accomplishments of the cripple should not be judged by those of the normal two-legged person, but by the accomplishments of those who have the same disadvantages as the cripple. In fact, the cripple may be a marvel of efficiency for a person so handicapped. He may get the same amount of satisfaction from the knowledge that he is using his equipment to the maximum capacity as his two-legged neighbour gets from doing twice the amount of work.

A man's capacity can never be determined by any scale outside himself. What is normal for one individual is far from normal for another person. The standard for comparison surely lies in the power latent within ourselves and never in that of any other person.

It is plain enough that we all differ in details of colour, size and form, and we usually accept these discrepancies without suffering from any great feeling of unfitness or inferiority. It is just as true, but not so easy to realise, that similar variations in our intellectual, emotional and aesthetic make-up ought not to interfere with our health and happiness.

An exact measure of our normal capacity, however, does exist. It is not that of the average person nor that of the exceptional person. It is the maximum degree of energy that we ourselves are capable of liberating without undue effort. In other words, every man's normal capacity is his maximum of *easily-produced* energy, for we always do well only that which we do easily. It is evident that what is one person's maximum may be another person's minimum and vice versa.

On account of poor eyesight Samuel Johnson would have been useless in the job of target-spotter on a modern battleship, and the keen eyesight of a first-class range-finder would have been of little help in producing a great lexicographer.

It is the physical as well as the mental differences in the individual that give each person his peculiar value and superiority. The Jack-of-all-trades excels in none.

We should, therefore, study our peculiarities—the ways in which we seem to vary from other people. Then we should use this dissimilarity as a starting-point to develop some talent, or to produce something that is better or different from anything we have ever produced before.

We often hear remarks about newly-married couples such as, "I wonder what she can see in him?" "What does he see in her?" "They have nothing in common". But so very often the newly-weds have in common one of the strongest points of attraction that can exist between two people—*their total dissimilarity*. These marriages are apt to be harmonious and happy because one complements the other and supplies to the partnership what the other one lacks.

### Law of Nature

Variation is a fundamental law of Nature. Botanists tell us that no two leaves and no two blades of grass have ever been found to be exactly alike.  It is also true that no two animals of the same species are without some slight differences in form and measurement.  Nature is not given to making things alike and the same principle of dissimilarity applies to human beings.

We may be sure that Nature has good reason for insisting on dissimilarity.  We do not set a bulldog to catch a rabbit, nor do we expect a St. Bernard to overtake the fox or the Pekingese to do the job of a Newfoundland and plunge into the water to bring out a drowning person.  But do we use similar good judgment in the expectations we have of ourselves, regardless of what Nature may have given us in the way of mental and physical equipment?

It would be just as much at variance with Nature's intentions to expect a man with tuberculous lungs to become a mountain-climber or get him to run in races.  And it would be quite as irrational to expect a man with a highly-developed brain to content himself with the job of a boiler-maker, or a prodigy of muscular development to enjoy poring over books and burning the midnight oil.  Each one of these individuals, however, is handicapped in a single direction only, for there is something that each one could do—and do particularly well— if only he would concentrate his attention and efforts on the talent he has, instead of using his strength to bewail his defect and to long for the impossible.

So, if we would turn our handicaps into assets we should first of all stop trying to be like others at the point where we are weak and be satisfied to develop faculties which will more than compensate for our defects.  It is no use trying to compete in a line in which we are beaten before we start.

What a list there is of never-to-be-forgotten men and women who have become famous, not only in spite of some overwhelming handicap, but because a deficiency in one direction actually spurred them on to increased efforts!

We doubt if literature lost much through the blindness of Dante, Milton or Homer; rather it would seem to have gained to the extent by which this affliction sheltered these men from the turmoil of their times.

Robert Louis Stevenson, Laurence Sterne and the poet Keats were members of that numerous company whose afflicted lungs fortunately made other occupations than writing impossible.

Nationality plays no part in determining these victories of mind over matter.  Talleyrand's crippled leg did not prevent that Frenchman from becoming the foremost statesman of his epoch.  Byron's club-foot, if it was not exactly an asset in his role of a Don Juan, certainly did nothing to detract from his excellence as a poet.

It is a strange sort of perversity that makes the majority of us prefer to excel in the lines in which we are particularly deficient. The brainy man with the atrophied muscles envies the blacksmith, and the boilermaker with the hypertrophied muscles would like to be a clerk or a college professor.

Byron, who was prevented by his lame leg from taking part in most of the sports of his university days, devoted himself with a perfect fury to horse-riding and swimming, with which the handicap did not interfere. He took more pride in these accomplishments than in the children of his brain, and this devotion to swimming was actually a contributing cause of his untimely death.

## We are all Variants

Fortunately the great majority of us are not handicapped by such serious imperfections. But thousands of men and women do suffer from slight deviations from the normal. Some of these defects may never be overcome, but they can always be compensated for by concentrating attention and effort in other directions.

These defects should not give cause for worry or disappointment, or be allowed to detract from the full quota of work that one owes to the world or from the quota of happiness that life owes in return.

Many of the slight variations from normal occur in those people who are nervously ill or maladjusted. Variants would be a good term for those people suffering from no organic or structural complaints. In one sense or another, we are all variants, just as no two blades of grass are ever found exactly alike in every respect. The majority of us are either above or below the theoretical average in some detail of functional or structural development. Those who are aware of the fact are apt to be discouraged because they are not "just like other people", forgetting that these other people are just as likely to be discouraged because they, in turn, are not like someone else.

Nine times out of ten, the variant's feeling of inadequacy, with the habit of morbid introspection, is the result of comparisons with other people who are supposed to be "normal", "average", or "above the ordinary". There is no better way of starting a first-class inferiority complex and bringing on a state of depression that makes its possessor a nuisance to himself and to everyone with whom he comes in contact, than this method of comparing oneself with others.

Nature dislikes repetition and uniformity in the vegetable and animal world; so there is no difficulty in finding someone who is richer, bigger, healthier, happier or better-looking than ourselves. These differences add to the spice and relish of life, and prevent us from degenerating into automata cut to machine pattern. Such diversities of endowment or acquisition should not be allowed to become sources of envy or jealousy.

Feelings of this sort often lead to the belief that we have been slighted by Nature in mental or physical equipment. It is then only a step further to concluding that we are abnormal or inefficient. And all this can come about through the use of a wrong standard of comparison in judging ourselves by this or that supposedly superior person.

Variety then is not only the spice of life but a fundamental principle of Nature. Yet there are many men and women who demand of themselves, to their own detriment, that they conform with the majority. They apparently do not realise that they need only conform with themselves.

It is true enough that we come by inheritance into assets and defects of bodily structure. There are family traits of vice and virtue, of health, sickness and crime.

Some inherit the broad, deep chest with its powerful lung machinery, others the flat type of chest with its constricted breathing-power, and yet others digestive organs with deficient ligaments and tone.

But it is also true that we all inherit something immeasurably greater than these—an eternal principle within—which endows us with *a limitless power to vary*, upwards as well as downwards, and gives us latitude wherein to save ourselves! And as Man is neither wholly animal, mind or spirit, but a balanced modicum of all three, so must he be studied and helped from these three sides of his nature.

# THE GATES OF THE MIND

"$H$E is so easily influenced—he has a weak character." How often we hear people pass this remark during the course of our daily conversation! We must admit that some of us are more easily influenced than others. People who are easily influenced are called suggestible; those not easily influenced are known as negativistic.

Children are usually more easily influenced than adults, and therefore we refer to them as being suggestible.

But the degree of suggestibility is not a fixed quantity in the case of normal people. This state is something which the average person may control and turn off or on.

We usually protect ourselves with a cloak of resistance—a temporary negativism—when we believe that someone is attempting to influence us to our disadvantage. We lower the portal of receptivity and actually invite more dominance on the part of the person who we feel is able and willing to influence us for the better. Those who would influence themselves for the better should practise auto-suggestion and lower the threshold of entrance for the beneficial suggestions. There are many things that help towards achieving this, such as the relaxation of all the voluntary muscles, limitation of movement, monotony, looking into the fire and listening to certain types of music.

A sudden refreshing, cooling breeze on a hot summer day lowers the threshold. Here also is the reason for the success which so often comes along over discussing business at a meal—the influence seems to come when we are partaking of the meal.

## Control Suggestibility

We should adopt the reverse procedure when we want to resist influences which we do not think are beneficial. We must not relax our voluntary controlled muscles; let us see that there is no great source of monotony; we should not deliberately fixate our gaze or listen to certain music which we know from experience tends to make us more suggestible. This explains many of the natural tendencies in our everyday life. When we tense the facial muscles it tends to keep us alert—guarding the entrance to the mind. This also may explain the reason for the impulse for us to keep moving and active when beset by unreasonable doubts and fears. It is a matter of great importance to control suggestibility or our willingness to be influenced. In order to control our own behaviour as well as the behaviour of other people we should be able, first of all, to control suggestibility.

125

There are, of course, other methods of controlling suggestibility, besides those we have already discussed. Alcohol and tobacco tend to increase suggestibility, while strychnine and coffee tend to decrease it.

Let us take, for example, prestige, which is so often used to increase suggestibility. Men and women, like sheep, tend to follow the leader and respond favourably to what has been sanctioned by those people to whom they look up. A guard should be kept against this type of influence. Just because some celebrity or other prominent person recommends a certain brand of cigarette or soap, it is not necessary that all of us should use it.

Perhaps we can now understand the reason why an indirect suggestion is more powerful than a direct one. A direct suggestion is apt to awaken the sleeping dogs that guard the entrance to the mind, thereby closing the avenues of entrance for every influence, irrespective of whether it is good or bad. The indirect suggestion is often too subtle to be noticed as it passes the portals of the mind and we do not recognise it for the influence that it is meant to be.

If we deliberately tell a person that he looks the picture of health, he is likely to ignore the statement. But if we ask him what is the secret of his exuberant health, that is quite another matter, because the question hides the fact that in a sense we have commanded him to believe that he is healthy.

How can we detect which suggestions are beneficial and which are harmful? There is no clear-cut answer to this question, because very often what is one man's meat is another man's poison. It is little benefit to the person who is already taciturn to talk to him about the value of silence. It can do very little good to a person broken down by over-activity to give him inspiring advice to be up and doing.

### Proof of the Pudding

What then can we use as our measuring stick in regard to the value of a suggestion? In the circumstances we cannot give a better answer than—*judge by results*. If, over a period of time, the results are satisfactory, then they argue for the value of the suggestions. It is understood, of course, that we use our common sense at the outset in choosing our suggestions based upon our own experiences and the experiences of others. We should try and preserve any influences which cause us to think, work and feel better.

Happy and well-adjusted people accumulate and make reservoirs of good suggestions. Favourite pictures, poems or melodies very often are spiritual resources; in fact, one might hold in reserve almost any controllable environmental influence.

There are many eminent people who have veritable mints of such material at their command.

One certain step along the road to self-improvement is in

consciously choosing our influences. On the other hand, the easy acceptance of each new fad and taste is apt to bring about degeneration. It requires great moral courage to ward off some of these negative influences. But if we approach problems from a positive standpoint, then there need be little difficulty, for we shall be so busy building up and reacting to the positive influences that the negative ones will fall into oblivion from sheer neglect. Reservoirs of good suggestions become balance-wheels of emotional stability and give the personality a lower centre of gravity.

The power of a single suggestion given at the psychological moment has very often brought success and achievement to many famous men and women. Individuals have been transformed from money-grubbers into philanthropists, from mere drudges into executives, and sick people have become examples of health by the magic power of right suggestion. If a single suggestion can be of such momentous consequence, then we may now begin to appreciate the power of the continued influences with which we are in daily contact. This will explain why a mildly unfavourable environment tends to "drag us down", why disposition and health suffer when we are employed in any work which is distasteful to us.

In order to avoid being unduly influenced by persons, conditions or places we should learn to control suggestibility. We should also:

Watch our muscular condition. Good muscles signify backbone and may do a great deal in preventing encroachments on our purposes and ambitions. When we tense our muscles it makes us more critical and thereby helps us to ward off undesirable influences.

Understand the methods of mental influence by studying books, courses and magazines dealing with practical and applied psychology.

Develop mastery. Mastery in one direction will give us confidence in other directions. For mastery is built on mastery. By developing our strong points we tend to sweep away our weak ones.

Beware of making excuses. "The meek shall inherit the earth", does not mean to convey that the world belongs to flabby-muscled, spineless and weak-minded individuals; it is simply a plea for reverence and humility in the presence of the great unknown.

# THE PIVOT OF LIFE

*"The strength of a nation . . . is the intelligent and well-ordered homes of the people".*

\* \* \*

IN our literature, in our prose and poetry, in song and story, there is frequent and continual reference made to "home". Nowadays, though the upheaval and disturbance of the past few years have created many exceptions, most of us take it for granted that everyone must have a home of some sort. It may be rich or poor, large or small, happy or unhappy, but it is a place from which we go out into the world and to which we frequently or infrequently return.

For a countless number of years, this home-making has been going on, until it is now an integral part of each human being. This applies to races all over the world, and life is built up around the theme "they built themselves a home".

Many centuries ago, primitive Man built himself a crude abode to shelter him from the elements and from wild animals, or dwelt in a dark cave or a rough shelter made from boughs, mud or the skins of wild beasts.

There, in time, he took a woman—a child was born and the home was started. Apart from the physical side the man derived a certain incomprehensible satisfaction from guarding the woman and child from the dangers of wild beasts. He found satisfaction, too, as he sped for miles in quest of food which he brought home to share with them.

The woman, in her turn, experienced satisfaction from the care she gave to the child and the man, and both almost unconsciously found release from the burden of loneliness. In more and more ways, they discovered increasing benefits from this way of life.

Even in the Bible it has been written: "Two are better than one, because they have a good reward for their labour. For if they fall, the one will lift up his fellow; but woe to him that is alone when he falleth, for he hath not another to help him up. Again if two lie together; then they have heat; but how can one be warm alone? And if one prevail against him, two shall withstand him, and a threefold cord is not quickly broken" (Ecclesiastes 4: 9–12).

So the home came to mean father, mother and family. It also stood for strength in unity, both spiritual and physical—inwardly and towards the outside world.

Even in those early beginnings of home-building, it was vaguely

128

realised that unity meant strength. Unity meant companionship—the banishment of loneliness. Unity meant satisfaction for inner urges and instincts, which more than compensated for any loss of freedom.

From these early days of mating and home-making, there developed the crude beginnings of that community of interest which is called civilisation.

Primitive Man doubtless lived a more or less isolated and solitary existence. But he was never without an elementary family life. With the evolution of the race, the gregarious instinct became more highly developed. It was met by the broadening of the family group. Children and grandchildren were kept together and families grew in size. Later, a number of families joined forces, founding a tribe for mutual protection. Then tribes joined in communities of interest and became known as nations. Laws were gradually imposed to protect the family and to maintain stability in society. Thus marriage became synonymous with home-making.

## Protection and Stability

Every normal young man or woman has a picture in his or her mind—a picture of a home. As the individual grows and develops, so does this picture grow and develop until the time when each person meets the individual he or she feels just fits into that picture.

The picture develops according to the sex of the individual and according to his or her tastes and interests. The actual picture may never be realised, but the dream is there on which to build, and faith in the success of the new home is the best and only lodger to take into any newly-weds' home.

Society and the continuation of our present civilisation depend on the birth-rate. Children are the future of the world; therefore creating new family groups is of major importance. So society protects the women and children in order to ensure its own stability. Women, too, seek marriage as a means of economic security, for only in the job of homemaking do women feel they are superior to men.

The Christian Church has supported society in its efforts to maintain a high standard of marriage and home life. It has sanctified marriage and raised the ideal to a spiritual height almost impossible of achievement. But even to aim at this ideal and only partially succeed means not only individual happiness, but order and stability in society instead of disorder, unhappiness and misery.

The superficial beliefs that are far too prevalent to-day, that marriage is purely for selfish reasons, for the satisfaction of physical desires, for economic reasons, for support or social success, are fated to be disillusioned, for that way leads only to disharmony, unhappiness and disappointment.

## Trial Marriages

How do we know that it's real love? How can we know that our choice of a life partner is the right one? How can we know that the one we select *is* the wisest choice for marriage? Will our marriage be a success? The answers that psychologists can give to these questions are not sufficiently well known. Hence the reason that some people advocate trial marriages.

Trial marriages, so we are given to understand, have been allowed in certain countries—with what success we have little information by which to judge.

Sometimes individuals have taken such a task on themselves, rarely, if ever with success. For it is only the rare individual who has the type of strength and personality to live happily while riding against the stream of social approval.

## Is the Home Breaking Up?

Trial marriage propaganda is only one of the causes behind what appears to be a threat to the home and the family unit. With the large number of divorce and separation cases, the thought must inevitably crop up, that home and family life is growing less strong and permanent. Though this may appear so at present, and it is something that is to be deplored and causes grave concern, yet the need for the security and warmth of home is greater than ever.

Apart from the greater ease with which divorce can now be secured, the incidence of two major World Wars fought over the countries of Europe, leaving thousands of children homeless through being orphaned, deserted or having their homes destroyed, has weakened the belief in an existence of family life. *But* it has not lessened the urgent need of the home, not only for children, but for adults.

## Causes of Disruption

Only as short a time as one hundred and fifty years ago, home was the social centre—life was smaller, narrower, extending only for a very few beyond the bounds of the village or small town. There were no large cities as we know them to-day. Few people travelled, for travel was difficult, expensive and often dangerous from bad roads, the elements, footpads and thieves.

The last fifty years have widened the individual's outlook and experience amazingly, and brought about far-reaching changes in everyday life. Cinemas and later television have brought to one's fireside the activities, interests and beauties, not only of one's own country, but of the whole world. Books and broadcasts stimulate interest. Many people, old and young, thirsting for experience and knowledge, are eager to see places and meet people first hand.

Holidays have become the accepted thing from the highest worker to the lowest. Communications and means of transport have been improved and widened by increased speed, improved comfort and lower cost. Transport is used not only for industry and business, but for pleasure—for those who are travel-conscious.

Work eventually takes children away from the home, while holidays more often than not mean that the home is deserted. The world is a much smaller place; thus the family tends to shrink in importance, the ties become less strong and vital.

There are, of course, many other causes which work against successful marriage. The test of a marriage lies, not in the first few months, but in the mundane routine of everyday life, in getting down to living in a world that is more often than not filled with the petty trials that are the lot of most of us in whatever status of life we may be.

It is as well before marriage to look at life with eyes wide open and feet planted firmly on the ground. After the first romantic flush of marriage has passed, one or both may become irked by a certain limit set upon one's freedom; selfishness steps in, lack of thought and consideration for the partner, and happiness is threatened.

Financial and economic reasons—usually too little money, though sometimes too much—can threaten the stability of marriage, childlessness or too many children often causes disillusionment and disharmony, while the sex relationship upon which wedlock is built, all too often brings about its downfall through ignorance or stupidity on the part of one or both parties. Sometimes ill health or the interference of relatives may wreck what may otherwise have worked out to be a happy, stable home life.

Marriage is one of the most difficult of all human relationships. *But* the rewards to those who have the love, patience and faith to win through are worth the struggle and the sacrifice.

There is no marriage that does not at some time, for some reason, pass through a period of difficulty and danger when its very structure is threatened. But problems can be solved, especially to-day, with the help that science, marriage guidance councils and psychiatrists can give.

If it is difficult for the individual to learn to live happily with himself, it is much more difficult to learn to live harmoniously-with someone else. But it can be done. And it is being done. It is a duty we owe to the world and to those whom we contact, that we should so strive to adjust ourselves. If we have a problem, we should not isolate ourselves, fill ourselves with self-pity, on the assumption that no one else ever had a problem like ours. Other people have experienced similar problems and are experiencing them now. Many have overcome them.

## Challenge to Home-makers

During the last World War, when men, especially very young men,
were existing under the most nerve-racking conditions in many parts
of the world, some of them cracked up.  It was found that men broke
more easily under strain who had no home, no home ties, bad homes
and in effect—no one who cared.  Those who came from homes where
there were unity, harmony and affection, even though they were poor
homes, possessed an unconscious spiritual strength which maintained
them through great hardship and strain.

What the home-makers need to-day and in the future, whether
they already have a home or are only planning or dreaming about one,
is faith, and courage to battle through the difficulties that arise in
every home and in every family.  If people would only put half the
energy and determination they put in trying to secure separation or
divorce, into trying to overcome misunderstandings and bickerings in
the family group, they would be repaid a hundred-fold by success,
peace and harmony.  And there would certainly be a far less number
of broken homes.

All threats to the family are in themselves a challenge to the home-
makers.  The need for the home and the family circle is still there—
strong and insistent.  It is an imperative need, for the individual, the
group society and the human race.  But it must be made so strong, so
attractive, so powerful in its influence and memories that it can be
felt across the world, and maybe later—through space!  Who knows?
For the home is still the root and foundation of all life.  It means
security, sanity, satisfaction!

# MAN'S GREATEST ASSET

THE greatest need of humanity to-day is peace of mind. The greatest tragedy of our age is that peace of mind is so rare.

Man, who was destined for mastery, is becoming a slave to inner conflicts that sap his strength, a prey to doubts and fears that rob him of his manhood, and reduce him to the level of the brute creation.

The human heart, like an angry ocean, seethes with discontent; morality and ideals are undergoing profound changes; and almost nowhere is there to be found the peace for which men and women yearn with every fibre of their being.

Man craves something better than a day-to-day existence fraught with anxiety and beset by conflict. From the depths of his innermost soul there comes a plea for deliverance from the heartaches and tribulations of life.

What antidote has psychology to prescribe for the poison of unrest that has entered our very souls? Before attempting to answer this question, let us examine what else is being done to solve the problem.

## Fed, Clothed and Sheltered

The basic needs of man are that he should be fed, clothed and sheltered. These are the bare essentials needed to maintain a minimum of decency and dignity for human life, to secure survival in the face of the rigours of Nature. There are those who would claim that once these needs are satisfied, the other requirements of human nature will take care of themselves. The welfare state has become a symbol of our reliance upon material provisions as a means of securing the happiness and well-being of disquieted humanity.

It is certainly true that unless these needs were satisfied, man would not long survive in his constant struggle against the hostile forces of his environment. While it is important that he should be fed, clothed and sheltered, this solution merely scratches the surface of the problem. It is the foundation-stone upon which we may erect the edifice of more abundant life. It is a means to the end of fulfilment. If we mistake the means for the end, however, we are falling into the gravest kind of error, and will be called upon to face the consequences of our short-sighted policy.

The emptiness of the human heart demands a nobler aspiration than bread, raiment, and a roof over our heads. The conditions for peace of mind are not guaranteed merely by satisfying the urge for survival on the material plane. The futility of supposing that man

133

shall live by bread alone is clearly seen in the mental distress that afflicts even those countries where the standard of living is highest.

In a world of changing values one fact remains unchanged, like a firm rock amid shifting sands: never before in history has so much outer achievement given man so little inner security. The times are marked by portents that men are seeking a way of life worthy of men, a gospel that will appease the yearning for peace and assuage the unrest of the heart.

In some human hearts the need is formulated neither fully nor clearly, but even the least sensitive experience at times the prick of conscience that assures them of greater possibilities, that endeavours to awaken them to a fuller awareness of their destiny.

"Man is capable of infinite accomplishment," declares Dr. Henry Knight Miller in an essay on "The Goal of Life", "once he awakens from his dull, sodden stupor, contacts the divinity slumbering within and launches forth in his quest of the sunlit summits."

### The Philosophy of Enjoyment

Many men and women who sense the yearning for a higher way of life have nevertheless despaired of the practical possibility of attaining it. Discarding peace of mind as an idealistic will-o'-the-wisp, they have persuaded themselves to exchange happiness for pleasure.

True, it has not been necessary to marshal many arguments to induce them to adopt this view and put it into practice, for the modern world holds no lack of incitements to pleasure-seeking. "Eat, drink and be merry" is the persuasive slogan of the hedonist's quest for satisfaction of the senses. Wine, women and song become for him the highest good of life. He pursues these pleasurable objectives not as a means of survival but as a philosophy of enjoyment.

It would be futile to deny the role of pleasure as a contribution to the maintenance of human life above the level of animal existence. Indeed, the view is held in psychology that man has learned the habits that constitute his adjustment to his environment by pursuing those goals that in the light of experience have yielded pleasure.

This theory plays an important part in psycho-analysis, which has perceived perhaps more clearly than any of the other biological sciences that by nature man follows the pleasure principle: he seeks the gratification of desire. It would perhaps be better to speak of the pleasure-without-guilt principle, since pleasure that makes a person feel guilty is generally unacceptable to him, even though he may feel compelled to indulge in it. For, in seeking this indulgence, the individual finds himself blocked by the dictates of his own conscience and the realities of his physical and social environment. Out of this situation arise the conflicts and tensions that disturb our peace of mind.

The limitations of the method of seeking happiness via exclusive abandonment to pleasure are commented upon by Dr. Sigmund Freud, the founder of psycho-analysis. In *Civilization and its Discontents* he thus voices hedonism's dilemma: "Its programme is in conflict with the whole world. . . . It simply cannot be put into execution, the whole constitution of things runs counter to it. . . . What is called happiness in its narrowest sense comes from the satisfaction—most often instantaneous—of pent-up needs which have reached great intensity, and by its very nature can only be a transitory experience."

Although the state of mind that we regard as our ideal is something of a more permanent nature, it would be idle to maintain that the philosophy of enjoyment contributes nothing to it. Bishop Fulton J. Sheen in his book, *Way to Happiness*, suggests that we can make it easier for our pleasures to contribute to our happiness if we follow a simple law. If we are ever to have a good time, he says, we should not plan our lives so as to include nothing but good times. The pleasure of achievement is like the beauty of midsummer: the one is conditioned by contrast with the hardship of attaining it, just as the other is set in relief by the sombre hues of winter.

## A Purpose in Life

If either looking after our physical welfare, or devoting ourselves to the pursuit of pleasure fails to satisfy us, how are we to attain the mental condition we envisage? Peace of mind is achieved only when a man develops the understanding that enables him to relate himself to the cosmos in a meaningful way, and to find for himself some satisfactory role to play in the great scheme of things.

Man's finite longings are pitted against the infinity of the universe. Unless he is to be overawed by the vastness of space and time, when he compares them with his own puny stature, he must see some purpose in his own existence. Each individual must answer for himself the question that his presence in the world poses. If he can convince himself that his life serves some purpose in the lives of those around him, his sense of futility and worthlessness will be banished, and he will know that in fulfilling that purpose he has the surest guarantee of peace of mind that the world can be expected to provide. Amid the buffeting of life's storms he will stand unshaken because his faith will be founded on a solid rock of affinity with the cosmos.

Such a man will know that he cannot achieve happiness and peace of mind by seeking them directly. His peace of mind will come as a by-product of his meaningful activity in relation to the world around him. "The happy man," says Dr. Karl S. Bernhardt, "is not one who is seeking happiness exclusively; rather he is a person who is busy doing something he thinks is worth doing. . . . He is losing himself in something he believes to be more important than himself."

L.C.—10

## Inner Harmony

We live in an age which is obsessed by the conviction that material needs are all that count. Many men and women sense within themselves a feeling that nothing matters but wealth. Their lives are meaningless for lack of a truly inspiring goal. The wage packet and the football pool are but the outward signs of an inner unrest that betokens a yearning deeper than money can satisfy. In the midst of things that are temporal and transient, humanity seeks a greater fund of abiding spiritual values.

The fundamental truths of religion are not always presented in a manner that commands respect for their merit. Too often is the common man left to flounder in a mire of misunderstanding and unpractical counsel that adds to his confusion of mind rather than releases him from it. Is it little wonder, then, that disillusioned man has turned in hurt contempt to the materialistic side of life, which promises him at least outward comfort even if his conflict continues to rage within?

The different ways in which this conflict is solved create the major demands that the individual makes on his physical and social environment. They also stimulate him to respond to the demands that the society in which he lives makes on him for his contribution to its continued existence. Men and women differ in their insistence upon their own demands and in their ability and willingness to answer the demands of others. Some are anxious above all for security, others are willing to take risks in the pursuit of pleasure, while others display a frank zest for achievement. The kind of security, pleasure or achievement desired also differs with the individual. These individual differences are probably due partly to heredity and partly to environment. To the poor man happiness signifies wealth. To the hungry it represents good living. To the sick it means health. Yet there are happy men who are neither rich, well fed nor one hundred per cent fit. What is the secret of their contentment? To all it proclaims the message that practical psychology echoes: the possession of inward harmony is the key to happiness and the secret of poise. Let a man be secure in the citadel of his own soul and he can steel himself to face with courage the tempest that shakes the world outside.

# MISGUIDED TOLERANCE

CERTAIN extreme idealists are remarkably fluent and voluble in offering advice calculated to solve most of the problems of mankind in one glorious sweep. These idealists are usually sincere enough, and they are to be admired for setting such high standards of human behaviour. The trouble is that many rules of conduct suggested by the idealists turn out to be sweeping generalisations. They may sound very nice in theory, but, unfortunately, they seldom work out satisfactorily in practice.

For example, let us consider just one "noble ideal"—a piece of apparently good advice given to us by well-meaning people.

"If only we were more tolerant, one to another," they say, "this world would be a much happier place."

We may agree with that statement, but is it true? Not necessarily. It is a loose generalisation; a half truth, and in some instances can be a very misleading piece of advice. It is true that we ought to show greater tolerance *in some respects*. It is equally true that we are inclined to be *far too tolerant* in other directions, and this can be very foolish or even dangerous.

We see, then, how unwise is the glib statement that greater tolerance all round will improve the world for everybody. It simply isn't true!

Just as actions shouldn't be judged without due consideration of the motives which prompted them, so tolerance shouldn't be hailed as a virtue unless we consider what is to be tolerated, why and for how long.

## One Extreme to the Other

Let us look, for example, at industrial relations. Years ago many employers exploited their workers by compelling them to work very long hours, often under appalling conditions and for a miserable pittance. Eventually the workers banded themselves together in Trade Unions in order to protect their interests and demand fair treatment. Who can blame them? Would continued tolerance of mean exploitation have been a virtue in that case? Surely not!

Now the pendulum seems to have swung to the other extreme. Instances have been reported where employers hardly dare dismiss a man for gross inefficiency, carelessness or trouble-making, because it would, in all probability, cause a strike.

Let's be fair about this sort of thing. Employers who pay good wages and provide congenial working conditions surely are entitled

137

to loyalty and good service from their employees. Why should any decent employer be expected to be almost blackmailed into the acceptance of bad workers or trouble-makers in his organisation? Why are some workers themselves willing to tolerate colleagues who refuse to do their fair share of the work? It just doesn't make sense. A chain is only as strong as its weakest link. The bad worker is a weak link in the chain of any organisation.

### Unreliable Service

Whilst on the subject of efficient service, a word must be said about the relationship between the general public and those whose duty it is to serve them.

In a recent case a business woman complained to a railway official that her train seldom arrived at its destination on time. This often caused her to be late for business appointments. Do you know the answer she got? "You could always catch an earlier train."

Now this just isn't good enough. The public are frequently being asked to pay increased fares for transport. There may be all sorts of legitimate reasons why a train is running late, but when a scheduled business train is persistently late the service is inefficient. It is no use officialdom trying to wriggle out of that one. The public who pay the fare are entitled to the service they pay for—or at least an adequate reason why they are not getting it. Why should such off-hand treatment as the above case suggests be tolerated?

Countless similar examples could be given of shabby treatment being endured by the long-suffering public. If you pay for a diamond ring you don't expect the "gem" to be a piece of glass—and no reputable jeweller would deceive you in this way. Why, then, should we tolerate those tradespeople who try to push off inferior goods at top prices, as they sometimes do? Why should we put up with bad workmanship, unreliable service or shoddy goods of any kind?

Nowadays, in fact, reliable service seems to be the exception rather than the rule. No matter what promises may be made, the chances are that they will not be kept. This is no exaggeration. It happens to us all, over and over again. There are, to-day, wonderful opportunities open to enterprising business people who are able to maintain *reliable service* as well as give good value for money.

### Domestic and Social Affairs

Now let us turn to family and social matters, and see how far tolerance may be exercised in these spheres.

Suppose a happily married couple find their lives suddenly blighted by chronic illness. Perhaps the wife becomes an invalid, for example. This is a case where tolerance on both sides is a supreme virtue. What would we think of a husband who lost interest in his wife because she had the misfortune to become an invalid? If a man loves his wife he will learn to tolerate all the inconveniences that her invalidism imposes upon him. Such a wife, on her part, should try to tolerate her own incapacity and all that it means. She should also tolerate any forgivable lapses in her husband's behaviour. What a blessing is tolerance in these circumstances!

On the other hand, there may be circumstances in marriage and family life where tolerance is a curse rather than a blessing. The wife who has a brutal, perhaps criminal husband would be a fool to tolerate him indefinitely, no matter what religion might have to say to the contrary. If she submits meekly to life with such a man she is *encouraging* him in his evil way of living. Many a good woman, through her misguided sense of loyalty and affection to a man not worthy of the name, has lived to regret her devotion. Tolerance is all very well on occasions, but *wrongfully directed* it is no better than selling one's soul for a mere pottage.

What about the gentle, inoffensive man who remains tied to a shrew of a wife whose bitter tongue and mental cruelty drive him to distraction? Is his tolerance of such an existence a virtue? A tolerant attitude in these circumstances can only do harm to both partners. If a shrewish wife makes no attempt to change her ways, then her husband would do well to teach her a few sharp lessons instead of tolerating her objectionable behaviour. What *good* does his toleration do to either of them? It merely condemns him to a miserable existence and does *nothing* to improve his wife's character.

In Juvenile Courts we often hear a child described as "beyond parental control". How can any child be beyond parental control, except because of the foolish toleration shown by its parents? Parents who continue to tolerate misbehaviour from their children are laying up endless trouble for themselves, for the children concerned, for the school teachers, the police and other responsible authorities, and for society in general. No wonder so many young people are vicious hooligans. Judging from some of the trivial penalties meted out to them, it seems that we are expected to tolerate almost anything.

Vandalism in cinemas, parks and other public places has become so prevalent that it is almost taken for granted. In one district the local Council tried to make the main road more attractive by planting young flowering trees along the footpath. Within a few weeks one one-third of the young saplings had been broken in half by irresponsible persons. Vandalism should not be tolerated in a civilised community. Those responsible should be brought to book with heavy penalties inflicted.

An unusual case was reported recently concerning a motorist who surprised a youth fumbling about in the boot of his car. Finding himself caught in the act, the youth whipped out a knife and lunged at the motorist. This motorist happened to be an ex-Commando, an expert in the art of self-defence. He wrenched the knife from the youth's hand, breaking two of the young thug's fingers in the process. The youth then tried to kick, but the motorist grabbed the lad's foot and twisted it so sharply that the shoe was pulled off. The youth managed to escape, but there's no doubt that his unpleasant experience will do him far more good than all the tolerance in the world. He won't forget that lesson in a hurry. Why should we put up with these vicious young hooligans? They need to be taught sharp lessons in the only terms they understand. They regard tolerance as weakness—and they will continue to terrorise all who tolerate their brutalities. No society can long remain civilised if it permits uncivilised behaviour. It must be quickly nipped in the bud, without any hesitation.

## Misplaced Tolerance

Even some sections of the Christian Church appear to be "sitting on the fence", uncertain what they ought to tolerate and what they ought to fight against. This is a most unfortunate situation, for we look to the Church for spiritual guidance.

Victor Hugo asserted, "Toleration is the best religion." The truth of his belief is open to grave doubt. Probably much nearer the truth was the philosopher who declared, "Toleration does not mark the progress of a religion. It is the fatal sign of its decline."

Many of us are puzzled as to why some Christian Churches are losing their appeal to the general public. Possibly misplaced tolerance has something to do with it. Has Christianity become too soft in parts? Is it losing the courage of its convictions? Is it too ready to compromise, shutting its eyes to certain wrongs in its anxiety not to offend public opinion?

For example, we have heard of certain leaders of the Christian Church who apparently raise no objection to the atomic bomb. They suggest that we should accept this terrible weapon as a necessary deterrent and learn to live with it.

Now from the *military* viewpoint, it may or not be true that stockpiling of atom bombs is essential for our protection. The majority of the general public may also approve of this theory. But how *any* minister of the Christian religion can support the manufacture and stocking of atom bombs is beyond many people's comprehension. There are some critics who have a strong suspicion that these same Christian ministers would readily condemn the sale of flick-knives because they know that public opinion is behind them in this.

With all due respect, a large and important part of the Christian Church seems to have lost much of its fighting spirit. So anxious is it not to *offend* the masses, that it has become much too tolerant of many evils in this world.

The preacher who attracts large congregations is not the one who mumbles platitudes from the pulpit or proclaims a milk-and-water philosophy, but the one who can preach a rousing, fighting, even controversial sermon. If the Church has good reason to disapprove of this or that, it should come out into the open and declare exactly where it stands, in no uncertain terms, regardless of whom it might offend. By tolerating the dangers that threaten our age the Church seems to be "playing to the gallery" in the hope of gaining popularity. But all it is likely to gain by these tactics is contempt. We are seeing many signs of this already.

Jesus didn't tolerate evil, he strongly condemned it. Though he was crucified for daring to defy the tyranny of his day and opposing powerful interests, his vital teachings have not only survived down through the ages but have changed the course of history into fairer ways.

### Careful Discrimination

This question of tolerance crops up in every sphere of life, and further examples may not be necessary in this article. They come to mind easily enough.

There is certainly plenty of scope for more toleration in many directions and circumstances. It is a question of careful discrimination. Youth should be ready to make allowances for the seasoned opinions of maturity and for the prejudices of old age. Parents should learn to tolerate the wild enthusiasm and high spirits of youth. Educated people should remember to show tolerance towards those who may display their ignorance. People blessed with sound mental and physical health should tolerate the presence of weaklings, knowing that medical science is doing all it can to help these people. Those of us who have firm convictions in one direction or another should tolerate the fact that everybody else has the right to equally strong opinions, even if they conflict with our own.

Nevertheless, having made allowances for all these and similar examples of the virtue of tolerance, we must recognise that *in certain cases and circumstances* tolerance can be a vice rather than a virtue.

Possibly stemming from war-time regulations which had to be rigorously observed, we are now inclined to adopt a docile attitude to most inconveniences and impositions. In short, most of us have become so accustomed to being pushed around that we accept it almost without question.

Whilst we do not advocate violence in any form except in dire necessity of self-defence, we do advocate a return of the fighting spirit, to be used with discrimination. Instinctively we know what we ought to put up with and what we ought to resist. Unfortunately, many of us seem to have become rather soft or indifferent—hence we tolerate far too much with no more than a murmur of dissent.

Let us resolve to be patient, charitable, kind and tolerant when the situation and circumstances demand it, according to our conscience and good judgment. But let us dig in our heels and fight against all injustice, cruelty, thuggery, sloth, iniquity, vandalism, dishonesty and other wickedness wherever it raises its ugly head.

What we do is usually not so important as our motive for doing it. What we *fail* to do is often more harmful than our positive acts. Misguided tolerance is a useless shield against the enemies of civilisation and all humanity.

# CHARACTER AND CONDUCT

*"A good character is the fruit of personal exertion. It is not inherited from parents, it is not created by external advantages, it is not necessarily an appendage of birth, wealth, talents or station, but it is the result of one's own endeavours".*

*     *     *

"AS a man thinketh—so is he!"

Readers of *Psychology* are familiar with this dictum and appreciate the fact that we can be made or unmade by our prevalent habits of thought.

But there is another aspect of the matter to which our attention should be drawn. We make ourselves potentially for good or evil, for success or failure, by our dominating habits of thought. As we think, in the main, so we become! But we should not overlook the fact that as we live our lives from day to day, so, too, do we make our own fortunes or encompass our own defeat. For action must follow thought; it is of little use to think nobly and constructively if we act contrary to the thought.

It has become all too common to ascribe our frailties to the accident of birth and environment, to blame our faults upon heredity or luck. The man who is timid, fearful, unenterprising, often asserts that his condition is due to mediocre parents or an unhappy childhood. The woman whose life is ridden by anxiety frequently blames it upon an unfortunate social environment in early childhood.

But we are the products not so much of our environment nor our heredity but of our own mental processes; we can overcome limitations imposed upon us by heredity and we can build new environments.

We are where we are, chiefly because we are what we are, and we are what we are because of the character of our habitual and accumulative thoughts. What we are to-day is the outcome of what we were *yesterday*! What we will be to-morrow depends upon how we think—*and live—to-day*!

## Self-development

The mastery of life largely depends upon character. And though we inherit certain tendencies and have no control over the good or bad circumstances at the start of life's race, nevertheless we build our own characters from day to day. The selfish character is the outcome of yesterday's selfishness; the weak character is the result of past evasion of responsibility; the sturdy, independent, fearless character is the result of the development of those desirable qualities acquired over the years.

We should, therefore, be careful how we spend our minutes, for we are in the process of helping to create our own destinies.

Ideal characters can help us to weather the worst storms of adversity, can help us to forge our way through set-backs and failures to eventual triumph and success. Character is the key to successful living.

Let us take, for example, two men with roughly equal abilities who have had more or less equal opportunities. The one with the strong, upright, forceful character will easily outstrip the other in life's race. And what is more, character gives one the ability to *enjoy* life.

When we have developed character, we are no longer at the mercy of baseless fears and groundless anxieties. It is the difference between an unmanned boat on a rough sea and a well-skippered craft. The latter will weather the storm, even use the power of the storm to drive the ship to port; the former will be at the mercy of wind and wave and will probably founder. Character is indeed one of life's rudders.

### Formation of Character

The saying that the Battle of Waterloo was won upon the playing fields of Eton is sufficiently well known. It is often used both to defend and to attack the British public school system; it is used to point to the tremendous value of schools with a tradition and also to show up the snobbery which is an ingredient of our make-up.

We are not concerned with the merits or demerits of the matter. While there is a great deal to be said both for and against the public school system, nevertheless, there is one point that can be emphasised in favour of it. The old English public schools concentrated on the *building of character*; whether or not they employed the best methods may be open to question, but they did at least realise the importance of character-building.

One often wonders whether present-day educationalists attach sufficient importance to this part of their work. Judging by some of the remarks we hear and by some of the results we see concerning these so-called modern methods, one perhaps may be pardoned for raising the query.

The fact remains that the development of mind, the training of personal qualities, is insufficient without the cohesive force of character.

The spoilt child is an apt illustration of this. Such a child may be brilliant, may score outstanding academic success—but he will be beaten by life unless he develops a sturdy, self-reliant, strong character.

Life asks more of most of us than that we should be clever. However well fate may treat us, even though we may have more than the average share of so-called "luck", life cannot be satisfying, worth while or noble without the sheet anchor of character.

## Co-ordinating Abilities

Perhaps we cannot progress very far in our discussion without first attempting to define "character". To some people the very word conjures up an image of an eccentric personality, someone who grows a beard, dresses shabbily or has some peculiar personal traits. "What a character!" is the remark applied.

But that is not what we mean to imply in regard to character. One of the most satisfying definitions of what we have in mind is:

"Character is the co-ordination of *all* our abilities to secure the *maximum* endeavour to reach a desired and worth-while goal by honest efforts."

There are many other definitions that can be applied, but the one quoted meets with most of the requirements for the purpose of our discussion. Let us look at it in greater detail.

*The co-ordination of abilities*, for instance. There is more in this than we would assume at first glance.

Let us take, for example, a man of lively imagination allied to a charming personality. Those very gifts can make either plausible rogues—or successful businessmen. It is character that can harness those gifts so as to enable them to use their abilities in the service of the community.

Another example is the boy who finds easy successes at school. He may not have to study very hard because he has an exceptionally good memory; he finds he has a "flair" for examinations. These very abilities, which could stand him in good stead in later life, can be his ruin unless he builds up a strong character that makes him tackle the difficult tasks, the menial duties, the unpleasant necessities of life.

Character keeps us on the rails when our gifts and abilities of themselves might make us enemies of society.

## Maximum Endeavour

We come now to the second point in our definition: *to secure the maximum endeavour.*

We have, time and time again, pointed out that many failures were due to the fact that men and women had not tried to achieve their objective *with all they had.*

As an illustration of this, there is the case of a young man who has become an accountant, yet all the time hampers his own progress by wishing he had been given the chance in another field of endeavour. He will not find full satisfaction in his career unless he likes it and goes into it heart and soul.

Then there is the case of the young married woman, disillusioned by the chores of keeping house, shopping and the many cares of the average housewife. She may wish with all her heart that she had remained single and continued her previous occupation. But that is no way to make her marriage a success!

Whatever we have started upon—whatever our major objective may be—it deserves the whole of our energies without any forlorn regrets or day-dreams of more pleasant enterprises we might have undertaken. We must bend *all* our efforts towards achieving our objective, harness *all* our resources, *all* our energies, *all* our abilities, if we would find satisfaction and success.

And character is the co-ordinating force that can bring and focus our strength and our ability towards the realisation of our self-chosen goal.

## Worth-while Objective

The third aspect of the definition we should stress is the factor of a *worth-while goal*.

Moral considerations apart, there is no reason why we should not set ourselves an objective that is anti-social. But it is character that ensures the choice of a life-goal that will be satisfying because our chosen goal should meet certain fundamental needs of our nature.

We shall not find fulfilment of our choice if our objective ignores the three demands of life. We must find fulfilment in work—we shall not discover it in idleness. We must seek success and happiness within the framework of social relationships—we cannot find success and happiness in the hermit's existence. And we must have a concern for the welfare of the community.

Success, achievement and the satisfying life will not be the lot of those who seek to reach their goal by utterly ruthless means or by taking a mean advantage of the community.

It is only by giving service to others and by the enrichment of the community that we can ensure life's most satisfying rewards.

Thus, character not only enables us to reach our life's objective, but takes a hand in the selection of it; discarding that which would bring disaster and choosing an objective which will give us personal success and satisfaction through service to our fellow-men.

## The Inner Voice

Character and that old-fashioned word "conscience" are very closely related, and this is an important point when we come to consider how to build up character.

For we do not achieve a strong, upright, forceful character by the way of wish-fulfilment. No! Character is being influenced slowly but surely, throughout the whole of our lives. Every single act of every day contributes in a large or small measure to the formation of character. The small selfishnesses in the home; the unworthy deed unknown to the world; the simple heroism in domestic life; the kindliness to our neighbours and friends—these are the elements that form character.

There is little doubt that, in the majority of life's problems, we know the right course and the wrong one. We may seek to make excuses for adopting the latter, but we have an inner voice that tells us the way we should go.

So let us do our best to act on the highest level; seek the right course of action; be friendly, helpful, unselfish—that is the way to form great, upright, powerful, impregnable characters—ideal characters that can lift us immeasurably to the summits of loftier achievement in all that makes life most abundantly worth while.

# WHAT IS TRUTH?

*This question has come echoing down through the Corridors of Time ever since Man first walked the earth.*

\*   \*   \*

ONE of the greatest questions foremost in the mind of Man has been "What is Truth?" It is a question that for ever holds the deepest interest of mankind, yet one that seems never to have been fully answered.

What is Truth? Is there an answer for those who eagerly seek it?

There appears to be no single mind capable of discovering or enunciating the entire truth, however highly evolved it may be.

Indeed, there is no subject on which Truth is likely to be known, for two very good reasons: First, no human being can have completed his evolution in a Cosmos which is still in a state of becoming. And secondly, the Cosmos being still in a state of becoming, truth is only relative.

We can study the records down through the ages only to find the same story: Whatever is accepted as true and final is denied in later years.

It is not always because the old truth has been found to be untrue, but because new light has modified it and given it another aspect.

In trying to find a solution to the problem we may have thought of something like this: Although it may not actually be that Man is born to trouble as the sparks fly upward, nevertheless, it is only through mistakes that he learns; only through unhappiness that he knows happiness.

Time after time Man sees examples of what is regarded as the inevitable on all sides, and, try as he may, he still is confronted with the idea that behind all phenomena there is a great purpose that moves in one direction and that it is useless to attempt to stop or turn aside.

He cannot throw off the notion and he sees his fellow-men banding together in little groups and adhering to some form of this conception —a form which will differ in name according to the society or group joined—yet nevertheless holding certain fundamental views of the Cosmos which are identical.

Thousands of books, written in all ages, by all nationalities, in all languages, support the views put forth by the various groups of human beings.

In other words, it has been assumed that there existed such a thing as *Truth*. In so many instances it has been possible to *prove* its

148

existence, and that it is predicated of all things, all thought and every phase of consciousness.

The very use of the word *law* is a tribute to this quality of truth which is supposed to be innate in all things.

Again, we have the term "cause and effect". If certain actions are set in operation, we look for and generally find certain results. Therefore, we contend that what we predicate of such actions is truth. What we call the Laws of Nature furnish us with further examples and confirm our notions of truth. So here we have a stereotyped conception of Truth in which like causes produce like effects and give rise to the science of logic—in fact, almost philosophy.

Every time a theory is confirmed we think we have clinched the argument for the existence of this subtle thing called Truth. It becomes our guiding star, our ideal, to which everything dear to the heart of Man is sacrificed.

## So-called Facts

Yet the purpose of life seems to be continuous advancement, and this necessitates the constant appropriation of the new and the constant elimination of the old. Does not one age decry the work of its predecessors? Is there a science (except mathematics, perhaps) that has not been turned upside down, that has not throw away its theories, its outlook, and adopted new ones forced upon it by so-called "facts"?

The presence of error seems to be universally admitted. To-day is a period of doubt and unrest in practically every country, in religion, politics, labour, art, philosophy. Wherever there are human beings to be found, the "millennium" or the "big change" is being looked for by most people. We suppose that if things were satisfactory they would be true, assuming that Plato was correct in regarding the good, the beautiful and the true as one and the same thing.

It is a moot question whether if such a thing as Truth exists it could do so side by side with error, and that error does exist will not be questioned by the majority of people.

## Man-made Theories

The trouble seems to be that what one generation terms "error" was the previous generation's idea of "Truth". The most horrible cruelties, barbarities and persecutions have, in the past, been defended on the grounds of Truth. Texts showing the world to be flat were quoted to deter Columbus from his so-called unholy effort to sail around it.

Some years ago, one of the big world-movements had as its motto: "There is no religion higher than Truth," but rival schools retorted, aping the time-worn question of Pilate: "What is Truth?"

Even Biblical records, despite all the efforts that have been made to harmonise them, do not always agree in telling the same story. In the Creation story in Genesis we find two separate histories by different authors joined together. Each gives a different order of Creation: one states that the animals were created first and that Man was created as the climax; the other says that Adam was created first and then the animals.

In the story of the deluge there are likewise two or more accounts joined together from different authors. One states that two of each kind of animal were brought into the Ark; the other records that two of all unclean and seven of all clean animals entered the Ark. One account states that it rained for forty days; the other that it rained for one hundred and fifty days.

The question, "What is Truth?" is still a real poser to many people of to-day.

*Is it possible that truth is what we make it?* This conception is opposed to the universal one that Truth consists of certain verities which Man can choose at will and with which he may act in harmony if he so wishes, or that he may reject them by following error and being punished for his pains.

It sometimes is assumed that Truth is some kind of vast force; harmony in the Cosmos, working for good, and rewarding its devotees by shielding them from harm or injustice or from the ignorant handling of the forces of Nature.

### Is Truth Unchangeable?

We often are told that Truth is unchangeable; it is always the same, otherwise it could not be Truth; that our conception of it is a matter of growth. The more experience we obtain the nearer we get to Truth, because "experience teaches"—and the thing taught is usually, somehow, supposed to be synonymous with Truth.

Truth is referred to as our guide, philosopher and friend. But if we give some thought to this vast subject—we may decide that a thing which is true at one time is not necessarily true at another, because of the element of change which is inevitable in every kingdom of Nature.

As we perfect our instruments of observation we see much more than we did when the instruments were crude and inadequate. Snow is not altered by looking at it through a powerful microscope, but our conception of it is, and very materially, too. Just as it is said that beauty is in the eye of the beholder, so truth is inherent in the person.

Hardly any two persons would agree about a certain sound, or an exact colour, because, although it would be precisely the same sound or colour, the observations brought to bear on each by different people would never be absolutely the same. We are made that way.

And this accounts for the opposite opinions so often expressed about the very same facts in politics, science and in those things we call "questions of taste".

It is the old story of the shield having two sides. A picture or a statue will differ according to the position of the person examining it, the conditions of light, the angle from which the person looks, the state of mentality and health of the observer and many other conditions upon which we need not enlarge.

In spite of the statements often heard as to the simplicity of Truth, it is, in reality, tremendously complex. Two and two making four is putting it on a basis which is not of much use to us in our daily lives, apart from which there have been mathematical demonstrations proving that two and two do not make four.

There did not seem to be any flaw in these demonstrations; yet there were many people present who, in spite of such reasoning, were far from being convinced.

## Alert and Open Minds

Now while we have been trying to find out what Truth is not, we are not going to try to define what it is. This is what so many people are doing and are contradicting themselves in the process.

If a person considers a thing to be true in his own case, it does not necessarily follow that it will be true to anyone else.

If there is constant growth, if evolution is a fact in Nature, then truth could be something which is always in a process of "becoming" to every human being; in other words, one person sees a thing in a certain light, whilst another sees it in an entirely different light.

So it seems that this question of "What is Truth?" is one which each individual should try to answer to satisfy himself. The vastness of the subject need not discourage us. There is no need for us to attempt to understand it all, for that would be a sheer impossibility.

We need alert and open minds on this question: "What is Truth?" And whether we find a Truth that satisfies us or not, we can at least free our minds from faulty traditions, supposedly divine imperatives, superstition, narrowness, bigotry and intolerance. We should not be afraid of following where our conception of Truth may lead. For there is no more ruinous dishonesty than intellectual dishonesty.

Let us learn by patient practice to think straight. Let us do our own thinking and not be influenced by false standards or build our hopes on dogmas that are dead.

We may not find the answer to "What is Truth?" but we can strengthen and enrich our lives by substituting knowledge for ignorance and reason for superstition.

# THOUGHTS AND THINKERS

LIFE—that is the spiritual life of the individual—has often been described as a perpetual struggle between Good and Evil. From a study of life and people around us and from those we meet, as well as from history, we realise that there have been, and still are, a few outstandingly good people and a few strikingly evil ones. The rest of us lie between these two categories, on various planes of Good or Evil, though the majority fluctuate round a mediocre, indifferent centre of colourless nothingness. We have neither the personality, the character nor the drive, to forge ahead of our fellow-men either in the direction of Good or Evil.

In other words our lives, instead of being positive, tend to be negative, which is by far the easier path to tread. Negative thoughts and actions seem to come naturally, while positive thoughts and actions require effort. Human beings, on the whole, are not prone to make effort, especially in thinking, unless circumstances compel them to do so for reasons of self-preservation. There are very few people who haven't, at some time or other, by their negative thoughts and wishes mentally committed many heinous crimes.

Men and women also do evil by words and actions that may cause harm to others. Many otherwise decent, respectable individuals feel fully justified in making themselves secure, or climbing the ladder of success, by intrigue, misstatements or negative suggestions which may prove detrimental or harmful to others. Who is to judge as to where Good ends and Evil begins? Is it for the individual to judge for himself, considering that each person has his own standard to live by? Then, too, there is a difference between spiritual Good and Evil as judged from within, and the Right and Wrong of man-made laws.

## Principles that Bring Reward

Evil may be termed a short-term policy. It is true that the evil doer often appears to profit and succeed by his mode of living. We have but to study history to discover outstanding personalities whose schemes for their own aggrandisement brought them success. *But in the later years of their lives, their wrong thinking, wrong living and actions, brought either directly or indirectly their own rewards.*

A tragic instance is that of Mirabeau. There is no doubt he was a genius—but a genius who had spent his youth in loose and immoral living. In time, it brought its own reward of disease. But more tragic than the physical ruin, was the regret and remorse he suffered when he realised that his illness, brought upon himself, prevented him by means of his personality and ability, from saving France from the horror and bloodshed of the Revolution. He died knowing what he must have been seeking all his life, that self-discipline is essential to final success because it brings each individual into line with the laws of the Universe. These laws are irrevocably ordered for righteousness, and Man cannot evade or escape them. It is the logic of life.

Good, therefore, is a long-term policy, and although many think that evil may "flourish as the green bay tree", the morally good acquire spiritual possessions, such as peace of mind, which, in the long run, the evil individual loses.

Apart from the actual evil or immorality of a few people, we are all more or less average individuals; there is some bad in all of us and, if we are honest with ourselves, we know and acknowledge our lower, meaner, baser selves. Often, however, there is too much emphasis put on the evil in the world and in Man, and insufficient stress placed upon the good. The decent, courageous things in life are, in any case, likely to win in the end because of the tremendous spiritual power they possess as compared with the lesser spiritual power of evil thoughts and acts.

It is important to differentiate between the individual who is influenced by, and concerned with, religious or ethical principles and the person who is not. If we claim, either privately or publicly, a belief in spiritual or ethical values, then we must acknowledge and accept certain responsibilities from which those who do not believe are free. Therefore, they are unhampered by such principles which forbid deliberate harm being done to others by such means as exaggeration, negative suggestion or misstatement.

Yet even the religious person or one who conforms to ethical principles is sometimes troubled by negative, harmful thoughts. He may lead an exemplary life, keep well within the laws of the community, give to charity according to his means, and frequently give some of his spare time to social service of one kind or another. But even those who are nearest and dearest to him do not know of, or even suspect, the negative, destructive, irreligious thoughts that sometimes disturb his mind concerning his fellow-men. His problem is to discipline these thoughts by replacing them with kindlier, positive ones, so that his attitude becomes more tolerant and his actions more helpful and sympathetic.

## Two Types of Thinkers

In all walks of life there are two kinds of people—positive thinkers and negative thinkers; those who think success and those who think failure.

Negative thinkers are afraid to venture anything in case "something goes wrong". There's the salesman who can't make up his mind whether to call on so-and-so because he "might not get an order". The executive who is afraid to air his views at the business meeting in case he "might make a blunder". The individual who, when faced with a problem at work, immediately goes to someone else with it because he "might make a mistake". The housewife with guests coming to tea who thinks, "suppose the meal doesn't turn out all right—won't it be awful?" The person who is certain that it will rain on the day of the picnic. The "wet blanket" at the party who refuses to join in the fun because he is afraid of appearing undignified. The procrastinators, the pessimists, the cynics, the do-nothing-about-it-types, the failures—these are the negative thinkers.

It's the positive thinkers who are welcome everywhere, those in whose company we find pleasure as against the negative thinkers who bore us. The positive thinkers are happier, more active, more alive, more adventuresome. They are the people who get things done. Of course they make some mistakes—they're bound to. But their successes are greater and more frequent than their mistakes; they are rarely criticised, but often applauded. The positive thinkers don't waste their time worrying—over things that very often don't happen!

### The Power of Thought

Thoughts are powerful—much more powerful than is usually accepted by the average man and woman. Our thoughts determine our character and the kind of thoughts which habitually pass through the mind eventually stamp themselves on the face of the thinker.

Thoughts are the foundation of all action. They can bring good or evil; lift us to the heights or lure us to the depths; raise us to lofty summits or drag us to destruction.

So we should guard well the thoughts we habitually entertain; see that they are properly controlled and directed. Although negative, destructive thoughts may invade the mind, it is up to us whether we accept or reject them. We may have but little control over the thoughts that flow in, but we can hasten the departure of the undesirable thought patterns. And the method of keeping the damaging thought patterns at bay is to flood the mind with thoughts of a positive, constructive nature.

This tremendous power of thought is not, even in these days of psychiatry and advanced study of the mind, fully appreciated by the average man and woman. We perceive our own actions and the actions of others, and sometimes we see the results. But thought remains still the main battlefield, for it is the starting point for the campaign that is to follow—of all that is to happen to the individual.

Only a small part of any individual's thought ever results in action —in direct, constructive action. It is in this way that mental energy is grossly wasted by lack of discipline and control. If the mind were so trained to entertain a greater percentage of desirable, positive thoughts, then much more mental energy could be translated into desirable and positive action, and so benefit the individual and others with whom he comes in contact.

We all of us, at times, fritter away our mental energy and in proportion as we do this, so is our usefulness and success in life increased or diminished. We should, therefore, direct our thinking towards action. So many of us find it difficult to get started on a project. We make up our minds to do something, then dwell upon the disadvantages of that course of action. We dilly-dally and find all sorts of excuses, instead of arriving at a decision and then acting upon it.

### Control Harmful Emotions

There are very few people who can honestly say that they have never wished ill to another. Some of us, who would even shrink from hurting an animal, nevertheless have occasionally been guilty of, say, wishing someone dead or wishing disaster or bad luck to someone who has crossed us or unwittingly aroused our antagonism. But as soon as we let reason, step in and control our thoughts and emotions, we realise that we are using thought power in wrong and wicked directions.

The control of careless, rebellious, violent thoughts, surely ought to be the aim of civilisation, for it would go far in establishing better and happier relationships throughout the world. Christian endeavour could do a great deal in this direction because, shorn of all the trappings it has gathered over two thousand years of trial and error, it is based upon thought control and mind training. Its founder, the Great Galilean, demonstrated clearly and unmistakably, that the way to a happier, nobler and better way of life was by transforming all negative thoughts and emotions into positive ones, so that in place of hatred, envy, greed, jealousy and bigotry, there would be love, understanding, self-denial, sympathy and tolerance.

How far have we travelled along the road of Christian endeavour in two thousand years? "Not very far," we may sadly or cynically remark. Yet what a happy transformation there would be in the lives of men and women throughout the world; what a wonderful change there would be in national and international affairs if only negative and emotional thinking were replaced by the gospel according to the Great Galilean.

### Habitual Negative Thinking

A great deal of negative and destructive thinking is largely due to slipshod, casual habits of thought, to *habitual* methods of thinking rather than *disciplined* methods. Self-control and self-discipline do not mean just disciplining and training the body and the senses. They must go much deeper than that to be really successful. They must go to the very root of our being and discipline our thoughts and emotions.

We should, however, be careful not to confuse discipline with repression. The two methods are entirely different. Repression is harmful and can even prove disastrous; discipline means the re-direction of thought energy, emotions and desires into channels that are more desirable, more beneficial to ourselves, to others, and in accordance with our religious or ethical principles whatever they may be.

The majority of people are easy-going and kind-hearted. If, however, their undisciplined and negative thoughts were literally translated into corresponding actions they would be horrified at the results. If it were possible to transmit these thoughts to paper unbeknown to them, and then present the written thoughts to them, they would in most cases deny the authorship.

Apart from any harm we may do to others by our undisciplined thought processes, our negative thoughts are flung back upon ourselves. While we entertain them, they form a bar or dam blocking the inlet of spiritual inspiration and making creative effort much more difficult. For it is positive and constructive thinking alone that can bring into activity the creative spirit.

More often than not, we are only partially conscious of our slipshod, negative thinking. This lack of control sometimes reveals itself in our speech. In fact it is inevitable that at times, in unguarded moments, the tongue is likely to translate some of our habitual thoughts into words. We take the negative thoughts one step further when we express them in speech.

## Make this Test

Here is a practical test which we can try out on ourselves. Suppose at the end of the day we write down all the things we have discussed, or heard discussed, in conversation. Were none of them heinous or harmful? Were there no embittered or envious remarks—nothing shameful or scandalous? No, maybe not. But—were the conversations negative or positive, destructive or constructive?

Weren't we grumbling about the weather—criticising the government or some political body—finding fault with our neighbours, co-workers, acquaintances and even with our friends? "Not very harmful," we may say. "Just what most people talk about in casual conversation." Yes, too true; but it was definitely not constructive; therefore it was destructive. We and all those concerned in such scrappy, critical, surface talk, have lowered ourselves mentally and spiritually. We didn't really think. We only passed the time away in casual, negative, critical remarks which come much more easily to the mind and lips than positive, constructive ones.

Why do we slide so easily, so aimlessly, into negative ways of thinking? It is habit. We think as we do, because we have formed certain habits of thought and we unconsciously follow those habitual mental grooves. Each time we think in a certain manner, the habit becomes more deeply impressed upon our minds. It is so easy to fall victims to such mental habits; it requires sustained effort to keep free from them.

Although negative habits of thought may be deeply ingrained, nevertheless we can root them out. But it is no easy task. It calls for controlled and sustained effort. It means refusing to think in the established groove by the sheer force of will and imagination, by shifting the attention, by auto-suggestion, or by any other method. In this way we shall greatly weaken negative habits of thought.

The next step is to set out to destroy them totally. Jot down on paper as many of the negative thought habits as possible. Then break them up; tackle them one at a time and substitute better thought habits for the undesirable ones. And finally, we should start at once to form regular habits of constructive, rational, wholesome thinking. Then, as we reach the stage when rich and positive thinking becomes habitual with us, our lives will be transformed and triumphant.

# GETTING TO KNOW OURSELVES

TOO much introspection is not good for us. It tends to cut us off from the society of others, it limits our knowledge of life, and we become self-centred. This isn't a healthy mental state at all. Nevertheless, we *should* devote some time to self-examination, because it can be of great help in enriching our lives. Periodically we should go into some quiet place for fifteen minutes or so, to do a little honest mental and spiritual stocktaking. If we do this conscientiously, we shall acquire a more comprehensive knowledge of ourselves as individuals and of the deeper realities of life.

After a serious attempt at personal analysis, we should emerge reinforced with a new vitality and determination. We should feel like giants refreshed, ready to do battle in a good cause. This good cause for which we fight is the ideal of self-improvement in every respect. Only in this way can we be assured of self-respect and peace of mind. Self-improvement not only brings us direct personal benefits, but it also helps to make the world a better, happier place in which to live.

As one individual—perhaps apparently insignificant among the millions of our fellows—we sometimes may feel frustrated, despondent and alone. Certain questions may arise in our minds, such as: What can *I* do of any importance? Who will take any notice of *me*? What does it really matter how I live my life so long as I can earn enough for the necessities and a few little extra comforts?

The fact is that you and I matter a great deal more than we imagine. Just as a chain is only as strong as its weakest link, so human society is only as healthy, happy and successful as the individuals who each carry their little bit of responsibility for the whole human species.

A healthy self-interest is not selfishness. Far from it! Self-interest is a noble duty, not only towards ourselves, but to the rest of humanity and to the Creator. Once we get this fact firmly established in our minds, we shall want to get down to the serious, yet exciting and rewarding business of self-knowledge, self-criticism and self-improvement.

### Suggestions for Self-analysis

At this stage we should understand that our desire for self-improvement must not be restricted to material ambitions, possessions and circumstances. In the process of self-examination, we should judge and assess many mental and spiritual factors as well as material

158

items. We must get tough with ourselves and face up to all that we discover, however unpleasant some of it may be.

To do this satisfactorily, it will be necessary to draw up a clearly-defined plan, based upon or similar to the following suggestions. We should write a list of the questions outlined, for this clarifies thinking. It enables us to see as well as to think, thereby bringing the various points into orderly system. We should commence with the broad picture of our past and present lives in general, and then examine minutely the many and varied details.

We should not try to force answers to the questions but keep our minds relaxed completely, for any sort of tension will block the flow of thought power. We must be realistic with ourselves, analyse our deficiencies and potentialities, and see things as they are and not as we would like them to be.

*What have I done with my life so far? Am I satisfied with my progress to date? What talents do I possess? Have I tried to make full use of them? Have I discovered any fresh talents lately? Do I work conscientiously each full day? Do I enjoy adequate relaxation? What are my plans for the future? What are my spiritual assets and aims? Will the world be any better because I have lived in it?*

Other pertinent questions could be asked and tackled, but the questions outlined above, are along the general lines to follow, in order to view the broad picture of our lives and to comprehend their shape and trend.

So let us deal with the above questions and think around them.

What have we done with our lives so far? Let us think back to the days of our childhood and youth. Remember the zestful optimism and the cherished dreams of those days of long ago? In those days we *lived* every minute of every day. We shared the joy of living with our brothers and sisters or with our school friends. We had lots of fun together; we played pranks, got into mischief, laughed at our elders, defied the authority of our parents and teachers. Almost every day was a great adventure; we lived each day to the full; went to bed tired and happy, and slept a sound, refreshing sleep. We were concerned only with our own little world and that satisfied us—if we were fortunate enough to be reared in a normal, decent home atmosphere.

Although we suffered occasional emotional upsets and physical ailments, we had few, if any, serious anxieties and problems. We were, in fact, not far removed from the lower animal kingdom. We accepted food and shelter from our parents or guardians, whose business it was to provide for our well-being; we had our childish pleasures—which were infinitely more important to us than our lessons and other inconveniences—and we took all for granted, without question.

When we grew old enough to understand more about life, we realised, with something of a shock, that one day we should have to fend for ourselves and take our share in "running the world". What, then, were we going to do about it? Plenty!

Up to this point we had discovered much to enjoy in life, but we also experienced an uncomfortable feeling that there was a whole lot wrong. Our elders seemed to have made a shocking mess of things, and we were not slow to criticise them and their ways. On the whole we were convinced that our elders meant well enough, they had good intentions, but they were a somewhat ignorant, blundering crowd. We were growing up, soon to take their place. *We* knew how to live; *we* could see clearly enough what was wrong with the world, and we would jolly soon put it to right directly we had a chance.

Well—have we done it? Are we quite satisfied with our handiwork? Is this world a much happier place since *our* generation has been in charge of it? Only our own conscience can answer this vital question. Probably we have, collectively, brought about certain improvements. We have also failed to solve many important problems—and we have even created new ones! Whatever has happened, for good or bad, we cannot honestly escape *our* share of the responsibility.

### Side-tracked and Diverted

What have we done with *our* lives so far? Have we pulled our weight? Have we given enough serious thought to personal, family, business and world affairs with a view to *improving* them? Have we paid due attention to our spiritual welfare and progress?

In the sober experience of middle age we are tempted to smile indulgently at the visions of Youth, or openly criticise them. Yet we had similar idealistic dreams at that age, and we knew that those dreams were unselfishly pure and inspirational. They were born of an honest desire to *do good* in the world, and we *knew* that our inspired desires were not only right, but feasible. Why, then, have we failed to materialise them in full measure?

Reasons—or excuses—for our failure to execute all our wonderful plans come readily to mind. There was a war—we got married—there was a business slump—we were too busy trying to earn a modest living and raise a family—we were not appreciated, we were misunderstood—our views were unpopular, etc.

If we live to a ripe old age we shall be able to add to our list of excuses. We had heavy responsibilities—health deteriorated—we deserved a rest—we're too old now, anyway. Let the youngsters have a go.

These reasons—or excuses—may appear fairly convincing, but the plain truth is that we have been side-tracked from our original, golden purpose. We have allowed outside influences to divert us from our course. These distracting influences are many and varied, ranging from intimate personal matters to prejudiced public opinion. For one reason or another we have lost heart. We have failed ourselves, and possibly denied posterity the benefits of our skill, determination and applied effort.

Consider the many labour-saving devices and the even more remarkable inventions and scientific discoveries. Select any one of them and delve into its origin and history. The chances are that the originator of the selected idea had to overcome tremendous problems, often unreasonable prejudice, discouragement, ridicule and perhaps downright persecution before his theories were proved and accepted.

It is true that these great scientists and inventors were blessed with higher mental powers than most of us, but these gifts would have been of little value without the courage, conviction, tenacity of purpose and sustained effort necessary to materialise dreams into realities. In short, the great personalities of our time, and right back through history, possessed the knowledge, self-confidence and determination to carry them through to their goal. Over and over again they were beaten back by opposition, but they never failed, because they never for a moment anticipated or admitted defeat. These men and women discovered and used their talents—not chiefly for their own ends, but for the benefit of humanity. Such intrepid pioneers are to be admired and emulated. We may not be mentally and physically capable of performing equally stupendous feats, but we can at least develop what talents we have and use them to good purpose. We can check our progress and decide whether it is satisfactory in relation to our abilities.

### Capitalising Natural Ability

Now when we come to consider our abilities we meet a further problem. What *are* our abilities? That is a tricky question. We may know that we have a natural flair for—say business, or art, or science. Our self-knowledge is such that we can subdivide these broad fields of activity and pinpoint our natural ability for a particular branch in any of them. For example, in business we may find that we are better as a salesman than as an organiser. If we are attracted towards the Arts, we may discover that we are more skilled at sketching than—say music.

Even when we discover these simple facts, we do not know until we try. Many a man, after spending fruitless years in one occupation, becomes so expert at his chosen hobby that it eventually becomes his profitable, full-time occupation.

Nobody knows *what* he can do well until he tries. So when we say that we have only a moderate talent in one direction, we are on very uncertain ground. Only by experimenting in a diversity of activities can we discover what additional talents we possess. So it is up to us to develop one or more of our new-found talents and increase our value to the community. By so doing we automatically raise our prestige, advance our knowledge and usefulness, improve our mental and physical health, and derive considerable personal satisfaction and happiness. All this is in addition to the possibility of raising our standard of living and material comfort. Aren't the results of greater self-knowledge well worth the efforts involved?

We should always strive to widen our mental horizon. There is always room for fresh ideas, improved methods, and the building of new structures upon old and sound foundations. A few minutes even, spent each day in concentration and meditation, can yield highly satisfying results.

### Physical and Mental Relaxation

Another important point to remember is that for mental health we should *vary* our mental activity as much as possible. Sometimes we meet an individual who is an acknowledged expert in one subject, but who is often ignorant in other directions! So absorbed is this person in his pet subject, that he exists in a narrow little world of his own. Certainly we must concentrate on one or very few subjects if we wish to become expert in them, but it just isn't healthy to exclude everything else from our thoughts. The mind needs relaxation as does the body, and the most rewarding form of relaxation is a *different kind of activity*. As a general rule sedentary workers benefit most by outdoor physical recreation, and manual workers are likely to find relief in interesting mental pursuits, or in merely watching sports and other entertainment.

In the suggested periodic examination of ourselves we must not overlook the importance of relaxation in one form or another. This doesn't necessarily mean sitting still and doing nothing, which soon becomes boring. Almost any change of activity is beneficial and relaxing for the mind or body.

In this connection also, we should bear in mind that only by doing a fair day's work in a conscientious manner, can we expect to derive the utmost pleasure from our relaxation. Therefore, during our self-examination we must ask ourselves: Do we exert our best efforts in our work every day?

If we can answer an honest "yes" to this question, our conscience will be clear. If not, we have here a clue as to why we feel vaguely dissatisfied with life, and why even relaxation offers little enjoyment. Nature always effects a balance. The more conscientiously we work, the more we can enjoy our leisure, and the more good it does us.

### Satisfying the Inner Yearning

What about the future? Do we know where we are heading and why? If we are not clear on this point, now is the time to give it consideration. Life and work can become somewhat distasteful and frustrating if we have no particular aim in view. Working merely to earn a living isn't enough to satisfy our inner yearning. It is far better to have a higher incentive; to set ourselves a reasonable goal and strive to reach it. When we get there, we can always aim a little higher and work towards the next step. It is most unwise, however, to allow an insatiable ambition to rule our lives and rob us of all other considerations, but without moderate ambition—something to look forward to—life can become very dull and futile.

Another point to consider is our place in society. Are we respected and well liked? If not, why not? What can we do to remedy the situation?

It is all very well to declare that we don't care a jot what other people think of us. Even the best among us can be seriously misjudged, but if we are frequently criticised about one or more of our individual traits, this is a good reason for a special check-up. It isn't at all easy to recognise one's own faults, or to admit them when others point them out to us. At least we should consider whether criticisms levelled at us are justified. If so, we can try to remedy any defect in our character or personality.

In this connection another curious fact emerges. What we dislike most in others is often present in ourselves. The probable reason for this is that we are subconsciously aware of this fact. Actually we hate *ourselves* for these weaknesses, and we project our disapproval upon others who display similar defects.

It is as well at this stage to examine our virtues. Many people are virtuous *to a fault*. So kind, thoughtful and generous are they, that other ungrateful people treat them like a doormat. Kindness and sympathy can be overdone in certain cases. The best way to help anybody is to teach them to *help themselves*, not to act as a leaning-post for them. God feeds the birds, but He doesn't throw their food into the nest.

### Summing-up

Before we can reach any conclusion as to whether the world will be a better place because we have lived in it, we must give some thought to the spiritual part of our existence.

Let us make no mistake about this. Life isn't only a matter of satisfying our material needs, even if we give good service for the money we earn. In taking stock of our assets and potentialities we have to consider our character, personality, emotional balance, philosophy and other intangible but important factors.

Life is all a question of balance and harmony. Wisely spent leisure *helps* to compensate us for the strain and stress of the working day, but we need other reliefs. For happy living and peace of mind we need a satisfying love-life and an acceptable philosophy of living.

When we finish the toil of each day we ought to be able to go home to an understanding, sympathetic, helpful and reliable partner. A happy home is a haven of peace and rest for those who work outside it. For the housewife it is a centre of great personal satisfaction—in spite of the responsibility and work involved.

The son or daughter who can return home to loving parents is indeed truly blessed. The husband who can unburden his problems to a sweet-natured wife is a very fortunate man. The wife who can feel secure, needed, appreciated and well-loved is a happy woman.

In assessing our value to the rest of the community—and therefore to the world—we must certainly consider our relationships with other members of the family. Are we being fair and considerate to each one of them? Are we accepting more than we are prepared to give? If so, here's another chance of self-improvement.

Obviously, we should take care to improve our general character wherever we detect a weakness. By doing so we increase our self-respect and keep our conscience clear.

Finally, we should meditate upon the Creator, the Universe, the whole human family and try to reason out the Great Purpose of them all. In this, Faith plays a great part. The human mind is incapable of grasping all the mysteries and wonders of Creation or comprehending all the wonderful forces of the Universe. We can, however, by intelligent observation and reasoning, reach certain conclusions which satisfy *us*—even if others are unable to accept our theories and views. In short, we must evolve our own philosophy of life, so that we can believe, as one philosopher put it:

"Yet, through all, we know this tangled skein is in the hands of One who sees the end from the beginning; He shall yet unravel all."

# CAN LUCK BE EXPLAINED?

WHAT is luck? To what extent should we rely upon it? Why do some people seem to be "lucky" and others "unlucky"? Can we attract or repel "luck"? These are some of the questions to be discussed.

My dictionary defines "luck" as: "Chances which come to a person, whether good or ill, a casual event or a series of events that affect a person's interest or happiness."

Luck is a highly controversial subject, about which it may be unwise to dogmatise. Whilst there does seem to be a certain element of luck in life, there are some people who harbour wrong ideas and even hold foolish beliefs concerning the matter. So that when an individual makes a success in life they say it is entirely due to "luck"— that there is some mysterious cause for his good fortune. Others believe in lucky stars, fortune-tellers and charms; that good fortune depends on the whims of fate, astrology, crystal-gazers or upon a rabbit's foot or a horseshoe! But surely life is not as simple or as easy as that.

On the other hand, there are some enterprising, successful "self-made" men, who declare that there is no such thing as luck! They maintain that success is the result of the particular qualities they possess, plus unrelenting effort and hard work. Some of these highly successful men and women go so far as to suggest that the failures of this world have only themselves to blame. Certainly there is some truth in this, in regard to certain cases, examples of which abound.

## Circumstances of Birth and Parentage

The young man, born of wealthy parents, who shudders at the thought of work and who degenerates into a useless playboy or worse, can expect to be blamed by society for his ultimate misfortune. Who can refer to him as being "unlucky"? Surely he has only himself to blame? This may be our first reaction.

But directly we consider such a case more thoroughly, we may be forced to revise our opinion concerning "luck". Was this young man lucky to be born into a life of luxury? We may at first imagine so, but the results of this hypothetical case prove that the circumstances of that young man's birth and parentage turned out to be a curse— *for him.*

Through being born with the proverbial "silver spoon in his mouth" such a boy must find it very hard to appreciate his "good fortune". He simply fails to imagine what life can be like without plenty of money to spend; without a sports car to dash around in; without leisure, travel and endless variety of entertainment. Moreover, if his parents spoilt him from childhood, as they probably did, he grew up with a distorted sense of values. Appreciation, mature discretion and possibly many other fine qualities were almost entirely absent from his character. Pity the poor "lucky" rich boy!

Nowadays, however, owing to a social revolution, there are very few "idle rich"—and a good thing, too, if only for their own sakes. It is extremely hard to be happy if one is too rich, as many have found to their cost.

Now let us turn to the other side of the picture. Consider the lad born into a squalid home, with no security or parental love. What luck—*bad* luck! The unhappy circumstances of this boy's birth were certainly not his fault. All the dice seem to be loaded against such a boy. Apart from the drag of his unfortunate environment, he may not have the intelligence or opportunity to raise himself up.

It is easy to understand how such a boy drifts into delinquency and comes to a bad end. In his ignorance of the dangers involved, he is only trying to compensate himself for his feelings of insecurity and injustice.

On the other hand, as we all know, there are many wealthy individuals and families who can be justly proud of their fine record of achievement. There are also frequent examples of children from poor homes and shocking early environment, who have become great leaders and thinkers and have risen to places of distinction and honour.

The circumstances of our birth and parentage represent our initial "luck"—good or bad. But it is not so much our start in life that matters, but the finish. It is not the environment in which we are born and reared, but the environment we build as a setting for our life's activities, that counts.

The quality of our intelligence is also often hereditary—or pure chance so far as we are concerned. But how we conduct our lives as we approach and reach maturity is not a matter of luck entirely. Our "good" fortune or "bad" is governed largely by *how we use* the qualities of character which we have developed.

## Taking Advantage of Opportunities

Whilst we must admit that there does seem to be an element that most of us regard as chance, running like a wandering thread throughout our lives, to depend on chance alone would be extremely foolish, because it is the most unreliable thing in the world. "Luck" comes very often by employing our powers of imagination, a rugged will to achieve and unremitting toil, industry and by being ready and prepared to seize opportunities.

Suppose we turn to the entertainment world for examples. A number of highly successful film, radio and television artists have, to some extent, a certain amount of "luck" to thank for their first big opportunity. A famous theatrical producer happens to see an original and talented act in an amateur show. He invites the performers to a special audition. Suggestions are made to give the act a little more polish. Rehearsals are arranged, and the performers are booked for their first professional show. But it is not due to "luck" that their turn "catches on" with the audience, and that, within a few months, the act "tops the bill". Months and months were spent by the performers, prior to the opportunity coming their way, in hard slogging, patient rehearsals in order to make their act perfect. They were equipped and ready to seize opportunity when it presented itself.

We sit enthralled as we listen, say, to a famous pianist. What would we give to play like this superman? We talk about his "luck". But the pianist says little about "luck". He tells of toilsome, weary hours, when with aching back, fevered brow and benumbed fingers he patiently paid the price of mastery long before the opportunity that placed him on the road to fame came his way. The romantic story of achievement is all too often but the unromantic story of hard work.

Countless similar examples can be given, not only in "show business" but in every other sphere of human activity. Opportunity is always popping up somewhere.

If we examine the life stories of many now famous men and women, we shall, in the majority of cases, discover some outstanding incident which proved to be the turning point in their careers. But whilst some may call such people "lucky", we very often find that they were constructive, positive, dominant, optimistic personalities, alert and ready to seize opportunities. And through the inexorable law of attraction they drew to themselves those circumstances, conditions and events which helped them towards achievement and success.

### Unpredictable Factors

In spite of the dictionary definition that "luck" and "chance" are synonymous terms, there appears to be a subtle distinction between the two.

Suppose, for example, a person draws the winning horse in a sweepstake and wins a thousand pounds. The fact that the person drew the winning horse in the first place was mere chance. But whether this event means *luck* for that individual depends upon what he does with the money and on several other unpredictable factors.

So it seems that luck is the *effect* of chance upon our lives. Moreover, chance is not the only element in luck. The other factor involved is *ourselves*. Whether and how a chance incident affects us depends upon how we *respond* to it.   The result—luck, good, bad or indifferent —depends, very largely, upon our own attitude and behaviour.

If we give a child a musical instrument to play with, he may never touch it again once the novelty has worn off.   Another child, however, may develop a passionate desire to play the instrument really well. He may even discover an inborn talent for music and become, in time, a world-famous instrumentalist.

It will be seen, then, that an initial chance may lead to good fortune or "luck", or it may make no difference whatever to our lives.   So many other factors are involved in what we call "luck".

We are unable to control chance, but we can often improve our "luck" by turning chance to our advantage.   This realisation is of great importance.   It means that we are, very largely, responsible for our own "luck".

So many people go through life with the conviction that they are "unlucky".   Every kind of misfortune seems to happen to them. Are they really "unlucky" or do they attract misfortune because it is, in the main, the externalisation of their own negative emotions and thoughts or because they make no effort to turn their so-called "bad luck" into good?   These "unlucky" ones would do well to consider the following quotation:

"There are no chances so unlucky from which clever people are not able to reap some advantage, and none so lucky that the foolish are not able to turn to their own disadvantage."

How true are these words!   Many a wonderful discovery in medicine and science and many a revolutionary invention have very often been the result of chance, accident, mishap.   But, in every case, the person involved in the chance happening realised its potentialities and got down to some intense thinking, further experiment, unremitting activity and hard work.

Certainly we should not drift aimlessly along through life waiting for chance, or luck, or merely hoping that something will happen or something will turn up to bring us a greater abundance of good things. We should, instead, be on the alert to seize every opportunity that comes to us and *use it* to every possible advantage.

Those who complain most about their bad or indifferent "luck" are usually drifters, mere flotsam and jetsam on the sea of life.   They accept life as they find it, will not help themselves and do nothing to improve their conditions.   This apathetic and indolent attitude invites continued disappointment.   For "good luck" tends to be attracted to those who make full and optimistic use of their highest qualities.

Conversely, psychologists have found that consistently "unlucky" persons behave in a manner that reflects their feelings of insecurity. If only these people would realise that there is no such thing as security. Nothing is ever 100 per cent. sure.   Life is full of risks.   Everyone is surrounded by them.   We cannot escape from them, however much we try. There's risk in everyday living. We're not even safe in bed.

No one ever succeeded without taking risks. There are risks involved in solving problems, in building up character. In all business there is an element of risk. The risk, of course, can be reduced by research, study and ability. But it cannot be eliminated altogether.

So if we would live successfully we must take chances. There is no other way, for that is the law of life. Yet risks add spice to life and make it more worth while. Life without risks would become drab and dull, meaningless and uninteresting.

Then we must associate with successful people if we want to succeed. We must steer clear of failures, pessimists, triflers and drifters. We often hear men and women grousing about other people's "good luck". They've had "the devil's own luck" is a common expression used everywhere—particularly by those who have got nowhere. They scoff and sneer at the individual who has succeeded, because they are jealous and envious of his success. No person gets very far who looks with scorn and envy upon those who have got to the top.

## The Value of Persistent Effort

There are many people who do not understand what luck means or they have wrong ideas about it. They think that "luck" is pure chance or that some are born "lucky" and others are not. But the successful men and women know that it is indeed very rare that "luck" is a pure accident or that "luck" is born and not made. They realise that life's "lucky" prizes are not awarded merely for the asking or by "luck" alone, but are the result of intelligently directed and persistent effort. These people accumulate all the knowledge and information they can get, study facts and figures, averages and percentages in regard to their chances of succeeding in whatever they contemplate undertaking.

There may be times when we meet with misfortune. It is then that we mustn't allow fear to rob us of our courage and initiative. If we retire into a quiet corner at such times, doubtful and fearful, we shall be well and truly "cornered" and beaten. If we permit our thoughts to dwell unduly upon our misfortune, it will become magnified out of its true proportion. Then we shall soon be saying: "It's no use—it's hopeless. This is the end. I'm finished!"

What, then, can we do to help counteract these depressive and negative thoughts? We should think along the following lines. We cannot succeed unless we can stand set-backs. Set-backs are the price we pay for eventual success. If we become afraid of failure, the more likely are we to fail. Then again if we didn't make mistakes now and then, we wouldn't make anything. The majority of successful people had their failures before they reached the top. We can profit by our mistakes and learn important lessons from our set-backs and failures, interpret them as having happened in order to discipline and prepare us for ultimate success.

We should also not make the mistake of trying to live a self-centred existence. We should consider the welfare of others and share our good fortune. Lend a helping hand, be generous, show tolerance, kindness and sympathy where and when they are needed. We should try to help others along the often difficult road of life.

There are some people, as we know, who are "lone wolves"; their guiding principle is to look after "number one". They are usually hard, ruthless, selfish characters who often are very clever and even brilliant. They sometimes have what appears to be a run of good "luck". But it rarely lasts and their ability and good fortune come to nothing—like seed falling on stony ground. There are very few individuals so strong, powerful or rich who can ignore public opinion or cut themselves off from their fellow-men.

Life is so strange and bewildering at times. Often it appears unjust, meaningless, fantastic. Real life contains far more weird and wonderful stories than are to be found in fiction. Yet, beneath it all there is a pattern based on certain universal laws and sometimes it would seem that these apply to "luck" as to everything else.

No matter how intelligent we may be we cannot always foresee what is best for us.

For instance, sometimes things happen to us which we consider to be due to pure "bad luck". But eventually, perhaps years later, when we look back, we find that the very things that happened were all for the best or for our own good, and often blessings in disguise.

Then again we may ascribe to sheer "bad luck" the fact that, unbeknown to us, we are travelling in the wrong direction in regard to whatever goal we have set or we are using wrong methods. We must learn to think straight, starting somewhere and arriving at a definite conclusion. Then act on our decision. We must learn to think inductively, building up our reason upon the facts of each case rather than upon mere hearsay, opinions and prejudices of others.

## The Law of Attraction

Finally, if we *think* that we are unlucky we shall be dogged by misfortune simply because we shall attract it towards us.

No doubt most of us, during our childhood days, played with a magnet. We would hold it over a pin, needle or other piece of steel, and watch the magnet draw to itself, with unerring precision, the object attracted. But when we held the magnet, say, over a piece of wood there was no response. The law of the magnet is that "like attracts like"; only the same elemental substance is drawn.

This same principle is readily illustrated in the mental sphere. The human psyche is, in fact, a great mental and spiritual magnet. It draws to itself, in accordance with this law of attraction with inexorable accuracy, the thoughts which we store in the Subconscious Mind. If we nurse thoughts of "bad luck", failure, lack or inability, they will invariably produce their kind in objective reality.

So we must cultivate thoughts of good fortune, ability, achievement and success, and the tendencies in these directions will be stimulated and multiplied. By changing our thoughts from negative to positive, we shall create a new set of physical, mental and spiritual conditions that can transform weakness into strength, lack into abundance, failure into success and defeat into ultimate triumph.

# FAITH IN THIS MODERN WORLD

*The most urgent need in the world to-day is a rebirth of faith. For faith is an essential to life, just as sustenance and shelter are requisites of physical survival.*

\* \* \*

THE men or women without faith in something or someone, and above all those who lack faith in themselves and the power of faith within them are doomed to purgatory. Their lives, their happiness, their success, their desire to live are ended.

And by faith we do not mean only religious faith. The power of faith and religious faith are all too often intermixed or confused in the person's mind. If we ask an individual what his faith is, most probably he will give the name of the particular religion in which he was brought up. Faith to him means orthodox creeds, ritual and worship.

To-day, these forms of religion seem to have gone, for good or ill, out of fashion. In our modern scientific days, we have gained tremendous and amazing knowledge of the heavens; we strive continually for power over the universe; we are rich in the majority of things, except faith. Faith is the quality that is now so often derided in an age that gives preference to scientific proof over spiritual awareness.

We have gained much knowledge of the mind and its power, made some progress during the last hundred years, yet we have touched but the fringe of the matter. It is doubtful whether we know more about the spirit than was known a century ago, yet its kingdom is infinite.

Acknowledgment of the power of the spirit has waxed and waned over the centuries. Like many gifts inherent in human beings, it is there lying dormant within, an endowment from the Creator, waiting to be developed and used. Like any other gift, it will grow only with practice and use. We need communion, which is spiritual contact, with our Creator, with Nature and with our fellow beings.

It is not necessary to attend a formal or conventional place of worship in order to have faith. Faith is essential to religion, but religion is not essential to faith. Religion has developed faith often to high planes, giving visions of hope and joy and peace.

Many people believe that faith cannot exist without religion; it absorbs it all. Surely this is a mistake. For faith touches the whole of life and, whether we will or not, it exists to some degree within each individual. Those on the brink of despair, those who reach the state

172

of suicide, those who fall prey to nervous breakdown or are driven for help to the psychiatrist—all these very often have let their storehouse of faith drop to a negligible quantity which can spell disaster and spiritual death.

Man first of all should have faith in himself, believe that he can find help within himself, for within is the seed of faith planted by his Creator when he made Man in His own image.

## The Divine Spark

Faith is the divine spark in each individual which makes Man the most important creation in the world, indeed, in the main, for whom the world was created. It is *how* we believe and not *what* we believe that is of vital importance. An individual's religion helps him, but it is of little account that one man believes one way and another man believes in a different way. The important thing is that he *believes*—that he has *faith*.

Suppose we pause a while and think about this matter. Isn't it true that even those who lack certain spiritual beliefs, at least have some sort of faith?—faith in life, that when they retire at night, the sun will rise in the morning; that at the end of a day's work, evening will come and the sun will set, bringing the promise of rest and peace to tired minds and bodies, and that during sleep the strength of body, mind and spirit will be renewed in miraculous, incomprehensible ways, ready for the work of the new day. Everyone has this kind of faith, for it is inherent in every man and woman.

But faith can mean much more than this. It can be used. It can be a flame which lights the torch of unlimited possibilities. It can be the driving force which spurs men and women on, to do and dare, blaze new trails, conquer the unknown. For the psychological significance of faith is that a strong conviction tends to register in the Subconscious Mind, and, if held with sufficient intensity, brings about the desired result.

We can enrich our lives by starting every day with an affirmation of faith. It was from this idea that sprang the now much neglected custom of morning prayer. Affirmations are well worth while cultivating. For instance, we could begin the morning by affirming our belief in those things which are near and dear to our hearts, or by affirming that life is beautiful and interesting, that there is abundance all around us in unlimited measure. Or any affirmation concerning the expectancy of good in regard to the activities of the day. Gradually our faith will help to bring about these conditions.

## Faith in People

We are sometimes unfortunate enough to meet an individual who has lost faith in people. He is a sceptic of the extreme type, whom life and experience have embittered, and who, through disillusionment, has come to judge all individuals by the few. He trusts no one, believes in no one. His creed is—"Do unto others as they would do unto you— *but* you do it first!" He believes in climbing up, if necessary on the backs of others, and then, having achieved a vantage point, he arms himself with a club with which he smites any who attempt to reach him in the struggle for success.

This individual ascribes only ulterior motives of gain or aggrandisement to any good deed or kindly action. Honour, a promise, sympathy, a helping hand are neither appreciated, accepted nor offered. Yet is it not true that "the man who lacks faith in other men loses his best chances to work and gradually undermines his own power and his own character?" It is a case of—"as you judge so shall you be judged". For the man who is a perpetual doubter of other people's motives and characters is in grave danger of his opinions rebounding on himself, so that others mistrust him and his motives.

Those people who may be in this category should begin their day with an affirmation of faith in people; in their families, their friends and their dependability; in their employer or employees. In this way their very belief can help to shape the people concerned along the lines they wish them to take.

### Faith in Youth

Faith in people turns our thoughts to the much discussed problem of to-day—the problem of youth. This concerns us all, but is no doubt nearer to the hearts of those who have children of their own.

When I was young, I heard much adverse and often scathing criticism levelled at youth from middle-aged and elderly people. And I thought that when I got older I would try to refrain from such bitter or extreme criticism of young people and instead try to understand and help them, and see their point of view. For after all, there *are* two viewpoints. Age, with its experience of life, sees one aspect, sometimes the result of suffering, sorrow and struggle. Youth has its point of view—eager, quick, impatient, arrogant, half lacking in confidence in their own ability to be fully grown men and women Eager to take their place and prove that they are adult, they often need encouragement and faith from the older men and women around them, especially those near and dear to them, who are only too often the ones to condemn them because youth does not follow the ideals and patterns of the older people.

Yet it was youth which answered the call and paid the price in World War I. And in the main, it was youth again which paid the price in World War II.

We should not despise or condemn youth, for the young people of to-day are partly the fruits of our creation—our training—our example. Condemn them and to some extent we condemn ourselves. They are our only hope for the future, for they *are* the future—the rulers, the creators of the future of the world and of mankind.

We should try, therefore, to look at them in a different light; build up faith in them; condone their exuberance, which is sometimes overdone as a result of the confidence of youth; overlook their arrogance, for it is the arrogance of those painfully ignorant of life and what it holds in store for them. And would we honestly have them at that age anything else but ignorant of the struggles of the world? Would it not destroy what is, after all, more than half the attraction of youth—their sanguine outlook—their absolute faith—in what the future holds for them and their ability to face and deal with it?

Their morals may be lax; their religion loose or uncertain or apparently non-existent. Yet perhaps they are working out a faith and a vision which may bring about a better civilisation in the years to come than ours has done. For looking at the world at large, what have we elders to congratulate ourselves upon?

So let us concentrate on the strong points of youth—perceive their optimism and practical frankness, and, above all, feel their need of our faith, help and guidance. Let us be prepared to be so magnanimous, so broad-minded, that we can still have faith in our children, even when they follow paths contrary to our own wishes or beliefs.

### Faith in Oneself

The people with the greatest faith in themselves find the greatest joy in daily living, the most outstanding successes and exhilarating experiences. One must also maintain faith in oneself before hoping to have faith in anyone else or imbue faith in others. And this faith means faith in the whole, the complete individual or personality—it implies faith in body, mind and spirit. For the individual is only complete as a trinity of these three. Faith in oneself is essential to health, to happiness, to success. It is lack of faith that often brings about so many suicides, failures, divorces and makes chronic invalids. It is lack of faith in themselves which sends thousands flocking to psychiatrists to help them from the slough of life in which they are floundering.

An individual must believe in the fitness and durability of his body, the quality of his mind, and the strength of his spirit, if he is to cope with life. He must do his best to cast out fear—fear of unemployment, of poverty, fear of illness, of oncoming old age and of inevitable death. The only way to fight fear is with faith. And faith can often be found here and now, on our own doorsteps, on our own hearths, in our own jobs and circumstances. Farthest fields may look the greenest—*but* how many have been disillusioned once they have travelled to the "green" fields? The dream of a lazy existence, of permanent leisure, whether of young or old, is indeed a legendary dream of bliss.

So we should have faith in ourselves and modify our present circumstances to coincide with the strength of our body, mind and spirit. And what is more important, we should have faith that we can withstand far more of the buffetings of work than we can the gentle lappings of leisure. Let us believe in the strength of body, mind and spirit—cease to concentrate on their weaknesses.

A great deal can be done and is being done by psychiatrists who, with their combined knowledge of the body and mind, bring confidence and peace to so many frustrated, harassed and bewildered individuals. But is this enough? It would seem not. We need the combined services of the minister and the skill of the psychiatrist. If religion, however wide in its scope and meaning, gave more support to psychiatry, and vice versa, if psychiatrists and ministers worked more closely together—became partners—there would be many more successes in dealing with countless people who need help with their problems.

If the individual needed the help of a counsellor in the things of the spirit, he would be sent to a minister; if he was troubled by mental tensions, frustrations and confusions, he would consult the psychiatrist. In this way the complete trinity of body, mind and spirit would be treated, welded and united, and would help to bring about the peace, happiness and fulfilment which all men and women seek.

### Religious Revival

The whole world to-day is in need of a spiritual revolution, because never before has the failure of material remedies for human distress made the need of a spiritual force, active and visible among men and nations, so obviously urgent.

In all large towns, outside all large hospitals, one sees appeals for blood donors to save life. More than ever, though still perhaps not enough, is being done for the physical welfare of people. But what is being done for the spiritual welfare of the nation or of the human race? The appreciation or acknowledgment of spiritual needs has fallen into the background and indeed is often ridiculed. Yet the trinity of body, mind and spirit is an indisputable fact.

If faith, through the power of the spiritual side of individuals, were developed, the efforts made to heal and perfect the body would be rewarded with 100 per cent. greater results.

Yes, we need blood donors. Transfusions have saved and could have saved many lives. But the race is in need also of a spiritual transfusion. It can only be given by, and come from, those who recognise and accept the existence of the Great Spirit in the universe and in every individual. Those men and women who believe in the spiritual authority of God are bound to use it in their everyday lives to help towards healing the ills of the world.

## A Spiritual Revolution

We need a spiritual revolution—a religious revival. We need spiritual guidance and leadership to keep pace with the present-day bewildering happenings in world affairs and with modern complex problems. Some branches of religion are awakening to this need. But others are still sadly lacking, inactive, uninspired!

Would it not serve humanity better if the religious leaders were to go out into the highways and byways and speak in the pubs, dance-halls and market-places? Why do they keep to their own little circle of devotees? Do they flinch at the thought of the mocking crowd? The laughter? The derision? The Great Galilean had to contend with all this as he preached throughout the hills and valleys of Judea, spreading his dynamic gospel among all sorts and conditions of people—saints and sinners, harlots, rich and poor, high and low, noble and ignoble—talking to vast crowds, to small groups or to individuals.

It isn't so much those *within* the churches who need help, guidance and inspiration. It is the millions *outside*. And if these people won't go to church, then why doesn't the Church go to the people?

The Gospel of the Galilean is just as applicable to our day as it was during the time He was here. For the world to-day has most of the scars of that world into which He came nineteen hundred years ago. There is the same despair, the same weariness, the same hopelessness.

Let religion arise again, renewed, refreshed, re-inspired through the suffering and misery of the past half-century. Let it be a newer, stronger, more natural, everyday religion to meet present-day needs— not, as it very often is, a hypocritical, psalm-singing affair for the self-righteous, well-dressed, well-to-do, conventional folk, many of whom practice religion only on Sundays.

## Day-to-day Religion

Surely religion should be of the spirit—for all ages and any age! For every day of the week! Anywhere and at any time! In joy or in sorrow, work or play, success or failure, or in the little everyday humdrum routine. There needs to be religion in the home as the housewife does her daily chores; religion as men go about their daily tasks; religion in leisure.

Religion could help to transform the dull routine of life to a higher plane filled with meaning and purpose. Work would become less arduous, play and leisure more enjoyable.

Religion need not, and indeed should not be a solemn, gloomy and depressing affair kept for special occasions. Jesus had his sorrows and tribulations we know, but too much stress seems to have been put on this part of his personality and life. Would a man of perpetually sad and gloomy counteance have attracted to him children who climbed on his knee and leaned against him? Isn't it more likely that his smiling, kindly eyes and the stories he had to tell drew them to him? He had his troubles, but also he loved laughter, fun, friendship, affection and the company of men, women and children. He enjoyed life and people. He went to parties and weddings; it seems that he found pleasure in watching people make merry. He believed that Sunday was made for man, not man for Sunday!

Religion does not mean robbing life of some of its joys and saddening the heart. Surely religion should bring a new zest and happiness to life, glorifying the body and all its faculties, enriching the mind and spirit.

Surely the way to realise all this is by a faith that can be the key to unlocking limitless powers of the body, mind and spirit. So let us nurture and develop this seed of faith and belief, not only in God, but in ourselves and our fellow men. For it is the power of faith that will conquer present-day chaos and make life richer and fuller. Let us have faith in our bodies, minds and spirits; faith in our ideals; faith in our jobs, however lowly they may be; faith in our families—in youth and the community. And finally, faith in the eternal verities of true religion and faith in the future.

# THE SHAPE OF THINGS TO COME

*Our imagination is staggered when we try to*
*visualise what life will be like in the future.*

\*    \*    \*

AMONG new words which have crept into the English language in
recent years is the word "Automation". To many of us this
strange word may have a menacing sound about it. It suggests not
only relentless production in industry with minimum human effort,
but an industrial revolution in which mechanical robots will be employed *instead of men.*

With this picture in mind, it is not surprising that a great many
people fear redundancy and unemployment as automation advances.
Is this fear justified by the facts?

Let us glance back for a moment and consider some of the changes
made, for example, in the building trade. Fifty years ago it was usual
for houses to be built with wooden sash-corded window frames, slate
roofs and plaster ceilings. Nowadays, many houses have steel-framed
casement windows, and most houses are built with tiled roofs and
plasterboard ceilings. Practically all kitchen units, cupboards, doors
and windows are prefabricated. Even roof trusses can be supplied
ready to assemble. It is quite possible that houses of the future will
be built with prefabricated, interlocking concrete slab walls instead
of bricks, and that windows will be "glazed" with some transparent
plastic material in place of glass.

If house-building is again transformed by the general introduction
of these news ideas and materials, what will become of the brick-
makers, bricklayers, glass-makers and glaziers? Will they all be
thrown out of work? Not necessarily. There will be a gradual
transition, during which a comparative few workers may be unemployed
for a time, but the overwhelming majority of workers will adapt
themselves to the inevitable changes. The more the brick-making and
glass-making industries decline, the more will the cement-making
and plastic industries flourish—and more workers will be needed in
them.

Although elaborate interior plaster work is seldom required in
these days, plasterers are kept busy fixing and skimming plasterboards,
often using materials other than plaster for walls. Other building
workers fix tiles instead of slates, while window frames, doors and
staircases reach the building sites ready-made for fixing. This is
inevitable—it is progress.

179

Years ago, several large distributing firms using thousands of horse-drawn vehicles, decided to change over to motor vans. All the van-salesmen were worried because they believed they would lose their jobs. What happened? They were all trained to drive motor vans. Not only did these men continue in their employment, but they enjoyed shorter working hours, made more calls and earned more money!

## Automation is Inevitable

These examples are worth considering, for they offer a useful pointer to the probable results of automation. The advance of automation is inevitable; it will mean considerable personal adaptation, but it is surely not to be feared. It should be regarded, not as a threat of forthcoming disaster, but as a promise of a higher standard of living and greater prosperity for all.

Although the examples given do not concern automation itself, the resultant changes will be similar. As automation advances, so will direct labour workers be replaced by maintenance men and plant engineers.

It must be remembered, however, that the progress to full automation will be gradual, over a number of years.

It is not beyond the bounds of possibility that one day the managing director of a company will be able to send a wireless message from his home to the works manager of his distant factory. He, in turn, will relay the message through a telemeter system which already can transmit through space more than five hundred different channels of information, such as speed, direction, acceleration, vibration, etc. A computer brain will then start the machines working—having calculated the exact amount of material needed to complete the manufacture of a given quantity of goods required. No human hands will perform the various processes, and the finished product will be ready for the market on time. It will all be worked out and executed scientifically.

Industry is moving rapidly towards this fantastic possibility, but before it is a common procedure, workers will be trained and adapted to meet the situation. Hard manual labour will no longer be necessary —and a good thing too, for those who might have had to do it!

All this, of course, will mean more leisure for future generations, and one important problem will be how to make profitable use of all the spare time available. A pleasant prospect, surely? Some of this spare time could be used by workers to train for more responsible scientific or executive positions. This will all be possible during time which is now occupied by most of us in earning a living.

As things are to-day, the ambitious young man has to work an eight-hour day for at least five days a week, and attend evening classes perhaps three or four nights a week in order to reach proficiency. Many of these young men are mentally or physically tired before they start their evening studies. A considerable strain is imposed upon them if they want to succeed at all in their chosen careers.

When automation is sufficiently advanced, we can envisage—say, a four-day working week with two "free" days for additional private study.

## Far-reaching Effects

Another interesting feature is likely to emerge with the advent of general automation.

Instead of the individual being required to adapt himself to this machine or that machine, it is more likely that machines will be adapted to fit the men and women who control them. Advanced technical engineering knowledge and skill could make this possible, on the advice of highly-specialised welfare executives.

Automation will eventually remove so much drudgery from work.

Just imagine, for example, one person in charge of several machines. The machines will be self-correcting for necessary minor adjustments. Suppose more serious faults were registered by the ringing of an alarm bell. In such a case the machine "operator" could sit and read a book all day or watch his favourite television programme until the automatic alarm bell warned him that his personal attention was required. This is not nearly so fantastic as it may appear to some of us now.

The effects of full automation may be even more remarkable and far-reaching. A new type of worker should develop!

Even to-day, there is a considerable amount of noise and an element of danger in most factories. Noise and risk of personal injury cause nerve-tension among the workers. When these two scourges have been almost entirely eliminated by automation, as well as the present manual drudgery removed, what effect will this have upon the factory worker?

No longer will he have to rely upon his physical strength, or the swift response of his muscles, to escape a sudden danger. He will not have to be alert to save trapping a finger in the machine or getting a steel splinter in his eye; his nerves will no longer be frayed by incessant noise. His mind will be in tune with the mechanical controls. Directly the danger signal goes he will be ready to spring to those controls and do whatever is necessary to minimise loss of production.

Probably the very air each worker breathes will be cleaner, and with adequate physical exercise during his increased hours of leisure, he should be a healthier and happier person.

Where may we expect automation to make considerable progress in the very near future? Experts who have already studied this question indicate that automation can be applied to about 16 per cent. of all manufacturing operations in the metal-working industries.

Automation already exists in one form or another in many other industries including chemicals, rubber, glass, pottery, paper, petroleum, refining, food and beverages, motor vehicles.

All these industries are planning substantial increases in automation at the present time. The motor vehicle industry is well ahead in this respect.

With labour and material costs increasing at an alarming rate, manufacturers are under great economic pressure to install automatic equipment which will increase production at reduced cost. Nothing can prevent this, no matter how some of us may fear the possibility of a temporary sharp rise in unemployment. At least there will have to be some reshuffling of employed persons, but workers will enjoy improved working conditions, with increasing responsibility for foremen and managers. There will be more need of highly-skilled technicians and specialists. Much of the manual labour at present employed will gradually fade out of existence, but the coming generation will not shed any tears over that!

Another interesting feature of the modern trend in industry is the labour-saving automatic office equipment such as the digital computer. These computers save money, time and labour in business houses, scientific projects and in certain Government departments. One chemical company reports that its computer produces in two hours a financial report that formerly took 320 man-hours.

The new "Datamatic" Electronic Data Processing System has been specially designed for business use to process mountains of complex paper work at a speed far beyond human perception. This giant electronic brain can devour all sorts of business information at a rate of 900 fully-punched cards a minute. It can step up the flow of this information to and from the central cumputer to a peak rate of 120,000 digits *per second*, or a sustained speed of 60,000 digits *per second*. Consistent with these almost incredible speeds this electronic marvel can print notices, reports, statements, etc., at the eye-blinking speed of 15 lines a *second* (up to 120 characters a line).

## Solving New Problems

As the danger element decreases in factories, owing to the use of machines instead of human hands for many operations, there is likely to be an increase in eye-strain among workers in general. Close work and concentration on office machines, control dials and illuminated panels, for example, will place additional strain on the eyes, apart from the leisure hours spent in watching television.

Furthermore, as more workers need to use less physical effort, there is likely to be an increase in the common ailments of sedentary workers.

It seems obvious that automation will gradually change the whole industrial environment. It will relieve workers of many present problems, but introduce others of a different kind—both physical and mental.

This, in itself, will open a wide field of industrial hygiene—which will, of course, require its own scientific specialists. With the aid of wonderful measuring instruments they will be able to sample and analyse sound, vibration, wind speed, air pollution, radiation. From these studies they will be able to predict the effect of various degrees and forms of automation on the workers.

In these days company managements are in any case paying far more attention to the health and welfare of their workers than ever before. This trend is likely to continue as automation becomes more widespread.

As automatic control takes over our factories and offices, there will be a greater demand for highly-trained specialists, scientists and technicians in new departments of industry. These "back-room" boys will concern themselves with such things as the recently announced "airborne digital computer". This small mechanical brain can solve mathematical problems in *one second*, as against *nine hours* which it would take a clever mathematician to work them out with pencil and paper.

In modern aircraft, automatic controls keep aircrews alive and fit at high altitudes; they keep planes flying when necessary by automatic piloting; they allow safe landing by instruments—and now being developed are split-second controls too fast for the human brain, to prevent collisions in the air.

### Fantastic Age of Progress

With these, and many other future developments, will emerge a *new race* of brilliant engineers and advanced scientists. They will be urgently needed in almost every industry one can mention. There will be new products, new processes, vastly increased production.

There is already a new X-ray machine which takes moving pictures of the insides of running engines. Think of the time and labour this one machine alone can save. Mechanics can see at a glance exactly where a fault lies, without taking the whole engine to pieces in order to trace it.

A similar industrial television instrument looks into difficult and dangerous places to give operators remote but continuous contact with operations and reactions. This contributes to safety and more efficient performance.

Sections of American railways have central panels of switch controls to manoeuvre waggons in the yards, thus saving lives and limbs. There is even a lift truck without a driver, which sets out on its rounds alone, drives itself into a storage section, picks up its load, backs out and delivers.

In one of the largest American steel mills, one closely-packed panel control is being installed. It will automatically direct the following *uninterrupted* operations. It will bring strip steel from a hot strip mill into an electric welding mill, cut the strips to the exact length and width desired, form each from a flat sheet into a tube, weld the seam, trim off the edges, anneal it, convey the tube through a number of cleaning and inspection stations and deliver it to the shipyards!

As for drilling holes of varying dimensions in the exact positions required, this is merely a matter of pressing the right buttons.

In dealing with these few mechanical devices of automation, we present just a glimpse of things to come in this fantastic age in which we live.

We are now only in the preliminary stages of the coming atomic age. If we will ponder for a little while, our imagination will be staggered as we seek to picture what life will be like in the future—atomic power for transportation, interplanetary space travel, electronic miracles to take the drudgery from daily living.

When we consider something of these wonderful possibilities that lie ahead for future generations, and even for this one, it brings home to us the incredible folly and the criminal stupidity of even contemplating an atomic war.

If this horror can be avoided, as we pray it will, a new scientific world of super-abundance will arise, a greater age of progress will come into being, with revolutionary changes that can multiply the happiness, comfort and well-being of all mankind.

# THE GATEWAY TO OPPORTUNITY

THE great difference between success and failure often is that one person sees opportunity where another sees only difficulty; the vital difference between the fulfilled individual and the mediocre misfit frequently is that while the one sees and makes use of opportunities, the other is blind except to his own self-pity.

Opportunity is a word the meaning of which we all think we know. But it is not such a simple word as all that. Many men and women fail to see opportunity because they do not know what it is nor recognise the guise in which it is presented. It is easy to see the grand opportunity that may present itself when the head of a department retires and the post becomes available for one of his former subordinates. One man applies for the position—and gets it. We reason that he has made the most of his opportunity.

But in point of fact, he probably grasped his opportunity several years before! He made the most of his opportunities when he trained himself to accept responsibility, when he improved his knowledge of the techniques of his job and of his firm. The opportunity for this promotion existed when this man—and his colleagues—first started with the concern as juniors. The one grasped the opportunity—worked for it. His actual promotion was but the culmination of years of making the most of opportunities. His former colleagues no doubt dubbed him a "lucky" person. But in fact he was a man who had grasped the small chances of every day.

The analogy, however, of the man and his job is not the full story. It merely emphasises the point that there are opportunities all around us every day. The great opportunities of life can be grasped only if we have made full use of the little ones.

Some people may dispute this statement and retort that there may be opportunities for clerks in offices; they can, perhaps, train themselves to become departmental managers and so on in due course. But what of the workman at the bench, the housewife in the home, the self-employed individual and a host of others? What opportunities are there for them?

There are a myriad of opportunities for all, every day, irrespective of age, sex or job. What we should realise is that *opportunities come to us in strange guises*; that the opportunity of a lifetime may appear at the outset as a calamity, that our best chances may come along as a result of very small things indeed.

For where there appear to be no opportunities in any day to make direct progress, an actual assault should be made upon the fortress

185

of our ambitions. There are bound to be opportunities for strengthening character, for developing personality, for toning up mind and body to grasp the major opportunity when it comes.

We have all known those days when everything seemed destined to go wrong. We fumed and fretted and apostrophised the fates. We spoke of "one of those days when nothing seemed to go right".

But what "those days" really offer us is the chance to prove that we are superior to set-backs, that we are above the petty irritations and mundane upsets. When we give way to irritation we have, in fact, missed an opportunity to build our characters—the very foundation-stone of success and happiness.

That is what we mean when we say that we are often blind to opportunity. We see the large and important opportunities but neglect the many small ones. *Opportunity comes to us in small things.* The chance, by a little extra effort, to do a job really well; the chance, by exercising extra initiative, to gain some new knowledge; the opportunity, by being greater than petty set-backs, to become strong enough to overthrow major obstacles—the chances that every one of us is accorded to live more fully.

When we think in this way, we begin to realise that opportunities are almost endless; *make the most of the small opportunities and the great ones will unfailingly come along.* But opportunities, however, do not always appear in the procession of the day's events.

### Making Opportunities

Most of us can *make* our own opportunities! And to illumine this point I cannot do better than relate the story of a man I have known very well for a number of years.

This man's parents were poor and his early years were unhappy ones. His education did not progress beyond a few years at a grammar school to which he had won a scholarship. Much as he would have liked to have gone on to a university, the family finances did not stretch that far. And so he was forced to try and find a job at a reasonably high rate of pay even in the initial stages.

To-day, as most of us will appreciate, such jobs with relatively high commencing wages are usually in the "dead-end" class. But this man was looking for work in the unemployment years of 1931–32; so some idea of his great difficulties will be more apparent.

In time he succeeded in landing a job as a door-to-door salesman on a commission basis only.

He told me, many years later, that he loathed the very prospect of it. He was of a shy and retiring disposition and his first day on the road was veritable hell.

He was in no way a "salesman" type—his interests were more academic, his preference and his training fitted him for a more scholastic type of work. But he realised that there were only two alternatives open to him now he had taken on the job. He could either make a go of it or else drag himself on dispiritedly from day to day until his earnings dwindled and the job disappeared; there were two choices—success or failure. He decided that he would succeed.

And so he tackled the job with all the imagination and courage that he could muster, compelled himself to find something of interest in it, forced himself to see its good points. He was, for instance, more or less his own boss; he met all types of people in the course of his day's work; he could learn a good deal about human nature from his daily contacts.

It was uphill work. It would have been that, even to one with a "salesman's temperament". But to him, in those days when unemployment was rife, the task was doubly hard, as anyone with imagination can appreciate.

### Giving Service .

He told me years later, that it was the most difficult fight of his life. There were times when he very nearly despaired. Even whilst he was making a fair success of the actual selling, he often felt like giving up the job. But he was resolved that he would succeed.

And eventually, by hard work, unflagging courage, always appearing cheerful even in the face of the most discourteous rebuffs, not only did he make a success of the job, but eventually overcame his deep repugnance and actually enjoyed meeting people and the selling angle. As he told me in later years: "I would knock at doors in my early days hoping against hope that no one would open them, so that I could go away with a clear conscience. Later on I would knock at doors with an eager anticipation, wondering what type of character I should meet and, at the first glance when the door opened and an enquiring face appeared, what split-second decision I should make as to the best opening remarks. Having got the introduction over, I based my whole approach *on the best way I could help the prospective customer*. When people realised that I was quite sincere in trying to be of assistance, and that my technique was not one where I wished to sell them something against their will, their response was usually most co-operative."

(This is not a treatise on salesmanship, but I would like to emphasise the words italicised. The man's success was due to his attitude of trying to help—of giving service; it is the keynote to success in any sales field.)

The part to remember in the case of this man is that he was forced into a job he did not like by pressure of circumstance, but he looked upon it not as drudgery, as most men would have done, but as an opportunity to get ready for something better. He did not bemoan the misfortune that had debarred him from college and forced him to "waste" his talents in an uncongenial job, but set resolutely about mending his fortunes in the best way he could.

I have gone into this phase of the man's life in some detail, because so many have shared at least part of his experience in being forced into a job rather than being able to select one. But by treating his misfortune as an opportunity, the man under discussion became a success, and after being successful at this, he felt he could blithely tackle anything else the world had to offer.

Shortly before the outbreak of war, the firm for which he worked promoted him to the position of sales manager, and in the short time before he joined the Forces he demonstrated in no mean measure his ability to handle men, to manage, to plan and control.

During his time as a salesman, he had not neglected the larger side of self-education. He had been unable to go to college, but as he told me in later years, *no man who has access to a good public library need be without a college education.*

During the war years, as the exigencies of the Services permitted, his "general education" continued. He spent most of his spare time in fitting himself for that better job which he was determined to secure after he had left the Forces.

Even whilst he was "on the road" as a salesman, he had decided on the post that he would like and even knew the firm for which he wished to work. His self-education consisted of a general form of all-round education, and also preparing himself for this specific post he had in view.

On his return from the Forces, he continued with his old job for a short time, but he had a plan in mind and when he had completed it, presented himself before a director of the firm in question.

He had no introductions, no previous experience of the particular type of work for which he had applied, but his undoubted sincerity, his general bearing, his success with his previous employers, all convinced the director that here was a man worthy of a trial. The man, in addition, told the director that he would be willing to work for a short time without pay in order to prove his fitness for the job.

He was engaged. To-day he is the general manager of that concern. He is in his early forties and has achieved what he set out to do. Not that he is without ambition for the future, but he has proved that a man may set a high objective despite initial set-backs, make his own opportunities and be the architect of his own success. Here was a man who converted his liabilities into opportunities.

It would seem superfluous to add that, as this man succeeded, so can the average individual. But the main moral of the story is that a person of courage can convert disadvantages into advantages and transform adversities into opportunities.

The circumstances of each individual may differ very widely from those of the man whose history we have recounted. But basically the problems are bound to be similar.

## Self-Advancement

Every day brings us opportunities for self-advancement. We should train ourselves to see such opportunities, have the courage to make the most of them, the insight to perceive disadvantages as opportunities in disguise and the faith to fight and the perseverance to keep on fighting. This is the way to achievement and success.

Apart from the moral of the story of the man under review there is yet another important point to remember. Opportunity is only the gateway to success, fulfilment and the larger life. Opportunity is not, in itself, achievement. The failures who have received no end of opportunities and who are still failures are proof of this.

To revert to the story we have recounted—the man landed the job that he desired—the type of work that he wanted, with the firm of his choice. But his difficulties were not over. An exacting task still lay ahead.

*He still had to make good!*

The gateway had been opened to him, but he still had to climb to the summit of achievement. The concern had given him his chance. Now it remained for him to justify the faith of the firm's director in him, to go on making the most of opportunities.

## Be Prepared for Opportunity

There are many men and women who merely sigh for a chance, an opportunity to do well, as if opportunity itself were the end of the road, whereas it is, in fact, only the starting-point of a very exacting race.

"If only I'd had a chance," they say. "If only I had better opportunities now."

Suppose these people had the chance, the opportunity for which they sigh. Would it find them prepared? If it is success in their work that they desire, suppose they were offered positions of managerial responsibility. Could they make a go of them? Have they the tact, the patience, the imagination for handling people? Would they have a thorough concept of the objectives of the firm? Would they gladly accept, or shy away from responsibility? Let these mere wishers for opportunities answer these queries truthfully.

If we wish for success and achievement, we should at once start to *deserve* them, so that when our opportunity comes, we shall not be unprepared.

The story of the man we have discussed could be repeated many thousands of times. Most of the captains of modern industry, the leaders in several fields of endeavour, the scientists, the writers and artists—to whom the world now pays homage—started under severe handicaps, without initial advantages or influence.

Again the story is repeated in the pages of history. Demosthenes is accounted to have been the world's greatest orator. *Yet Demosthenes stuttered!*

Beethoven, the emperor of the world of music, wrote his finest work when he was deaf.

The most mature work of John Milton was dictated when he was blind.

And there, in the far distant past, stands the Galilean Carpenter. He was born in the manger of a stable in an obscure locality and lived his young manhood as an itinerant preacher. He faced insuperable odds and overcame innumerable obstacles. Yet he created new worlds, recast the drama of civilisation and changed the course of history into fairer ways.

Success in a given business or profession may not be our major aim in life. Our life's objective may be something entirely different. But the opportunities are still unlimited and are to be found everywhere. And the prizes are waiting on every hand for the men and women who will grasp these opportunities and who will dare and do!

# THE NEED FOR INCENTIVE

*Without the driving force of incentive, Man must perish. For we are so made that, without the drive towards evolutionary development, we must inevitably slip backwards; unless we press forward, we retrogress towards extinction. In national, no less than in individual life, there must be the incentive to strive, fight, persevere towards some worth-while goal.*

\*　　\*　　\*

WE hear more and more these days about incentives, whether in industry or in the classrooms. We are nationally conscious of the fact that we need some form of a spur to urge us on to fresh endeavours and new conquests, that we need some bait to lure us on to new achievement.

But though we may hear so much about incentives in many forms, there is so much muddled thinking on the matter that it would be well to consider it fully, for the subject of incentives has individual as well as national significance.

The main talk about incentives centres around some form of reward for extra effort or efficiency in industry. It is, very largely, the question of extra rewards for extra effort. In pre-war times, we did not hear so much about rewards that followed extra effort. We heard more about the penalties that followed the lack of effort. Before the war, employers in general relied upon the power of unemployment in order to induce workers to work as well and as efficiently as they could.

To-day, in view of over-employment, the pendulum has swung to the other extreme, and there is more attention given to the rewards allowed for more successful work. It is the old story of the stick and the carrot. Prior to conditions of full employment, the stick was used to urge onwards any reluctant worker. To-day, the carrot is dangled in front of the reluctant one so as to tempt him forward.

Now I want to make it quite clear that I am not particularly in favour of either technique, nor do I wish to dwell too long upon this as an industrial or political problem. Nevertheless, it is necessary to look at it for a while longer in order to get our thoughts clear upon it, and before we come to discuss a more fundamental psychological matter than the mere question of the stick and the carrot, punishment and reward.

In industrial concerns to-day, it is quite usual for the management to introduce some scheme whereby workers can earn extra money by more quickly and more efficiently, by studying very closely the movements made in certain operations, and scientifically training operatives to eliminate waste movements and thus secure more *productive* work. Such systems have, often enough, proved phenomenally successful.

On the other hand, the introduction of such schemes is looked upon with disfavour in some quarters. There is even a certain amount of feeling abroad that workers should receive the rewards without achieving the actual results that extra production would bring.

Another way of looking at it was recently expressed by a certain business man. He had inaugurated an incentive scheme in his factory. It worked very well. Over-all production had been greatly increased. The average earnings of the operatives were up by £2 or more per week, without overtime.

The workers were satisfied except that they grumbled about the amount of tax they had to pay on the extra earnings.

The employer had every reason for contentment. He was getting extra production that would not otherwise have been possible, except by investing heavily in additional plant and extra labour. Under the incentive scheme, the additional production was secured at an economical rate.

But the employer did have some misgivings. As he expressed them: "My grandfather would have been horrified. All we are doing in effect is to pay the men an average of £2 per week extra for going all out—something they should really be doing for their regular wage as an honest day's work."

He went on to add: "Financially, I have no grumbles. But I am not too happy about the fact that the moral fibre of some of our working population is such that they do not honour a contract of employment without being bribed by incentives. I am worried about the effect of this on the future."

I do not propose to dwell too long upon the moral of this story. It points to a weakness, perhaps, in the relationship between employers and workers in industry to-day. And if it is true that we cannot get full production from our labour force without the carrot of incentive or the stick of under-employment, it is a factor that augurs ill for the future of the nation.

### The Giant on Our Backs

But this is not the end of the story. The workpeople had earned an extra £2 per week under the incentive scheme. Their efforts and their efficiency had been rewarded. But each individual's actual wage packet was not heavier by £2. Income tax had to be deducted, leaving him probably just over one-half of his additional earnings. And even with the extra money he had left after deduction of income tax, what can he buy? Very little that is not taxed again! If he spends a £1 of it on tobacco or cigarettes, he will, in fact, receive less than 5s. worth of actual tobacco. The Inland Revenue has again stepped in and taken the balance. There is little doubt that taxation is a severe brake on effort, is seriously hampering our progress and threatening our standard of living.

The result of to-day's intolerable taxation is also to be seen in the case of the men who are really ambitious, training themselves up to take over managerial responsibilities. These are the men that industry needs so badly. Yet they are often crippled even more heavily by tax burdens. The man who works his way up to an executive position may earn a great deal more than those he controls. But the crushing rate of income tax, plus the necessity of maintaining some status in the community, will probably leave him with less actual cash than the people he supervises.

We are urged to work harder, produce more, become more efficient. But there is very little incentive to do so. For the greater the efforts we put forth, the more we produce, the more tax we pay.

People work and plan and organise because of the rewards of their labour. If these prizes are snatched away from them, they will not give of their best. Why should men and women work hard, take on added responsibilities and worries, when they know that the rewards of success will go to the Inland Revenue?

Taxation has now become intolerable. It is paid by everyone. Even the child who spends a few pennies on sweets is taxed. Our shops have become tax collectors, for we pay taxes on whatever we buy. Clothes, pots and pans, tobacco, beer, entertainment—all have been enrolled in the ranks of tax gatherers. We collect taxes from one another. We have become a nation of tax collectors.

While we are struggling to build up our overseas trade, we are being weakened and knocked down by this merciless, insatiable tax collecting.

We are being crushed and our assets looted in a legal and respectable way. Taxation has destroyed businesses and property that were built up by the toil and sweat of our forefathers.

The more taxes that are paid, the less capital there is left. Only by earning and saving can capital be accumulated. Capital cannot be created by the printing presses. That would make our money still less valuable, and eventually lead to national bankruptcy. If an individual's savings are taken away from him in the form of taxes, he will have none left for capital. He will then be unable to invest any money or increase his deposit at the bank, extend his business or employ more people.

Taxation has now become such a heavy burden that it is not only taking our savings, but it is eating into our reserves as well. The inheritance that was left to us by our forefathers is steadily being destroyed. There is no protection for the rights and money and the property of the people.  By no standard of ethics is it possible to justify the present excessive and oppressive rate of taxation.  It has become legalised plundering.

The process is surely suicidal.  It is slowing down the work of the country and will bring Britain to a standstill unless in the near future it can be checked.


## Incentive is Necessary

Though it is now generally accepted that taxation in some form is necessary, most of us feel that a great deal of the money filched from us is being squandered.  There seem to be no limit to national expenditure and very little control over it.  The bill for every crazy scheme comes to the taxpayer from the squeeze and squander departments.  On the other hand, opportunities of earning more money or making more profit are being cut down.

These are the facts.  Political extremists and arrant demagogues may prefer either to evade or ignore them or to under-estimate their importance, but they do reveal a dangerous state of affairs.  When effort is penalised by heavy taxation, the level of effort will fall.  When the profit of enterprise is taken away, then individuals will refuse to take risks.  Incentive is necessary to men and women.  People must be stimulated, not pauperised.  And one of the best stimulants that has ever been known is the right to keep what is earned.

*Psychology*, however, is not so much concerned with the industrial or political implications of this.  Its concern is with the effect upon human beings.  And if effort is penalised, if enterprise cannot enjoy some real form of reward, then the very foundation of our industrial and social life is in peril.

By all means let us extend our social security measures.  Let us ensure that the best in educational facilities is available to all, irrespective of class or income.  Let us ensure that the aged, the infirm and the misfits are properly cared for.  Let us wage an extended war upon want and disease.  This will cost money and must come from the common pool.  We must all contribute towards these desirable objectives.

But men and women are so made, that they are not content to have a big slice of their earnings taken away from them by taxation, leaving merely sufficient to pay to be housed, clothed and fed.  To-day's heavy and oppressive tax burdens could be very considerably lightened without reducing social security schemes if rigid economies were made in the administrative departments.

But this, maybe, is a matter more for political discussion. *Psychology* merely points out a grave danger in the present set-up, which, because of intolerable taxation encourages loafing, indifference and inefficiency. Men and women must be encouraged to give of their best, to be more efficient. They must feel that there are worth-while rewards and objectives they can reach by real effort. This is the only way that any nation can forge ahead to greater over-all prosperity.

## The Inward Spur

We have discussed so far incentives that take the form of some material reward. Such incentives cannot be ignored, and there is no cause whatsoever to decry them. But though incentives spur the majority of people on to real effort, there are a few individuals for whom work alone is sufficient incentive. They work because they are influenced and inspired by an inner urge. They feel that they have found fulfilment in their work, happiness in their endeavours and satisfaction in their labours. They believe that by developing their latent powers, life becomes more meaningful, that they are able to see more clearly the needs of their fellow men, and contribute fully to the general weal.

Such men and women have found the high road to successful living, for it is along that road that true fulfilment is found. The material rewards may be greater, the social success may be on a larger scale, but the greatest reward of all is that inner feeling of satisfaction, that consciousness of living every minute to the limit that can transform mere existence into meaningful life.

Far too often, however, some people talk as if the two approaches to life were incompatible; they consider that the man or woman swayed by the desire for material rewards alone can never reach towards the larger goal of self-fulfilment. This, of course, is nonsense. A man originally may be driven by the thought of material reward alone, but may later discover that this is only the first step to more effective life.

There is nothing at all wrong in desiring the material rewards for our labours. There is nothing evil in a man or woman confining his or her aim to that level. But to do so solely on that basis means missing a great deal in life. For it is by broadening our goal towards that of fulfilment that we find true happiness. The purely material reward alone may prove disappointing or disappear. But the treasures of the spirit are imperishable and come to those who set their sights higher.

## Freedom is Paramount

To-day we are witnessing an ever-increasing encroachment upon the freedom of the individual. We are living in times of mass organisation and regimentation, in which the individual is all but submerged.

We are not allowed to manage our own affairs. We can only eat and drink when we are permitted to do so. We cannot buy from the shops after a certain time. We spend our days filling in forms—answering questions that are often stupid, absurd, impossible. We are inspected, supervised, obstructed and ordered about by hordes of officials.

We are tied up with red tape. The more competent, progressive and ambitious an individual is, the more the "red tapers" harass him. There is not a single trade or industry that is not being regulated by the bureaucrats.

These insidious ideologies impose upon us a false standard, a false view of life, by seeking to prove that Man as an individual is an anachronism, that progress is only possible by subordinating the individual to the mass.

Yet all true progress comes from the individual. Every step from barbarism to civilisation was originally taken by one man or woman; we do not see the actual movement until the whole community falls into step; but the original incentive came from one personality, and any tendency to put a brake on this is retrogression—Mass organisation *never yet* created anything of worth.

Some forms of social organisation are, of course, a necessity. The destruction of these would throw Man back to the chaos of savage and unbridled individualism. But all organisation should be made subservient to human freedom, happiness and growth. Organisations should be for the benefit of the individual and *not* the individual for the benefit of the organisations.

The great need of to-day is for the recognition of individual rights, to set people free from all unnecessary restrictions and give them the exhilarating sense of worth-while incentive and true freedom.

# THE LAW OF SURVIVAL

LIFE is a battle—a dramatic struggle—a survival of the fittest! Ever since Man first drew breath on this planet he has been preyed upon by all the forces of Nature, heat, cold, tornado, rain, flood, fire, earthquake, pestilence.

To primitive Man the struggle for existence was bitter, cruel and relentless. His instinct for self-preservation, however, drove him to battle against these mighty, hostile forces which threatened to annihilate him.

Although the battle against Nature has become much less severe since the days of primitive Man, mainly as a result of Man's inventive ingenuity, nevertheless the survival of the fittest still remains the Law of Nature. It applies to plant life, insects, fish, birds and animals as well as to men and nations.

This Universal Law, on the surface, may seem to be unjust and cruel, and certainly not very beneficent to mankind. But if we probe further into the matter, we shall find that there is a great deal in favour of this Law of Survival—that it often seems good, just and wise.

## Strongest Survive

When good seed is sown in rich soil and is tended by an experienced farmer, we can expect a bumper harvest. If a few inferior seeds manage to germinate at all, the resultant plants will be frail specimens. Let there be a drought or a frost, and these weaklings will be the first to perish. Does this matter very much? If these inferior plants had survived, the fruit they would bear, if any, wouldn't be worth gathering. And what would the seed of that poor fruit be like? Certainly not worth sowing!

How do we get a good racehorse? Only by breeding from the finest stock available.

The same Law of Nature applies to Man. Let us begin at the beginning. In the act of copulation a large number of male seeds are released for action. They encounter hostile conditions from the moment they are released, and only *one* out of a great number reaches its destination to fertilise the female egg. Which one? The strongest, the most active, the most persistent one. All but that one perish. If it were not for this wise and wonderful law, the human race would have deteriorated and become extinct thousands of years ago—soon after it began!

Now what happens to those who survive the further perils of

197

childhood and adolescence and reach manhood or womanhood? Some are sadly neglected by foolish or ignorant parents, and if they are denied love and wise guidance, they may grow up with a twisted conception of life and responsibility. A few may drift into crime or become enemies of decent society.

Others with an equally unfavourable start will recognise the danger signals in time. They will refuse to be bogged down in the morass of their environment. With their heads held high, and their eyes on nobler and better things, they will struggle onward and upward to become worthy citizens, whose own children will be given a very much better opportunity of happy, successful living.

Fortunately, the majority of us have known the blessings of reasonably kind and loving parents. We have received sound advice from older, more experienced people. We have been educated to the limit of our inborn intelligence, and been launched into the world with a fair chance of survival and progress.

### The Game of Life

What have we done with these precious gifts which have been so generously provided? Have we nourished and protected the good seed, or have we, by our own neglect, apathy, idleness or other moral weakness, thrown away our golden opportunities?

Never let us forget this fact. The Universal Law of Survival of the fittest applies to us *now*—as always from the beginning. We cannot afford to overlook the relentless reality of this Law. We dare not allow ourselves to be weakened by wishful thinking.

We cannot over-emphasise the importance of this Law which we have discussed and demonstrated by example earlier on in this article.

We live in a troubled world. Not content with the *natural* "wastage" of the weak, in accordance with the Law of Survival, some of the strong are exerting every effort to crush the weak by brute force. Certain totalitarian states are committing inhuman acts for the lust of power. Their passionate desire seems to be to trample upon the weak, dominate and use them as slaves to their own will and greed.

Ever since the last war, nations have been at each other's throats in the dangerous game of power politics. Some are not willing to "live and let live" and because of this, others are fighting for their very survival as free people. And what is life itself without freedom?

The wisdom of a Solomon is needed to sort out the prevailing world-wide muddle, brought about by so-called political diplomacy. It is not, however, our intention to introduce political arguments into the pages of *Psychology*. Let it suffice for us to say that the politicians will continue to play their stupid and dangerous games, with the masses used as pawns on the chess board of the world . . . so long as they are allowed to do so.

Life *is* a gigantic game of chess. Ordinary men and women seem
to be the pieces on the board, each on his or her own square. Some
individuals in certain exalted positions of authority may be likened
to the "kings", "queens", "knights", "bishops" and "castles" in the
game, with the masses as the pawns.

There is, however, a vitally important distinction between a game
of chess and the game of Life. In real life, every single "piece", even
the humblest "pawn", has an intelligence of its own. Whether we
decide to *use* this intelligence or not is another matter. We can remain
idle, like the wooden pieces on a chessboard and allow ourselves to
be pushed around, or we can watch for a suitable opening and move
ourselves! And we should remember that "pawns" can overthrow
"kings" to win in the game of life.

In life, although the survival of the fittest is the Law, brute strength
isn't everything. It is quite easy for a slip of a girl to throw a powerful
man *if* she happens to have an adequate knowledge of ju-jitsu. By
the "fittest" in life's game we mean those with the highest development,
not only physically, but mentally and spiritually.

In order to face up to the problems and dangers now threatening
mankind all over the world, and help to win a victory for reason and
sanity, we must identify our weaknesses, learn how to correct them
and then utilise our new found strength to the full.

### Resist or Die

In general, the weaknesses most apparent among us at the present
time appear to be pessimism, fear and apathy. We are so sick and
tired of all the international discord, so disillusioned by the antics of
alternate Party politics, so bewildered by one economic crisis following
another and so burdened by restrictions and taxation that we are in
danger of losing heart altogether. Many of us begin to feel so weary,
frustrated and puzzled by to-day's happenings that we are almost
becoming complacent and indifferent to them.

But a dull, sullen subservience or an unthinking passive submission
to such things is fatal to the progress of the individual. We need to
remember that constant struggle and effort are the price demanded
for physical, mental and spiritual growth. We must fight repression
and oppression wherever it is found. We must resist or die!

We must acknowledge the Law of Life—survival of the fittest!
We must see to it that we *are* fit, in the widest sense of the word.
Then *use* all our fitness in positive, dynamic, persistent effort. Even
if we have been "pawns" for too long, we must wake up and put forth
mighty efforts and fight for human rights.

We must be strong. The world has little use for the weak-kneed,
the timid, the faint-hearted. To gain recognition and support we
must earn respect. Nobody respects weakness but even an enemy

will respect the strength of his adversary. It must, however, be the strength of wisdom, high ideals, and moral courage, born of a genuine desire to serve humanity.

The brutal, material strength of a selfish tyrant will never earn the respect for which he may yearn—and the reason is obvious. The despot cannot for long hide his ulterior motives. Sooner or later, the world sees the vision of truth which eventually shines through all the clouds of deception. It is then generally realised that what appeared to be strength is, in fact, a lamentable display of weakness and fear— a desperate attempt to survive at the expense of any who may dare to oppose.

· Only among the lower animals does physical strength alone maintain survival. The higher up the scale of life we ascend, the more does survival depend upon mental qualities. To be fit enough to survive in this modern world, Man must rely upon mental and moral qualities of the highest order. These do not include pessimism, fear and apathy, all of which are woefully apparent to-day among large sections of the community.

Only the weak need be pessimistic, afraid or submissive in their hopelessness. There is no virtue or honour in moral weakness.

We are all aware of the many problems and difficulties around us. The world is in a mess and the future of mankind seems to uncertain. It would be foolish to minimise the dangers confronting us or to shut our eyes to realities. But the greater the task, the finer the opportunity, and the richer our reward—*if we are strong, materially, mentally and spiritually.* Now is the time to get rid of that deadly trio—pessimism, fear and apathy and in their place instil faith, hope, courage, activity and tenacity of purpose.

So many of us to-day are wearing misty and distorted spectacles. We see only menacing shadows and we imagine evil dragons that may turn out to be harmless mice. Too many of us believe that because we do not occupy high positions of authority, there is nothing we can do to help in the battle for freedom and progress. How wrong is this negative attitude! How foolish and how dangerous!

Every age has produced men and women who, born in obscurity, disciplined by poverty and hardship, without influence or position, have helped to break the shackles of oppression from the masses and led them forth from tyranny to universal democracy.

### Attitude Counts

We are as great as we *believe* we are. We are capable of doing only what we *think* we can do. This does not mean that we should acquire an exaggerated sense of ego. All we need is that quiet, inner *realisation* that we have within us vast resources of physical, mental and spiritual power that we may never have used or even discovered.

We cannot find and use these powers until we realise they are there, within reach, waiting to be used.

Millions of people spend a lifetime, yearning for happiness they never find. Why? It is, in the main, because they fail to realise that happiness is a state of the mind. It is not conditioned by, or dependent upon persons, places or things. It comes from within and from our attitude towards life.

If we wish, therefore, to secure and maintain a reasonably happy and contented existence, our attitude towards the tangled and perplexing problems of national and international affairs is of supreme importance. Admittedly, it is sometimes difficult not to become depressed and anxious in these troubled days. It is easy to lose heart, grumble about the present state of affairs and voice gloomy predictions of the future. Some people go so far as to predict that there *is* no future worth looking forward to, especially in this country. The number of our people emigrating to Canada, Australia and elsewhere is increasing rapidly. "This country is finished," some of them declare.

It would be unfair, unkind and unwise to blame those who have decided to start a new life in growing countries which offer more scope and better opportunities. It is good to know the traditional British spirit of enterprise and adventure is still very much alive in our younger generation.

But what of those of us who are remaining behind? As more and more young, healthy and intelligent people leave the old country, we who are left behind must shoulder greater responsibilities to safeguard our present and future. What should be our attitude? How can we prove ourselves *fit for survival* and even continued progress?

First of all, we should make every effort to overcome the negative emotions of pessimism, apathy and fear, and replace them by positive feelings of optimism, enterprise, tenacity of purpose and courage. We should also encourage these virtues in those with whom we come in contact. We are not trapped rats in a sinking ship. We are soldiers left to guard the fort. In common with all who enter battle, we may experience fear *before* action. But we need not be ashamed of that. There is nothing like *action* to counteract fear. The biggest mistake is for us to creep into a corner, cringe and tremble and imagine the worst.

### Man's Inalienable Rights

In the shadowy beginnings of the human story, Man was very much of an individualist. From this point, we have witnessed the ever increasing encroachment upon the freedom of the individual. To-day we live in a world in which the individual is all but submerged. The accepted principle that individuals have certain sacred and inalienable rights has, to a great extent, been forcibly and callously overthrown.

We should fight this insidious encroachment upon the rights of Man. For it is only by battling against repressive and oppressive dictates that we can win freedom and progress, preserve our own individuality and be true to our own ideals and standards. We should not infringe the rights of others, but we should not surrender to the dictates of others and permit them to do our thinking for us and prescribe the mode and manner of our lives.

If we would be fit to survive the ordeal of the future and be worthy to help to build a better, fairer and happier way of life, we must be willing to make temporary sacrifices. We must have stamina, grit, be strong, bold, positive, decisive. We must be prepared to fight against seemingly insuperable odds and cut our way through all opposition. These may seem hard facts to expound. But when we come to think about them perhaps it is all for the best. Maybe the world's hard attitude, the necessity for keeping up with life's swift procession, the bitter struggle in which the unfit go down in defeat are the very things that spur us on until victory crowns our efforts.

# THE HIGHWAY OF ENDEAVOUR

*"Two men looked through prison bars:*
*One saw mud, the other stars."*

&ast; &ast; &ast;

LIFE is, in the main, a prison-house only if we make it so; for whatever the conditions our minds can be free. Freedom is nothing more or less than the right use of mind. One of the greatest tragedies in human life is the limitation that men and women impose upon themselves.

With a rich, infinitely interesting world around us, with the vast potentiality for a rich and full life, so many condemn themselves to the solitary confinement of a restricted, uninteresting, unsuccessful existence. There is unending treasure all around them, yet they sit moping under the tree of dejection, too apathetic to reach out for the limitless wealth which surrounds them. In the midst of plenty they live starved, emaciated lives.

And such people are not, unfortunately, a minority! They form a majority in almost any society. They are the pathetic legions of the half-alive, the pitiable regiments of the unrealised, the dreary millions of the disillusioned.

I believe in the dictum that "It's better to have tried and lost than never to have tried at all." Furthermore, I believe, and experience underwrites my belief, that no one who has really tried has ever wholly failed; that usually no individual who has attempted something worth while regretted the attempt; that rarely does a person pursue an ideal and though he failed to achieve complete realisation, is not infinitely the better for his attempt.

Admittedly, there have been magnificent failures. They have failed, perhaps, in so far as they had such a splendid vision that a single lifetime was too short to see the ideal fully realised. It is possible that the world may assume a man to be a failure, when in fact his inner being thrills to the realisation of victory. Outward appearances are deceptive. The Cross, which appeared to be the symbol of utter, abject, irredeemable defeat, was, in fact, the Standard of Complete Victory.

And what is more important still, the life devoted to a great objective is a full and satisfying life, irrespective of whether the objective is achieved or not. There is glory in the attempt as well as in the achievement; in the labour as well as in the triumph.

A man may stake all on a great and worth-while enterprise, devote his life and energies to a specified life aim, but does not quite achieve all he had planned. Does that mean that he has failed? By no means!

A man may have lived to the limit, enjoyed the time spent in his endeavour, and found infinite satisfaction in effort. He may have found glory in the attempt, reward in the hardship and triumph even in seeming failure. He may not find complete and absolute realisation of his objective, but he may find the pearl above price in personal realisation and fulfilment. It is as if a poet had attempted to reach the level of Shakespeare and only achieved the immortality of a Milton. Nevertheless, he has scaled the heights and blazed his name across the horizon of unborn centuries.

### The Half-alive

What a difference between such a man and the *half-believers in our casual creeds*, whose lives are a dreary routine of work and sleep, punctuated by short bouts of enervating pleasure-seeking, darkened by a feeling of insufficiency and insecurity, blighted by frustration— bogged down in the quagmire of the unthinking and unaspiring ruts in which they live. And let's be honest! Isn't that the life that so many men and women lead? The world seems filled with the drifters who drag through life on a plane of dull, drab mediocrity.

Some grumble that life has little to offer, without ever having attempted to secure even that little by way of personal endeavour. They grouse that they are handicapped and limited by birth and education, without having made any honest attempt to break the shackles of faulty heredity or the manacles of unfavourable environment. Far from expecting too much of life they are satisfied with too little. They ask only for a few physical comforts; they seek only the fundamentals of security. Yet life seems to deny them even these few simple things.

Of course it does!

For life does not hand out blessings on a plate. Man is not an animal to be fed by a beneficent fortune, to be fattened by a benevolent destiny. There is no kindly fortune to smile on us and hand the prizes of life to us merely for the asking. There are no free passes. No scholarships. The rewards of life demand self-sacrifice and patient and unremitting toil.

The trouble with our half-alive men and women is not that they have failed, but that they have never really tried. They look to the heights of achievement, consider the cost and are unwilling to pay the price.

Life's bounties are only earned as a result of intelligently directed and persistent effort. Yet the unwholesome philosophy of something for nothing still prevails.

This is illustrated very dramatically in our national tendency to

gamble.  And let's face it, we do gamble on a phenomenal scale.
It is only in an insignificant number of homes that at least one member
of the family does not have a "flutter" on the horses or the pools.

Why this colossal spending on the altar of the Goddess of
Chance?

We are not here concerned with the moral issues of whether it is
a good or a bad thing for the nation or the individuals concerned.
We only ask: "why do people do it?"

Various answers can be given—the hope of reward without effort
or the desire to get rich quickly.  But maybe the fundamental reason
is that the men and women concerned feel that they have *attempted*
something, that by staking their small sum on such a venture, they
have tried to do something creative.  Naturally, the hope of the
magnificent return is a big incentive.  But it would seem that one of
the main urges is that of doing *something*, of having made some attempt
to lift life from the mundane to a higher level.

But what a poor attempt it is!

We are not decrying these things entirely.  By all means, let us
have our "flutters" now and then.  But we shouldn't let the selection
of a few football teams, or the picking out of a couple of horses, serve
as a genuine attempt to improve and ennoble our lives.

It is so easy to sit back and fill in a coupon.  No effort is called
for; no great amount of imagination is needed; no real endeavour
is involved.

And we may be sure that life generally will pay no great dividends
for such heartless and pathetic attempts.

On the other hand, if we decide to learn a new language, master
a specific subject—anything from astronomy to accountancy—no
matter whether we become fully proficient astronomers or accountants,
there are rich rewards awaiting us in the shape of a more satisfying
life, a livelier appreciation of values, a sense of well-being that arises
out of using our faculties.  Nor need our rewards be confined to this
general feeling of self-esteem.  We can direct such efforts to enriching
our lives, ennobling our characters, building the personalities that we
wish to be.

That is the road to the fulfilled life.


## The Misfit

Let us take the case of a certain young man.  He was an attractive
youngster of twenty-two or twenty-three, of fine physique and pleasant
manner.  He was employed on a sales job with a large industrial
company and doing reasonably well.  But he confessed that he had
moments of deep depression, when he hated and loathed his job, and
when he could hardly face up to the need of meeting people on his
daily round.

He was asked what he did in his spare time. "There's nothing much to do where I live," he said, "only the pictures and a dance now and then. And that's expensive."

Unwittingly, no doubt, he had revealed one of the major causes of his *malaise*. He was of average intelligence, but with no genuine interests outside his work. He barely read the newspapers, except to digest the more sensational news; even the cinema was merely a form of temporary escape. The programmes he turned to on the wireless and television were the variety shows, and he showed but little approval of and no enthusiasm for these as a means of recreation. He hardly ever read a book, except possibly a thriller to while away a train journey.

Now, we are not setting up this young man's case in any way as an example of modern youth; yet his case is not unusual. There are far too many young men and women in his plight; some of them continue such a purposeless existence all their lives; others degenerate into social misfits and nuisances, often popularly termed "maladjusted" or "delinquent".

There would seem to be far too many young people who have failed to find satisfying, creative interests, and who lead stunted, inhibited lives.

And so unnecessary!

It is easy to ascribe the fault to over-indulgent parents, or to a mollycoddling Welfare State. Perhaps both have some bearing on the production of the type of young people we are discussing.

But the cause is not our main concern. It is the remedy. And the remedy can very largely be found in that word "recreation".

Usually none of the hobbies or pastimes of these young people are truly creative. They are but aspirins to dull the pain of boredom. What these people need is the fresh air of some worth-while task, the inspiring effort of a truly worth-while hobby, the medicine of a clearly defined objective.

What should the young man to whom we have referred do? What should any young man or woman in a roughly similar case do, in order to achieve a greater sense of satisfaction in life? What would we do if we felt that we share to some extent at least the young man's symptoms?

## Some Practical Suggestions

There are certain minimum steps we can take. They are easy and are enriching far beyond the efforts entailed. They are common-sense steps; steps that can be taken straightway.

In the case of the young man, he can set aside a few hours a week to study the particular job in which he is employed. There are some excellent books on the selling technique which he can buy or borrow from the public library. He will be amazed at the number of things he will learn, and make infinitely more interesting his meeting and talking to customers in the future.

But not only should he study his own part of the job, which is selling, but he should get to know more about his particular industry, acquire more knowledge of the product he is selling, become fully conversant with the productive methods employed and the general administration of his company.

In this way, he will find life more interesting, he will do a better job and will earn the reward of his greater efficiency.

But that's not all he should attempt.

His job is meeting people. So he should take a real interest in people generally, in their jobs and their hobbies; cultivate a variety of interests so that he can talk sensibly on a number of topics. There is no need for him to become a politician in order to discuss some aspects of politics interestingly. Nor need he become a sports enthusiast in order to converse on that subject. There's no necessity for him to make a specific study of such subjects. But he should keep his eyes and ears open to acquire all the knowledge he can. He should ask questions and on those occasions when he finds he knows little about a given topic, he should honestly admit it. Many of his prospects and customers will be only too willing to enlighten him and he will earn their goodwill in the bargain.

He should study the newspapers sufficiently to keep abreast of current topics and events, and to form intelligent opinions on the various subjects. In this way he is using his mind instead of clogging it with boredom.

He will also find that cultivating the habit of observation will pay rich dividends. No doubt he travels around a good deal at his work. What signs of human activity are there in the places he visits? Perhaps a new school is being built in a certain area; a road is being widened or a new housing estate is being erected in a certain part of the town. All these form topics of conversation at the very least. And they may serve as a means of increasing his sales with regular customers and extending his sales to new ones. But what is really important is that he will be using his mind to take an active interest in people and things, developing his powers of observation and driving out by mental *activity* the sense of apathy and frustration that mental inactivity produces.

### Getting a Grip on Life

What about the young man's recreation?

It should be something that will revive the tired mind and jaded spirit.

Physical activity, even if only in the form of long country walks with their sights and sounds, will refresh and invigorate both mind and body.

The reading of a good book, studying some of our splendid poetry, watching an interesting play or listening to soothing music will revivify his spirit.

> *"The world is so full of a number of things*
> *I'm sure we should all be as happy as kings."*

It's only a fairyland jingle we know but it embodies a wealth of good advice.

We have only outlined the minimum steps that one can take towards becoming more alive, more interesting, more active—steps that can at least help the individual to get a better grip on life.

But these steps on the road to the fuller life can only be likened to the first stumblings of the baby. For if we would know true adulthood, if we would breathe the atmosphere of the summit of more successful being, we need to set out with a firm and determined gait along the broad highway of endeavour.

It will require great sacrifice. Time now spent on self-gratification will need to be spent in physical and mental toil. The transient must be sacrificed to the permanent. The superficial must surrender to the abiding.

### Map Out a Course

Finally, we must map out our course and follow it relentlessly. We must not be deterred from it. We must turn a deaf ear to the myriad allurements which seek to keep us from that course.

Like the ship which is sailed through tempest and calm, through surging billows and inviting tropical streams, past siren calls, we must keep our eyes fixed inflexibly and unwaveringly upon the goal that leads to the harbour of more successful living.

> *"One ships sails East and another sails West*
> *With the selfsame winds that blow.*
> *'Tis the set of the sails*
> *And not the gales*
> *Which determines the way it shall go*
>
> *Like the winds of the sea are the ways of fate*
> *As we voyage along through life:*
> *'Tis the set of the soul*
> *That decides the goal*
> *And not the calm or the strife."*

# THE WILL TO WORK

*I believe in work, for work brings joy of accomplishment.*
*Every discovery, every achievement, is a registration of work.*

\* \* \*

WORK is not very popular among some people these days, but it is an essential element in the scheme of things. Surely most of us realise that work is a necessary and desirable activity. It is a positive action suggesting production, progress, independence, security, satisfaction.

Very few of us are in the position of not having to work, and if we were, it is likely that we should find life so boring, that only an absorbing hobby could save us from melancholy, poor health and ultimate despair.

In a world that is far from perfect there will always be jobs that are unattractive, and there will always be people who have to do them. We are not living in Utopia and never shall be!

We must remember, however, that different people have different ideas as to what is congenial work. Various forms of work are not necessarily repellent in themselves—it is our attitude towards any particular type of work which is so important.

Individual temperament has a lot to do with our attitude towards a particular job. A man whose absorbing interest is nature study and who loves the open country, is not likely to feel happy in the deafening environment of a steelworks. The man with a clever, active brain will not be content to spend his working days doing a repetitive mechanical task in a factory. He might be much happier as a draughtsman.

Somewhere there is just the right kind of employment for each one of us. I once knew a mortuary attendant who was so happy in what most of us would regard as a gruesome job, that he would not change it for anything else in the world!

## We are all Workers

It is difficult to understand why the term "working man" suggests to most of us only a manual worker, or why so many manual workers seem to imagine that the great army of clerical and professional men and women should not be regarded as "workers" in the true sense of the word, or that their work is not at least equally important to the community as a whole.

Equally disturbing is the attitude of certain "intellectual" snobs who look down their elegant noses at the man who works in greasy overalls or who swings a pickaxe for his living. It might be very amusing to see a professor of history trying to dig a trench for a water-main, or a shipyard riveter attempting to navigate an aircraft, but the probable result would be equally unsatisfactory.

It takes all sorts to make a world—fortunately for each one of us! Every individual has special talent in one direction or another. You may have been hopeless at mathematics and most other subjects at school, but later you discovered a natural flair for mechanical repairs and assembly. You may have ruined scores of expensive pieces of wood in the school carpentry lessons, but now you are making good progress in an accountant's office.

### Work of Infinite Variety

No matter how you earn your living to-day, you probably regard it as useful and hard enough *work*—and rightly so, whether you are a bricklayer, school teacher, motor mechanic, shop assistant, housewife, scientist, bank clerk, or even an editor!

There is work to be done in infinite variety, and somewhere there is just the right niche for *you*. If you have not yet discovered your ideal job of work, lose no more time before you find it—and then do it with a will. If you feel you are in a rut doing office work and fancy yourself as a commercial traveller, by all means get out on the road at the first opportunity. But you should realise that good salesmanship demands a suitable personality, a special technique, a fair knowledge of psychology, an undefeatable spirit, good health and other qualifications.

If you are doing distasteful manual labour and dream of becoming a newspaper reporter, go ahead and study for your dream-job. But to-night, as you relax those aching muscles, try to realise that the mental and nerve strain of news reporting is every bit as tiring as your present job.

Whatever you do or wish to do, it is all *hard work*!

Since there seems to be no escape from work for the vast majority of us, let us consider why it is necessary at all.

Even in prehistoric times, Man's dominant instinct was self-preservation. Stone Age Man had to eat and drink in order to remain alive. To sustain his body, primitive Man was compelled to search for water, gather berries and hunt and kill animals for his food. He needed suitable containers in which to carry and store a supply of water; he required weapons with which to kill his meat—and his enemies; he wanted shelter and skin clothing for protection against the weather—which was probably as erratic and treacherous as it is now.

These bare necessities of early Man had to be searched for, or fashioned by his own hands.

To preserve the human race, another primitive instinct, the prehistoric male had to select—and no doubt fight for, a female mate. Even if he demonstrated his powers of persuasion by knocking his beloved over the head in a futile attempt to subdue her, we presume that he afterwards exerted himself to feed her as well as himself, and to make her reasonably comfortable and safe in their cave residence. His wife, in gratitude, probably fashioned his simple garments as well as her own, and tidied up the cave before her man returned home.

Later, when these two became parents, we can imagine them both busily engaged in rearing and training and protecting their off-spring.

This picture of prehistoric humanity which I have tried to present has, you will appreciate, *work* as its theme. We have examined only one dual reason for work—individual and racial preservation.

## Life becomes More Complex

Fundamentally, life is not so different to-day, is it? We work to eat and for shelter and security, to preserve ourselves and our families. Life in modern times has become infinitely more complex and worrying, but through all the years that have passed since the Stone Age, the necessity for Man to work has not, to any appreciable extent, diminished.

Such is human nature, however, that mere preservation of self and the human race is not the *only* reason for work.

There is, within Man, a creative urge which demands satisfaction beyond procreation of the species. He is prompted by the desire to produce an ever-increasing variety of items for his sustenance, protection, use, comfort. Man also continues to *improve* what he has produced and make it available for more and more people. Inventions are born, goods are made, improved upon and, in due course, in many cases mass-produced for the benefit of everyone. This is the march of civilisation, for good or ill.

We have seen that work is necessary, not only for individual and racial preservation but also for the continued progress of civilisation itself. All this is on the material plane, but work, too, has a *spiritual* value.

Those of us who are old enough to remember the dreadful days of mass unemployment have retained in our memories the tragic picture of unemployed husbands, fathers and sons queueing up at the employment exchanges day after day for weeks, months and even years. There they were, this shabby army of unwanted men, hoping and begging for the *opportunity* of work, which had then become an unexpected privilege for the lucky ones. As time passed, with still no hope of work on the horizon, these men slowly became demoralised, physically, mentally and spiritually. Their eyes became dull, their faces haggard, their shoulders drooped, and they shuffled about like so many lost souls.

Eventually many of these unfortunate victims of economic depression lost the ability and the *will* to work. They were no longer healthy, happy men, but frustrated, dispirited, broken throw-outs on a human scrap-heap.

Make no mistake about it—this is how men deteriorate when deprived of work for long enough.

### Personal Satisfaction and Progress

Work is not only essential for the material needs of humanity, but also for our physical, mental and spiritual welfare. Work not only enables us to have food and drink, clothes, shelter, money, comfort—and perhaps luxury. Work brings with it those intangible yet precious possessions, personal satisfaction through progress towards our ultimate ambition; peace of mind; a sense of security; the knowledge that we are useful members of society. This general mental and spiritual harmony and satisfaction encourages an altogether healthier state of mind and body. In short, we cannot live a complete and wholesome life unless we work.

Let us consider further our *attitude* towards work, for this is of vital importance to our happiness. To-day many people do not so much dislike their own particular work; they dislike the very *idea* of working!

We can enjoy work, endure work or detest it so much that we refuse to do any at all! The man who enjoys work can usually find plenty of it, and he is a happy man. Many people regard work as such a tiresome burden that they do as little as possible—and that grudgingly. These people can be found in every trade and profession—the moaners, "column-dodgers" and clock-watchers. There remain only the few who positively refuse to do any work, that mysterious fraternity, the professional tramps—and there are still some of them, even in this Welfare State.

The professional tramp is worth a mention in this article on work, for he is at least an honest rebel against work—and possibly *because* of his honesty in this direction he is *happier* than the man who dodges the work he is paid to do and who invents all kinds of ingenious excuses for *not* doing an honest day's work.

Yes, in my opinion, the professional tramp—although he does no work at all—deserves more credit than the dishonest work-dodger and industrial agitator.

The genuine tramp has no desire to work, or intention of working.

He believes that only fools work, and he manages to live contentedly *without* working. Of course, very few of us would be willing to endure the discomforts or hardships of a tramp's existence in order to share his freedom from work. We may think of the tramp as a homeless waster, and despise him on that account. But the professional tramp does not consider himself a homeless good-for-nothing. He is *always* at home on the road, and he is proud of his skill in extracting a crust of bread and a few coppers or shillings from respectable, kind-hearted folk like us.

What this little side-light on a tramp's life should convey to us is that one's *attitude* to work is all-important, and that we should be honest about it.

If we do not intend to do an honest week's work, we have no *right* to demand a full week's pay every Friday from our employers. There is no room for the slacker in any business. He is being unfair not only to the boss, but to his own workmates who pull their weight.

Some people, who should know better, have curious ideas about the value of work and especially about its place in economics. Listen to this for example.

"Who wants to work anyhow? We do not care if they sack the lot of you, so long as they pay you the same wages as when you are working."

This is not a passage from a schoolboy "howler", but the reported words of one of the leaders of a well-known trade union! Did you ever hear such pernicious nonsense?

### For the Common Good

The worker who imagines that the only result of his work is to make the wealthy employer richer, can see no further than the end of his nose. A prosperous business tends to expand, to produce and sell more goods at home and possibly abroad. This country depends for its very existence—above the starvation line—upon its exports. The more we produce, the higher becomes our standard of living. What does it matter if the employer does grow richer by our work, so long as we are better off in proportion?

We should not regard work as a necessary evil but as our right and privilege; our invaluable physical, mental and spiritual exercise, which helps to lift us to higher and better things, towards a fuller, nobler life. We should look upon our work as an important service, not only to a sometimes irritable employer, but to ourselves, our families, our country and to humanity itself.

If work, to you, is nothing but an irksome burden, the chances are that you are in an unsuitable job. It is up to you to discover your special talents and to work where you can express yourself to advantage.

Happy is the man who loves his daily work—but there is no reason why he should not be YOU!

If you are unable to work were your heart is, it may not be impossible for you to put your heart into your work. Try to realise that your work, whatever it is, represents an important *service to somebody*. There is joy and satisfaction in service, once we recognise the value of that service to those concerned.

Into the changing pattern of this modern world a new word has emerged—automation. It is an ugly word and it suggests, to many workers, an ugly future. Their fear is not without foundation, as we have seen already in the case of one particular concern.

This firm found it necessary to install modern machinery which led to the dismissal of over two thousand workers from its pay-roll.

It is ironical that besides the majority of willing workers who may become redundant owing to automation, there are the work-dodgers who were so clever in the past at finding excuses to down tools.

Yes, the advent of automation is bound to cause temporary hardship among the workers of certain mass-production industries, but let me quote the Prime Minister's comments on this controversial subject.

"Automation gives us the chance to do better work, and to produce more. It increases our industrial efficiency, and our ability to compete. . . . Our keenest competitors do not regard automation as their enemy, but as an ally, and we must learn to to do the same. We just cannot afford to be left behind."

### Slackers are in Danger

Life is always changing, and values change. Society has hitherto honoured the conscientious worker, and in spite of automation there will always be plenty of opportunity for him. Those in most danger are the slackers—the moaners who cling to their negative attitude towards work. When the time comes for more and more machines to replace men, the first men to go will be those who have been unfair to the employer by dodging the responsibilities for which they are paid. The employer will be able to dispense with the services of men and women who do not pull their weight. He will not be forced to carry "passengers" in order to get any work done at all.

It is obvious, then, that not only in the present, but more so in the future, the "Weary Willies" of this generation must adopt a healthier attitude towards work. They must realise their individual responsibility and feel proud to be doing their share in strengthening our economic position in the world.

Improved methods of production, including automation, are bound to cause some redundancy among workers for a period, but this will give way to full employment and perhaps a shorter working week.

Nobody will complain about *fewer* working hours, at higher rates, so long as all men and women work hard and efficiently when they *are* supposed to be working. There must be a greater mutual trust and friendship between employers and workers. All the stupid bickering such as who shall drill holes in what material—with complete disregard for the millions of pounds' worth of business being lost— must stop. Such fantastic situations should never be allowed to develop, and a little commonsense could prevent most of these squabbles.

There should be less thought given to the "employers' side" and the "workers' side" in industry.

We are *all* workers, and it is in the interest of us all to work together in harmony, for the general good of the human race. Let us be proud to give of our best.

We can enjoy ourselves in our work, and our best tasks can bring forth our greatest enjoyment.

As Tolstoy rightly said:

> "*Work is the inevitable condition of human life,*
> *The true source of human welfare.*"

# DARE TO ASPIRE

*It is not that men cannot do what they would wish;*
*it is that they don't know what they would wish to do.*

\* \* \*

THE above is not a proverb but it has every right to be so regarded. It embodies a fundamental truth, sums up a philosophy that we would do well to heed.

The words were not recorded by some well-known sage, but by a simple man, whom I have known for many years. The world has not heard of him, but he long ago decided what he wanted most of all; he has reached his objective. He is one of the men I most admire, a simple, kindly man, yet one who bears testimony to the fact that the individual can be greater than the sum of his environment and heredity, a man it does one good to know, a man who has found life satisfying, who has found fulfilment.

Let us examine his saying more closely. "It is not that men cannot do what they would wish to do." That implies that men and women can, in the main, do *anything* that they set their hearts upon doing. Is this true?

The immediate reaction of the average person, conditioned to accept some things as impossible of achievement, is that the statement is exaggerated. He may admit some fundamental truth in the assertion, but he cannot accept it as it stands. He would qualify it by saying, "Man can do anything he wishes—within the bounds of physical possibility, within reason, within the limits of his mental capacities"—and so on.

For instance, someone may retort sarcastically that a man may wish to travel to the planets but his wish would not get him there. Is my friend's statement, therefore, to be accepted as a trite saying, a parable full of sound meaning but impossible of acceptance in its ordinary form?

What has Practical Psychology to say?

Its verdict is on the side of the philosophy we have quoted. It states that there are few known limits to Man's achievement, that the impossible of to-day becomes the realised fact of to-morrow; practically all that we desire and dream of, that, too, we can accomplish.

But what of the dream of interplanetary travel? A fair question! Since Practical Psychology makes very few conditions to the assertion that Man can do anything, it must say yes to the possibility of Man travelling to the moon or Mars.

216

But what of the more modest ambitions of the ordinary man and woman? They may dream of and desire financial security, success in some chosen vocation, achievement in some selected sphere or a happy and balanced existence.

Let us clear away some of the possible doubts that they may have about realising their hopes and ambitions. Practical Psychology avers that, in the main, they can succeed, that what they desire to be, they can be in reality.

## The Will to Triumph

This is where we must now consider the second part of the quotation with which we started this Chat—the statement that most men and women do not really know what they wish to do.

Let us take an example. An individual perhaps dreams of wealth, or of success at work, or of fame and achievement in some activity. But let us examine these day-dreams honestly. Aren't most of them forms of escapism, half-hearted *wishes* rather than virile desires; aren't they hazy and shifting rather than clear-cut ideas of what the person means to do?

There are many who would like more money in order to live a fuller life. But how do they propose to achieve their objective? If they are honest with themselves, they will admit that their day-dreams suggest that their desire will be fulfilled by a lucky break, a win on the pools or the legacy of a rich (hitherto unknown) relative.

Isn't this often so? It is a vague, ill-defined, ill-considered day-dream that fades away in the merciless light of reality and leaves the people concerned depressed and dispirited.

The dream can be realised only if it is desired with intensity and pursued relentlessly, by planning a campaign thoroughly and taking active, determined steps to reach the goal; if, by their own efforts, unaided by capricious Fortune, they mean to reach the objective about which they dream.

Let us examine the case of the woman who dreams of success perhaps in the world of literature. At the moment, all she does is to sigh for achievement, the recognition and the satisfaction that this would bring. Does she put pen to paper? No! Does the ambition electrify her whole life? No! But in order to succeed, the desire to be a writer must change her whole outlook, should be the very foundation of her daily life. It should sharpen her eyes when she is shopping, should attune her ear when she is conversing with friends, should impel her, however busy she may be, to write and write and to go on writing.

Only with such a determined attack can she succeed.

To summarise, so many men and women day-dream of fame and achievement; yet they hardly ever crystallise their desires, make certain iust what they want to achieve and then bend their whole energies towards reaching it. Yet that is the secret of success!

## The World at Large

This defect is seen most clearly in the social scene. No one will dispute the fact that there is a deep, restless longing in the heart of mankind for peace, prosperity and plenty throughout the world. There seems to be a hunger for universal brotherhood, a genuine wish to rescue the backward nations and set them upon the high road to a fuller social life.

All this, in the main, exists; there is a vast fund of goodwill, neighbourliness and genuine social awareness. Yet we move but slowly towards the Golden Age, and even our painful stumbling towards the ideal is made hideous by the spectre of world famine or the catastrophe of atomic war.

To-day we have the means almost to transform the very globe had we but the will. We have the power to conquer disease, penury, want and war. The reign of universal brotherhood, the total liberation of humankind, is within our grasp.

Why then do we fail? Having the power, why do we tend to use it for evil rather than for good? Having the means to salvation why are we in danger of employing these for our destruction?

The answer seems to be fundamentally the same as in the case of the individual who wishes to succeed, yet does not concentrate his energies upon a firm and clearly defined objective.

In other words, the world appears not really to know what it most desires. The universal desire for peace apparently intermingles with a strong desire for undisturbed nationalism. There seems to be no pooling of energies to achieve the peace and plenty that are possible. It would appear that nations do not realise clearly that the good of one can lead to the good of all, and that energies that are dissipated in bickering could be better employed in creative reconstruction.

We do not wish to imply that the world's problems can be easily solved. Far from it! That is not the point we would make. But provided mankind as a whole could have a clearly defined idea of its objective, stated in precise terms of common weal, peace and progress, then these objectives eventually could be reached.

The lesson is the same if we take the national unit as our subject for study. We are not sure what we desire, even for our own country. There is a clash of ideology, often merely camouflaging the fundamental unity of aim.

If only a prophet could arise to express and crystallise the heart-longing of the nation, to picture for us the ideal dream, to objectify for us a worth-while goal, then within a few years our land would be the envy of the world.

But it is not the purpose of this Chat to carry the analogy of the social scene and the individual too far. It has only been referred to in the larger sphere in order to bring home our point more forcibly, namely that if we dare to aspire, if we can picture clearly the objective we would reach, then eventually we shall win.

At the same time we should beware of the treachery of our conscious faculties; beware of the sceptical whisper from within, "That's impossible"; and not be betrayed by the inner fear that asserts, "It can't be done."

### A Clear and Definite Picture

Let us think for a moment of a new-born baby, a helpless morsel of humanity, completely and utterly dependent upon its parents, incapable of speech or purposeful activity.

Have we ever thought of the amazing progress the baby makes even in the first three or four years of its life?

It learns to balance and to walk upon two feet; accomplishes this against the whole drive of natural instinctive posture, which indicates progress on all fours. It acquires the miracle we call speech, how to communicate in words to make its wants known. It masters an incredibly complex vocabulary. From birth to the age of four the child makes fantastic progress—progress an individual unacquainted with the human species would state unhesitatingly to be impossible.

From the age of four to seven or eight is another period of unbelievable achievement.

Fancy trying to teach a child to read and write! On the face of it—if we consider it seriously—it should be a task that would take a lifetime. Yet in a few short years the child can handle a pen dexterously and read with fluency. Its vocabulary now includes abstract terms, that is, its words do not merely represent concrete things such as food, play, toys, but it has a dawning conception of such things as love, truth, honour and justice.

If only we could continue developing at the same rate as the child develops at up to the age of seven or eight, we should by the time we reached middle age almost be demigods!

Yet is there any reason why we should not continue such development? Why should we suddenly put the brakes on at a certain age and in all probability stop developing altogether a little later on? The main reason that development slows up at a certain age is that, up to that age, our rapid development is partly the result of mimicry. In other words, we are in close contact with our older brothers, sisters and our parents and we have an overwhelming desire to become like them. *We have a clear and definite picture in our minds of what we wish to become.*

But having reached a certain stage the disparity between ourselves and our elders lessens and disappears. We now seem to have no clear picture of what we can become.

What then can we do? *We can make a picture for ourselves!* If we can do this, if we can form a clear picture of a larger, better, more developed self, we can make rapid progress towards enlarging our characters and our lives.

Before we say to ourselves that our personal dreams are impossible of fulfilment, let us consider what others have achieved.

Helen Keller was blind, deaf and dumb, yet she mastered these overwhelming handicaps to lead a rich and satisfying life.

Beethoven was stricken with deafness at the height of his power, a blow that would have crippled the faint-hearted, yet he lived to create music that has held untold generations enraptured.

Or let us recall the plight of our nation twenty-two years ago, bereft of arms and facing an enemy of whose might the world had never seen the like before, alone, defenceless, yet undefeated. But with courage, tenacity and a dream of victory, we triumphed.

History abounds with glorious examples of ordinary men and women who have dreamed, who have dared, who have conquered. They had only the same faculties as us; their talents did not in many instances exceed ours; their advantages were, often enough, considerably less than those that we possess. They had but one thing that so many of us do not possess—*a clear picture of what they wished to become.*

The story of Adam and Eve's fall can be likened to a parable rich in suggestions for modern Man. The Garden of Eden held everything for which man or woman could wish. But Eve was tempted; Adam did not resist; they were cast out of the Garden; they were banished from perfection into an imperfect world.

We will only refer briefly to the first moral we can draw from this story, and that is, that the "fall" was, in fact, humanity's first opportunity to develop and to triumph. Maybe the banishment from Eden wasn't a curse but a spur that has prodded Man on to re-create the world and to fulfil his destiny.

### The Enemy Within

Let us place emphasis upon the temptation itself. An inner voice whispered to the denizens of the Garden of Eden. It was this voice which made them dissatisfied and unfulfilled. It suggested that they were merely mortals, that they were not one with the Divine.

It is that voice of betrayal which holds so many of us back to-day. It echoes within our inner consciousness. It whispers that life will have to be dull, unsatisfying; that our dreams are mirages. We should refuse to listen, refuse to be tempted—for that way can mean our banishment from realisation.

Let us think for one moment about what we would wish to be, imagine ourselves as we would be if our dream came true.

We would, metaphorically, be of greater stature. So our doubts and misgivings would be replaced by serene self-confidence; the niggling little troubles of every day would be seen in true proportion —gnat-bites—not the calamities we may regard them as to-day.

We should build this picture of ourselves still further; think of the home we would live in, the idealised conditions under which we would work, the type of people we would meet and mix with should our dream be realised. Then we should sketch in the background of this new idealised existence!

Now, assume that we have that picture clear in our minds—a reasonably clear mental image of the men and women we wish to become.

We can make that transformation possible, not by magic, but by our own efforts and with the help of Practical Psychology.

By now that word "impossible" probably occurs to us. But we shouldn't let it fool us. Our grandparents would have said that flying was impossible.

### The Right Perspective

How do we set about realising this dream?

First of all, we should get that picture of the ideal clear and see it vividly in our minds. Then fill in the picture with as much detail as we possibly can.

Let this picture be the first image we call up on waking; let it be the last that the mind holds before we drop off to sleep.

Now, for the next stage. The person we aim to be has certain qualities of character. What are they? Each one of us can readily enumerate them if we have a really clear picture of what we want to be. We should strive day by day to cultivate those characteristics. It may not be easy at first. It is not an easy matter for the baby to formulate its very first words. But progress is very rapid afterwards.

We should learn to think big; learn not to be discouraged because unexpected obstacles crop up. They are very often not deterrents; they may serve to test our strength, to help us build up the characters we wish to become.

Day in and day out we should act as the ideal character at which we aim; develop the confidence, the awareness, the quick eye and mind of our ideal.

Then let us bring the Unconscious to our aid. By the methods we have advocated time and time again in previous Chats, we should impress the picture of what we wish to be upon our Inner Mind.

### Mental Attitude

"And how long will this take?" some may ask. A great deal depends upon how far away we are at present from our ideal. But, in general, we should not concentrate upon this problem of time. For if we are in earnest, striving towards our goal, the time element will seem unimportant.

An over-anxious concern upon how long it will take, how far we have to travel, can be detrimental to our progress.

If we are walking along a long straight road and we concentrate upon the fact that we are only at a certain spot and the journey's end is almost on the horizon, the journey will be apt to daunt us. Furthermore, if we start counting the number of steps we have to take, the energy it takes to make each step, we may become exhausted before we have travelled very far. The thing to do is to swing out bravely, take an interest in the scenery, and whilst keeping our eye upon our destination enjoy the walk that will get us there.

It can be a mistake to make too close a comparison between what we are and what we wish to become. For it ignores one essential point. We are, in actual fact, much nearer to our ideal than our Conscious Mind supposes. We have within us a power that moves not by painful and hesitating steps, but that operates by creative action, so that the transformation from the pessimistic persons we may be to-day to the buoyant optimistic individuals of to-morrow is not such a great step as we might suppose. For we have the energies, the creative powers slumbering within us. Let us call them to life; get the inner dynamo working. Let our slumbering powers activate our lives until our dream becomes reality.

Some of us may have heard the story of the man who was, one day, completely down in the dumps. He felt miserable and sick at heart; the world and life generally seemed so dreary and hopeless that his mind began to dwell upon self-destruction.

He dwelt upon his private miseries, the unpaid bills, his disappointment with his children, his dissatisfaction with his wife, the uncongenial nature of his job. There was nothing really worth living for.

On his way home, sunk in misery, a lady he knew called to him and asked if he could help her. It was only a question of filling up some official form, but when he had shown her how to do it, she was profuse with thanks and said: "You are always so cheerful, Mr. B, you always make me feel better after I have talked to you."

Mr. B left her in a completely different state of mind. His worries and problems remained, the world and his job were exactly the same, but there was a new spring in his step and the outlook did not seem so hopeless.

The conditions of his life were unaltered *but his attitude had changed*. He felt he had to live up to the picture the lady had painted of him.

A simple story but it illustrates a great truth. It is that *our mental attitude is the transforming power that can lift us from the slough of despond to the loftier heights of exuberant being and convert our dreams into aspiring reality.*

# THIEVES OF HAPPINESS

NUMEROUS articles have been published in *Psychology*, inspiring readers towards success and happiness. Many of our readers, by following the sound, psychological principles so often expounded in the magazine, have achieved success and the increased happiness it should bring. But like many other men and women, these readers have found that as with everything else worth while, there is no easy or royal road to achievement and success—they demand a price.

The cost and penalties are numerous and varied. There are obstacles to be surmounted, set-backs to be overcome, sacrifices to be made— these are but a few of the countless difficulties encountered before the summit of achievement is reached. Even after an individual has climbed the steep and rugged path to success, he then encounters the envy and hostility of many easy-going, mediocre people. For the more material success a man achieves, the more possessions he acquires, the more enemies he makes—and the more enemies he makes, the more difficult it is for a successful man to find the happiness he imagined material success would bring him.

Many of the enemies surrounding a highly successful individual are often unknown to him. They assail him just because he has dared to succeed and because they envy his success. These jealous-minded enemies of every successful man or woman may even be unknown to each other, yet together they form a kind of "fifth column" underground movement trying to sabotage the achievements of their successful quarry.

These misguided, envious individuals use every possible weapon in their secret armoury to hurt their often unsuspecting victim. They vilify him by spreading false rumours against him; they ridicule his achievements; they try to outmanoeuvre him, not only by legitimate moves, but often by trickery. They do everything in their power to undermine the successful man's prestige, and secretly, they would delight in his downfall. Every successful person should be aware of and as far as possible guard against the activities of his spiteful enemies, even if their identities are unknown to him. It is not only his business rivals who may be jealous and envious of his success; some of his own relatives may envy him, as well as certain neighbours and so-called friendly acquaintances!

## A Common Human Failing

Of course, the successful business man is only one example of the individual who often becomes a target for the shafts of envious people, for envy and jealousy abound in all walks of life, are found in all kinds of situations and masquerade under all kinds of guises.

Reference is often made to women concerning their "cattiness" born of envy, but men are equally guilty of envy in one form or another. Just watch the face of the man next door when his neighbour buys that new car, for example! Or listen to the comments of almost any group of workers, male or female, when any individual is promoted to a higher position than they hold.

There is only a thin dividing line between envy and jealousy. Many a husband is secretly jealous of his own children because of the love and attention bestowed upon them by his wife. Wives are sometimes jealous of their husband's career or his hobby, because it claims so much of the time and attention they feel should be devoted to them. Keen gardeners may envy the grand display of flowers blooming in a neighbour's garden. But when this envy prompts a rival to ruin prize blooms due to be shown by another competitor at the local flower show, envy has turned to jealousy.

There are so many different reasons for envy and jealousy. We have the traditional and accepted jealousy of lovers, and the common jealousy of a "plain Jane" directed against a pretty girl or the rivalry of junior office girls for the attentions of the handsome young executive.

We are all apt to notice the signs of envy in others quite often, especially when we are not directly concerned. Yet how many are there who can honestly say that they have never been guilty of envy of some sort? Who has not experienced jealousy?

One curious feature of jealousy is that we are usually ashamed to admit it in ourselves. We try to conceal it, not only from the person of whom we are jealous, but from our own conscious minds. We can lose our tempers and feel somewhat pleased with ourselves for getting a grievance "off our chest"—but we are almost ashamed of any jealousy in our hearts, and would be most reluctant to admit it to others.

This streak of envy or jealousy in us all is not only an individual and personal weakness. It is also present in various groups, organisations, clubs, teams and even nations. The present rivalry in the "space race" is a typical and topical example of the kind of ambition that very easily can create envy among nations.

### Negative Emotional Reactions

Desire, envy and jealousy go hand in hand. They are almost inseparable companions. Envy can be described as a feeling of discontent when we begrudge another his good fortune. And this is where desire enters the scene. If we are envious of the possessions or good fortune of another, we ourselves must desire what the other person has.

When we feel envious of others it is because they have something that we desire but do not possess. It may be wealth, prestige, power, good health, a desirable wife, beauty of face or figure, or even a washing machine.

Unreasonable and uncontrolled desire is the driving force that may make us envy another person. Then, quite unfairly, we are likely to project a feeling of malice towards the person who has got what we want. We are tempted to believe that the victim of our envy does not deserve what he or she has. If he is a successful business man we almost convince ourselves that he must be more than a little "crooked" in his dealings. If we envy a beautiful woman, we are apt to think that she must have low morals or few brains. If we envy a middle-aged man who has a lovely young wife, we may believe that he must have taken advantage of her innocence to lure her into his clutches. From these malicious thoughts and feelings it is but a short step to the spreading of unkind rumours about the object of our jealousy. These are but a few examples to illustrate how easy it is for the individual who possesses something we would like but haven't got, to attract the jealousy and envy and even the vindictive feelings of others.

There are some feelings of envy which although they may seem to be harmless can so easily degenerate into jealousy, though the dividing line is somewhat obscure. It is quite possible to envy another person who is more fortunate than ourselves, without feeling any animosity towards that individual. We may have a passing recognition of envy and say to ourselves, "He's a lucky fellow. I wish I had his good fortune." When we react in this mild and abstract manner it is reasonable enough, if we let the matter rest there. If, however, we brood and fret over the other person's good fortune and begin to resent it, it can only lead to unhappiness and wretchedness. For what could at the outset have been no more than a passing and harmless envy, is likely to become jealousy—a more personal negative emotional reaction.

### Desire—a Gigantic Force

Now let us take a look at desire. Desire in its rightful place is only human and as true to nature as anything could be. It is the essential driving force in life, the spur to endeavour, the impelling motive in all progress, individual and racial. But desire must be properly controlled and directed. The desire to make a success of our lives; to serve our fellow-men; to love; to travel; to be happy and to make others happy, such desires are indeed worth while and praiseworthy. But negative and uncontrolled desire can lead men and nations to their doom. This gigantic force of desire can lift us to the heights or lure us to the depths, can raise us to lofty summits or drag us to destruction.

### A Negative Primitive Instinct

Envy and jealousy may be described as the twin, illegitimate children of negative, uncontrolled desire, with jealousy the ugly sister. If jealousy is allowed to develop it can become a definite threat to a person's whole personality.

Jealousy is a primitive negative emotion that can—and often does —become a harmful and even dangerous obsession. In its simplest form, jealousy in animals is worth studying. Jealousy seems to be inbred in animals, just as it is in Man. It is, in both cases, associated with the instinct of possession and acquisition. Again, as with Man, some animals are extremely jealous, whilst others show very little sign of it.

When a dog is hungry it is natural for it to protect its food from other hungry dogs. But many a dog, having eaten all it wants, will not permit another dog to eat what is left.

In his book *Jealousy—A Psychological Study*, Dr. Boris Solokoff tells the tragic story of a jealous bulldog.

This dog was devoted to its mistress, and followed her everywhere. It showed signs of jealousy of anybody who tried to go near its mistress, and was even jealous of her husband. Then the woman had a child, a little girl, and although the dog was not neglected in any way, it became very morose and sulked. As the little girl grew older, the dog snarled at her every time she tried to pat it.

One day the dog grew very angry, because its mistress was playing with the little girl and paying no attention to it. Later, when the child tried to fondle the dog, it flew at her throat and killed her before she could be rescued.

This extreme example of jealousy in an animal shows how dangerous excessive jealousy also can be in human beings. Just as dogs can be trained to control their jealous instincts, so can humans learn to control this morbid and often dangerous emotion. The urgent need of such control is obvious, when we consider the unhappiness and misery caused, and the variety of crimes that occur through jealousy, including murder.

### Parents' Responsibility

Jealousy is evident among children very early in life, and parents who do not correct it are failing in their duty. Prevention, however difficult, is much easier than attempts to cure a chronically jealous disposition which has been allowed to develop by neglect. Parents who ignore signs of jealousy in their children do not realise that the whole future happiness of the jealous child is at stake—apart from the welfare of others who come in contact with the child later on in life.

As every mother should know, it is common for the first child to feel jealous of a baby brother or sister. A child should always be prepared well in advance, to look forward to the new arrival and to accept it as part of the family. The mother should be most careful not to give too much attention to the new baby in the presence of the older child. As soon as possible, the older child or children should be invited to help mother with the baby and to share interest in it in every way.

In fact, no child, whatever the excuse, should be shown more love and consideration than the others. An excess of mother-love directed towards one child—even a weakly child—can be harmful to *all* the children in the family. The children who do not receive so much affection or attention will begin to resent the mother's over-devotion to the favoured child. Moreover, the favoured child will grow to expect special treatment, not only from the mother, but from everybody else right into adulthood. So are the seeds of jealousy and egotism sown.

If one child for any reason (usually poor health) does require more attention than the others, this should not be made too obvious by the parents. Instead, they should do everything to inspire the sickly child to have courage and self-confidence, so that he or she can cope more readily with life ahead.

Older children are sometimes jealous, one of the other. For example, an unattractive girl can easily become jealous of her pretty sister. Or a boy of average intelligence may become jealous of his clever brother. Any signs of jealousy in these cases should be openly discussed by the parents with the children concerned. They should be taught how wrong, foolish and dangerous is jealousy.

Parents have a tremendous responsibility for moulding the characters of their children, and this should never be overlooked or neglected. Once jealousy has been allowed to grow, it distorts the whole mental outlook of a young person and haunts him or her all through life.

### Self-examination

What can an adult do about his own jealous disposition if he recognises it and admits his weakness?

First he should subject himself to a searching self-examination and try to discover the underlying cause of his maladjustment—for that is what it is. In all probability he will find his jealous nature originated in childhood, and once he realises the *childishness* of this emotion he will be well on the way to conquering it. He will realise that he is not a child any more and must put away childish behaviour.

The next step is for the individual to readjust his sense of proportion. He must make every effort to avoid undue exaltation of the ego. He should never over-emphasise the importance of *any* individual, and that includes himself.

It is essential, of course, that he must have a reasonable amount of self-confidence without being ruled by arrogance and egotism. A certain amount of legitimate and reasonable desire is also necessary, otherwise ambition, incentive and achievement would be stifled. *But he should keep these things in proper perspective.*

## Accepting Life's Realities

And finally, but of vital importance, the person concerned should not believe—as so many people do—that the world owes him a living. In fact, *he should realise that he is indebted to society for his existence.*

Once such a person faces up to and accepts this reality in life, he will refrain from expecting all the good things to come his way, with little or no effort or at the expense of somebody else. No longer will he be envious of another person's success. He will realise that he can get *his* share of prosperity without wasting his mental energy envying and resenting another's share of prosperity. He will accept some of his limitations, keep desire within reasonable bounds and be content with the rewards that come to him, realising that he gets what he earns—no more—no less.

Those men and women who are envied by others should always remember: To be an object of envy is the sign of success. Apart from protecting his own interests, a wise man who is aware of the envy of others, should take no more notice of it than the moon does of the howling of dogs.

The only answer to such envious people is to be like the moon and continue for ever to shine on.

# THE REWARDS OF PATIENCE

*"Still achieving, still pursuing,*
*Learn to labour and to wait."*

\* \* \*

WHETHER or not we are patient ourselves, most of us admire patience in others. We realise instinctively that patience is a virtue, and a somewhat rare one at that!

One dictionary definition of patience is "The quality of enduring or suffering calmly; perseverance". From this it will be understood that patience demands courage. In fact, one might say that patience is a form of courage, therefore lack of it is cowardly.

The great scientist Sir Isaac Newton declared: "What I have done is due to patient thought".

Benjamin Disraeli regarded patience as "a necessary ingredient of genius".

It follows that if patience is necessary to genius, it is quite indispensable to the success of the average man or woman. It is, indeed, the secret of success.

We cannot all be great, but we *can* all be patient—and unless we are, we shall never make much progress in any sphere of activity.

If we turn to Nature we can learn many things, and patience is one of them. History tells us that King Robert the Bruce of Scotland learned the value of patience by watching a spider spinning its web No matter how many times a spider's web is damaged, the industrious little creature will repair the fault, and then wait patiently for as long as necessary for a fly to fall into its trap. The insect world, in particular, abounds with remarkable, living examples of patience, or—as the dictionary definition adds—*perseverance*. If insects can be so patient, Man should feel ashamed not to be at least *equally* patient.

Gardeners soon learn to be patient, or they may as well give up gardening. Nature will not be hurried. The processes of propagation and growth are slow but sure, and the gardener just has to wait patiently for the result.

One of the finest examples of patience is that of the patient invalid, who suffers pain, discomfort and inconvenience, perhaps for years, with hardly a complaint, and often with a friendly smile. Who can fail to admire such courage and perseverance? But how many of us learn this lesson of life and profit by it? Patience sweetens the temper, creates contentment within us, and greatly enriches the character.

Patience also often protects us from danger and even from an

229

untimely death in these days when speed is worshipped. To illustrate this point we have only to consider *impatient* motorists and the tragedies they cause. How many of these lunatic road-hogs have brought death and destruction simply because they refused to be patient for vital *seconds*?

In spite of the proved value of patience in most circumstances it has been said that there is a limit at which patience ceases to be a virtue. This is true when patience has degenerated into cowardly submission to gross injustice, exploitation, oppression or other evils. When patience is imposed upon by ruthless or defiant characters, to the danger of civilised society, then no right-minded person or authority can be expected to remain patient enough to endure such wrongs indefinitely. Apparent "patience" in these circumstances would be stupid *condonation* of a wrong. As with every other virtue, patience must be guarded by discretion, otherwise patience itself becomes prostituted. Certainly the exercise of patience implies forgiveness, but not the acceptance of a known evil.

Patience is no longer a virtue when it is used unscrupulously for a wrong motive. Before we say that this isn't possible, let us remember the vindictive person who *waits patiently* for revenge. Let us consider the criminal who patiently plans his crime in advance. Such patience is hardly a virtue, but there are exceptions to every rule—even to the golden rule of patience.

### Loss of Patience

Having considered the value of patience, we now turn to that common human weakness—losing one's temper. Here we must recognise the fact that whereas the naturally ill-tempered person is wearisome, the normally patient man can be really dangerous when he *does* lose his temper.

It is wise to be cautious of the "quiet" man when his wrath is aroused.

Among the penalties we pay for living in this modern world are mental anxiety, nerve strain and consequent irritability. We are constantly irritated by all sorts of things and conditions. We are annoyed by stupid people, difficult children, impudent teenagers, unbearable taxation, excessive noise, inferior television programmes, selfish motorists, inefficient workers, ungrateful employers, dissatisfied wives, thoughtless husbands and a host of other aggravations. Many of them, regarded individually, are no more than petty irritations. Collectively, however, they have an accumulative effect which frays our nerves and impairs our general health.

No wonder we all lose our temper at times. We should have to be plaster saints—or fools—to remain completely unruffled at all times and in all conditions.

When we consider the possible results of losing one's temper too often and too violently, we must realise the value of self-control. It is said: "He that ruleth his spirit is greater than he who taketh a city." It is something to rule a city, but to rule oneself is one of life's noblest attainments. The road to self-mastery is extremely difficult and calls for great effort. But the rewards are rich indeed.

### Repression is Not a Solution

Having acknowledged the dangers of not controlling one's temper, it might seem to be a logical step to bottle up a rising temper; to "bite one's tongue", as we say, and to subdue any tendency to "go off the deep end".

This is often a natural reaction, but here we are treading on dangerous ground. When we fly into a temper we discharge a lot of pent-up nervous energy. In fact, we release a safety-valve. This very often relieves *us*, however much it distresses the unfortunate person at the receiving end.

The following extract from Dr. Louis E. Bisch's book *Your Nerves* is well worth quoting:

"Noisy nerves are not necessarily weak, unstable, dangerous nerves. Among the worst cases of neurosis I have ever seen were men and women whom you never would suspect of possessing nerves at all. What's more, the more explosive the nerve force—the more apparent the nervousness, in other words—the quicker, generally speaking, the cure. . . ."

"There must be outlets for the dynamic force and power of the feelings. The nervous possess such emotional energy in a plus way. They have so much more than average, calm, adjusted folks and it's simply *got to come out*."

Where do we go from here? We *know* it can be unpleasant or even dangerous to lose one's temper. Yet here is a famous psychiatrist telling us, in effect, that it is equally dangerous for us to try to bottle it up!

The answer to this apparently conflicting evidence is simple enough.

Those of us who are "explosive" in our quick and perhaps violent temper must learn to divert or sublimate our excess nervous energy.

People's temperaments vary a great deal, as do their viewpoints, beliefs and prejudices. Otherwise this would be such a dull world, and we should be driven to avoid the society of our fellows altogether. Alternatively, we should all perish of boredom.

We are not wholly responsible for our individual natures. It has so much to do with heredity and environment.

If we have quick tempers we may secretly admire—or envy—the person who never seems to be ruffled by anything or anybody. Yet it may be as natural *for him* to remain calm and collected as it is *for us* to rear up in anger at the slightest provocation. All the same, there is no reason why we should not learn to control our temper—not by bottling it up, but by diverting our excessive *nervous energy* into healthier channels.

For all we know to the contrary, that placid man or woman we admire so much may have been as hot-tempered as the worst of us earlier in life. He or she may have *learned* the art of self-control by using well-tested and reliable methods of practical psychology.

### Discover Fundamental Causes

Let us examine a few cases from real life, to illustrate the causes and effects of an uncontrolled temper, and to discover how this weakness can be overcome.

A classic example of a domestic upheaval was reported in the newspapers some time ago. It could have suggested a stage comedy, yet it ended tragically.

The husband in this case frequently came home the worse for drink. Unfortunately, too much alcohol invariably made him develop a truculent mood in which he often bullied or beat his long-suffering wife.

On the occasion in question this man came home very drunk. His condition led to the usual family arguments and loss of temper all round. The elder daughter of the family happened to be upstairs when the commotion began to get out of hand. She seized a big flower-pot full of earth and dropped it over the banisters on to her father's head. This quietened him right enough, but it also fractured his skull and he died from his injuries.

Common sense and self-control could have avoided this tragedy— as they could many others.

In this case the husband couldn't control his drinking habits, the family couldn't control their tempers, and the daughter who, in a fit of frenzied folly, dropped the flower-pot, didn't stop to realise the possible consequences of her rash act.

No doubt all members of this unhappy family had good reasons for losing control of their emotions. There must have been some deep, psychological reason why the husband became a drunkard in the first place! If only we knew more about *ourselves*! The common, basic cause of this tragedy must have been the *misdirection* of nervous energy.

The sensible thing for anybody to do when conscious of *any* weakness of character or unstable emotions is to discover the *fundamental cause* and learn to remedy the defect in a sensible, scientific manner. Here, a study of practical psychology is of great help.

How often do we see a mother spank her child for running into the road, or even for stumbling and falling over? The child is already scared or hurt. Why does the mother spank it? Only because she has momentarily lost her temper. Her display of anger is caused by her fear for the child's safety. This mother is finding an outlet for her pent-up emotion—her nervous energy. This may be helpful *for her*, but not for the child. It is unwise and unfair to lose one's temper and frighten a child into being more careful. But we are all too human, and often we allow our emotions to rule our heads.

In any difference of opinion, argument, debate or contest, the person who loses his temper is always at a disadvantage. He can no longer think clearly, and if he loses self-control too much he can easily do something stupid or dangerous. Not only is he likely to hurt somebody else, but—directly or indirectly, himself as well. Typical examples are: the man who, in a fit of temper, puts his fist through a window; kicks a stone angrily and injures his own foot; punches another man off balance and cracks the man's skull on the pavement; drives a car dangerously in a fit of pique and then swears at a policeman for correcting him.

Countless examples could be given, and women are as equally guilty of this human failing. In fact, owing to their more highly-tuned nervous system, women are more inclined to "go off the deep end" at a minor irritation. They believe they just have to relieve their tensed-up emotions.

Anger can be sparked off by fear, jealousy, frustration, ridicule, embarrassment, injustice, deceit, criticism and many other various causes. Almost always, the person who loses his temper believes that his ego has been undermined in some way. Consequently, the egotistical individual is always getting upset by somebody. Nobody else thinks he is as wonderful as he believes himself to be, therefore the egoist is always having his ego battered. This annoys him, and he quickly loses his temper.

The person with very little ego doesn't "stick his neck out" so much. He is passive and phlegmatic. He *doesn't care* what other people think of him, so he isn't so likely to lose his temper through feeling slighted in any way.

### Emotional Outlets

We have studied some of the reasons why people lose their tempers, and we have touched upon the harmful and even tragic results of uncontrolled bad temper. We can add to these reasons the often unrealised fact that the person who too readily loses his temper upsets his own health. It is true that by "letting off steam" he may perhaps avoid neurosis, but the man in a temper imposes an undue strain upon his heart and raises his blood pressure. He is being foolish to himself as well as hurtful to others.

Powerful emotions must be released and exercised, but there are much saner and healthier ways of doing this than by acting like a smouldering volcano, ready to erupt at the slightest provocation. We are all a bit "touchy" at times, but do let's be reasonable, for everybody's sake.

Self-confidence is certainly a great asset, but we must not allow our ego to become so swollen that we become a source of annoyance to others. If we do, they will always seem to be irritating us, either unknowingly or deliberately. We should always remember that, however important we are in our own estimation, we are not of such importance in the eyes of other people. When we realise this, we shall not expect too much attention. We shall at least *act* a little more modestly and thus become more attractive instead of antagonising people.

The "touchy" person should mix freely with people and try to fit himself harmoniously into their company. We must expect to get hurt, snubbed, even pushed around a bit at times. Instead of losing our temper we should allow even unreasonable, provoking incidents to bounce off us, and *prove by our actions* that those incidents are not deserved. In time, we shall not even *feel* hurt or annoyed.

Another great aid will be found in the cultivation of a sense of humour. We shall be able to laugh at things that used to make us angry, because many of our troubles and animosities vanish when we laugh at them. There are so many incidents that have their funny side.

If we *feel* angry, it is better to *express* our anger than to bottle it up. This doesn't mean that we should punch the offender on the nose! It is much wiser to leave his company in a dignified manner and go and punch a cushion to relieve our feelings. A game of golf, football or cricket will also relieve emotional tension. A few good whacks at a ball will soon get rid of a bad temper, even if the motive doesn't improve one's game.

These simple suggestions may appear to be rather silly, but they give most effective relief. All sorts of little tricks can be devised directly anger begins to rise. We can make an excuse to leave the company of the person who has given the offence; change the topic of conversation; go for a walk alone to simmer down; laugh at ourselves for a change. Best of all, however, is to learn not to *feel* angry so easily in the first place.

## A Wholesome Philosophy

In a special category are the people who, although normally calm when their own ego is offended, get deeply angry over cruelty or injustice to others. This motive for anger raises a somewhat controversial issue. Is anger justified in these circumstances? Is anger *ever* excusable? One philosopher puts it this way:

"*Be ye angry, and sin not; therefore all anger is not sinful; I suppose because some degree of it is inevitable. It becomes sinful, or contradicts the rule of Scripture, when it is conceived upon slight and inadequate provocation and when it continues long."*

People who experience a strong sense of justice, often become aroused to anger when they witness injustice or cruelty. It is very difficult for us to criticise them for this reaction. Nevertheless, these good people would do better if they didn't lose their self-control, even in such provocative circumstances. They should do something constructive to put right the wrong concerned.

For example, if we see a child or an animal being cruelly treated, we should report such cruelty to the appropriate authorities and leave them to invoke the law to protect the victim and punish the offender.

Anger, if felt at all, must be expressed in a healthy manner, and never suppressed and concealed until it degenerates into hatred with thoughts of revenge. William Blake clearly illustrates this in the following simple verse:

> *"I was angry with my friend:*
> *I told my wrath, my wrath did end.*
> *I was angry with my foe:*
> *I told it not, my wrath did grow."*

In these lines the poet exposes a danger. Anger should know no aftermath of persistent ill-will or unrelenting bitterness. When resolute action has restored equity and justice, the hand of forgiveness and forgetfulness should be extended so that lasting harmony reigns supreme.

# REVIVE THOSE LOST IDEALS

TO-DAY we live in a vastly changed world compared with the world of a hundred years ago. And with the changes that have taken place—they could almost be called upheavals—have come the inevitable problems.

A century ago life was fairly simple compared with life in the modern world.

For instance, the population of Britain was then rural, but the majority of the population is now urban.

Owing to the relentless pressure of modernity our lives have become increasingly artificial. The lure of material comfort, better business prospects, variety of entertainment, higher wages and the more exciting social life has tempted men and women to flock to the larger cities and towns. Whilst these centres have grown bigger and richer in a material sense, they have also become noisier and dirtier.

The cities and towns have better amenities than the country districts can offer. There are more attractive and convenient shops, bigger and better theatres and cinemas, well-lighted streets, smooth pavements, better public transport and more shelter from the elements. The town-dweller has indeed many advantages. But what do they all amount to in terms of happiness?

The forward thrust of civilisation is a two-edged sword. One edge has cut away the jungle of primitive, unhygienic existence, the other edge has hacked deeply and dangerously into our physical, mental and spiritual welfare.

It is true that owing to the ignorance of many of the laws of hygiene, exposure to the elements, ramshackle housing and inadequate medical facilities, our forefathers' expectation of life was considerably less than our own. There were large families of children, many of whom died young, but those who survived were as sturdy as the forest oaks. Men worked hard and long; so did the women, for labour-saving devices were unknown. Education was sadly neglected and manners were as crude as everything else.

We have so much to be grateful for in these modern days, yet what do we find?

## Feverish Activity

Just watch the hurrying crowds travelling to city offices, factories and workshops. The majority of these people look thwarted and repressed, harassed and despondent. Their faces have dull and sullen expressions with the deep-set lines of anxiety and worry written there.

Nobody bothers to look at anyone else; all are hurrying along, each with his or her own mental preoccupation. The casual observer can only guess at the secret fears, frustrations and anxieties which lie hidden behind those "dead-pan" faces. Only here and there, like a rare jewel resplendently shining forth, do we behold a face reflecting tranquillity and happiness.

The majority of us are so geared up to the feverish activity and the fast pace of modern life, that we have forgotten how to relax; we are tense, restless, vaguely discontented. In spite of the wide variety of fascinating interests all around us, we quickly become bored. Life itself often seems pointless and unsatisfying.

Let us consider more thoroughly the general pattern of our existence from the cradle to the grave. From the time we are old enough to observe and understand what life is all about, we are conscious (if we are fortunate) of the love bestowed upon us by good parents. But this happy state of consciousness is quickly counteracted when we discover that parents also wield authority over us. We are not permitted to do what we like, when we like, and how we like. Instead, we are corrected, restricted, frustrated. The livelier our spirit, the more daringly original our ideas and desires, the more heavily does the hand of restrictive authority fall upon us. We are expected to submit to the will of the parents who brought us into this strange world without any option on our part. There may be brothers and sisters in the family, and due consideration must be given to them. We have to share the love of our parents with them, share our precious toys, share our time and further restrict our own personal freedom.

During childhood, of course, we need a certain amount of guidance and correction, but too much of this is apt to warp our outlook later on in life.

We go to school and are now subjected not only to the authority of our parents at home, but to the colder authority of the teacher and the even more frightening authority of the headmaster. We have to cram our brains with a lot of facts, few of which really interest us. We have to compete with other boys and girls for supremacy in the class-room and even on the playing-fields. We enjoy and share a certain amount of companionship, and fun, but we also suffer many indignities—quite apart from the nerve-racking experience of school examinations, which those in authority over us consider so very important. Far from enjoying more freedom as we get older, we find ourselves even more restricted and frustrated. Here again a certain amount of discipline is necessary and good for us, but all too often is overdone.

## The Inner Self

Somewhere inside ourselves we are aware of a personal, individual and unique spirit, which we instinctively realise is our Real Self, and which often rebels against so many of the needless restrictions and frustrations heaped upon us. Nobody else appears to know of the existence of our inner Spirit-Self—certainly nobody else respects it nor cares what is happening to it. Yet we know it is there, imprisoned like a wild bird in a cage. This Inner Self struggles and fights to get free. Our Real Self, that indefinable spirit within us, clamours for experience and complete freedom of expression. We would gladly release it and let it carry us on the wings of adventure, but alas—everybody and everything around us conspires to keep our restless, restricted and frustrated Real Self trapped in its cage.

Even when we go out into the world of commerce, trade or profession, it is still difficult to express ourselves with anything like the freedom for which the soul yearns.

In most cases, as employees we are expected to obey orders; to work to rule; to conform to Trade Union principles, or to observe professional etiquette. If we are in business on our own account, we may have a little more personal freedom, but at what cost? We may be able to take a few more holidays each year and perhaps maintain a higher standard of living, but—more than ever to-day—we are hemmed in on every side by countless restrictions. In fact, if we have the initiative and ambition to establish our own business, the numerous petty frustrations are all the more irritating! The inspirations of our Inner Self are still bubbling and bursting for freedom of action and expression, but where can we discover the freedom we need? We seem to live in a world of "Thou Shalt Nots".

As the years pass, most people learn to adapt themselves to existing restrictive conditions. The youthful spirit of adventure, with its frequent disregard of convention, almost withers and dies. Promising talents, often unappreciated and unrecognised, are allowed to fade into the background of our lives. We perform our daily tasks almost mechanically, merely to earn a living or, in the case of the housewife, to please and satisfy the marriage partner and family. Most of those treasured dreams and ambitions of youth have been obliterated in the process of economic and conventional necessity. We exist rather than *live*, while life itself remains an enigma—a rather pointless and meaningless affair.

## The Artificiality of Life

A great deal of this, of course, remains hidden from the world, for it is too intimate and personal. We may even consider it unique, abnormal, something of which we ought to be ashamed. Other people seem to be reasonably happy and content with life. They smile and chat when they meet us, they do not complain much about anything or anybody, they maintain a fair standard of living and enjoy a reasonable amount of pleasure. So we smile and chat to keep up appearances.

We don't wish to be considered an "oddity", a neurotic or a bore. Secret problems, worries and fears may continue to nag at our minds; frustration may be bubbling up inside us, but we present a brave, cheerful face to our family, friends and our colleagues at work.

All this is not meant to suggest that most of us are miserable and unhappy, and that we think life isn't worth living. No, the chances are that we suffer from a curiously subtle malady, difficult to define. The symptoms include a vague feeling of discontent, uncertainty, irritability, peevishness and languor. We are perhaps only half alive, often find it difficult to concentrate or take a keen interest in anything. We feel that we are in a rut—our own diagnosis may be "nerves". Perhaps we need a tonic.

Often, especially at certain times of the year, we do require a tonic, though not necessarily in a bottle from the chemist.

Let's remember the artificial kind of life most of us are forced to live. Circumstances may have pushed us into unhealthy habits. Who wants to walk anywhere if he can ride? How many of us would choose to study the flora and fauna of the countryside, when we can sit in a cosy armchair and watch chorus girls on television? Are we able to enjoy the sting of rain and wind against our cheeks or do we prefer the warm, scented atmosphere of the cinema?

Do we ever run, swim, play football or cricket or take part in any other vigorous game, or are we content to sit and watch others exercising themselves?

We may read hundreds of articles and scores of short stories and exciting novels during the year, but have we ever experienced the thrill of trying to write one? We use a wide variety of tools, ingenious gadgets and labour-saving devices. Have we ever *invented* anything useful, or even bothered to try? Take a walk around the art galleries, examine the countless sketches, paintings, pieces of sculpture. Some are delightful, some are puzzling, fantastic, bizarre. Have we ever tried to create a picture, to capture a scene or a character with pencil or brush?

No matter what excuses we make, no matter how few talents we imagine we possess, this is the sort of question we should ask ourselves if we want to escape from boredom and discontent. Having asked ourselves these questions and admitted our guilt—for we are *all* guilty to some extent—we should then get down to some really *creative* thought and work.

## Creative Imagination

As children we lived in a world of imagination. If we have forgotten those exciting days of the now dim past, just let us watch a few boys or girls at play. A normal, healthy boy can ride in a rough, old soap-box on wheels, with a piece of string for steering, and imagine he is a famous racing motorist, winning the coveted trophy in competition with all rivals. He can paddle an old tin bath across a pond and imagine he is navigating a shark-infested ocean on a raft. He can hide in a hollow tree and pretend he is a secret-service agent in peril of his life. He can put a space helmet on his head and fly to the moon in his rocket-ship.

A little girl can play with her dolls and in the twinkling of an eye she is a harassed mother, a hospital nurse or a teacher, according to her fancy. She can gather leaves, seeds and pebbles from the garden, imagine that they are essential foodstuffs and become a shopkeeper for a change. She can drape an old lace curtain over her head and become a beautiful bride.

What can we learn from these childish games? We can learn that in each one of us there is a *creative instinct*, an endless flow of *imagination* which can transport us from the ugly realities of a mundane existence to the glorious panorama of life in a new world. We can learn that our happiness need not depend upon our physical appearance, nor where we live nor the material value of our possessions.

Our happiness, our mental and spiritual satisfaction, and to some extent our physical health, depend chiefly upon our *creative imagination*, and the wider expression of our Real Self.

Some readers may be tempted to reply: "These flights of imagination are all very well for children. They have no responsibilities; they have plenty of spare time to indulge in their fancies; they know nothing about the bitter experiences and the grim realities of life. They'll soon get that nonsense knocked out of them when they grow up and discover what life is really like!"

Yes—that is the tragedy. When children "grow up", they are taught a different set of rules, a new code of ethics. Many of the human characteristics they were taught to regard as virtues are now said to be unpractical ideals, and unsuitable for progress in the outside world.

### Shattered Ideals

For example, as children we probably attended Sunday School, where we learned that selfishness is something of which we should be ashamed. According to religious teaching, unselfishness is one of the noblest of virtues. As we "grow up", older colleagues with greater and wider experience of the world ridicule any demonstration of unselfish consideration—unless they themselves benefit by it! "Don't be such a fool," they advise. "Look after 'Number One'—self first is the best motto," they say. If we ignore their advice, as we may be inclined to do, we soon discover that many people are ready to exploit our unselfishness. They will take as much as we are prepared to offer in thought, time, money, service; they will sponge upon our generosity —and then they'll not care what becomes of us.

This callous treatment is apt to make us harder, less tolerant, more suspicious, more selfish—and less Christian in our attitude towards life. Then the materialists of the world—and they are legion—will refer to us as clever, shrewd, business-like persons who should make our way to the top.

It is the same with virtues such as honesty, humility, honour, morality—even love. These qualities are to be expected in monks, nuns, priests and children, we are told, but in business, politics and professional life generally the same virtues, except in very small doses, are called great "handicaps", if not "weaknesses".

Suppose we turn our thoughts back to childhood for a few moments. Remember all that a loving mother taught us? Remember the good advice of the local vicar? If we listened at all and were sensitive and anxious to live a good life, were we not shocked and bitterly disappointed by the rough-and-tumble realities of the outside world when we were launched into it? And did we not eventually mould ourselves into the accepted pattern as the years passed and as we gained experience of manhood or womanhood?

The chances are that, if we tried gallantly and sincerely to cling to those principles taught to us as children, regardless of popular opinions and advice of the "men of the world", we should be regarded as fools or cranks. Nobody likes to be treated as a fool, or to be exploited and imposed upon constantly by these "smart guys" with whom one has to mix.

So, emulating the common herd, we probably effected a compromise by lowering our stands of behaviour in order to compete more favourably in the world. Let's be honest about it all!

## Popular Thoughts and Actions

At some time or other most of us have been forced to the conclusion, "My trouble is, I'm too conscientious or perhaps too kind, generous, modest, scrupulous, honest or trusting." We see others around us with less intelligence, integrity or legitimate skill "getting away with it". They are winning promotion, making more money, enjoying more material comforts, even gaining respect and gratitude that we know they *do not deserve*.

Why should we be left behind in the race for money, power and prestige just because of our perhaps old-fashioned ideas and principles? After all, we tell ourselves, an occasional "fiddle" isn't really dishonest —everybody does it. There are times when there is no harm in speaking the truth, but there are other occasions when a lie is merely "diplomatic" and much safer. "All's fair in love and war"—and in the ruthless, cut-throat competition of the world to-day why should we have any scruples about pushing other people down to gain favour and personal advantage ourselves?

Thoughts and actions like these seem to form the general, popular, cynical, materialistic attitude towards life. So long as they remain on the right side of the law, many people are not troubled by the moral issues. Spiritually they wear blinkers, so that their conscience is not troubled by the light of truth. They are not criminals or even obvious cheats, but they are trying to cheat life itself.

This example of moral cheating is typical of what goes on in every walk of life. As we grow out of childhood our creative instincts are subdued and frustrated by influences and circumstances around us. Eventually we are forced into an unnatural, unethical way of life and even our formerly cherished virtues are scorned by "men of the world". In order to compete against others in the material sense we all too often lower our own moral standards rather than "lose points" by sticking to our highest principles.

If we conform to this popular pattern of "growing-up" and stray away from our earlier concepts of truth, integrity, fidelity, trust, generosity, love or other virtues, we are not only guilty of cheating others, but we are cheating *ourselves*.

If we fail to make practical use of our talents, if we allow our creative instincts to be stifled, if we silence the inner voice of conscience, we not only rob the world of all we have to offer, but we also rob ourselves.

## The Miracle of Spring

After the bleak desolation of winter, comes spring—an ever-recurring miracle of new life. Surely spring is the most wonderful season of the year—the season when we see the mystery of the Resurrection manifested everywhere. Trees and hedgerows, fields and woods, flower-beds and grassy plots quicken with new-born life. Blackbirds, larks and thrushes pour out their song to herald the arrival of spring. Sunshine and showers, high blue skies with wisps of gauzy clouds—everything gives a sense of new life and movement—the very air seems like wine, sparkling with life, with joy, with song, with the promise of fulfilment.

What about us? Surely the miracle of spring should make us catch our breath and gasp with wonder at the beauty and mystery of life; surrendering ourselves to the uplifting influences of nature, looking forward with expectancy to the days which lie ahead with the urge to be up and doing, to adventure, to create.

If we are unable to feel in complete harmony with nature during this season of rebirth, what has gone wrong with us?

Perhaps in "growing up" we have drifted away from all that really matters. Perhaps we have forsaken most of our hopes and ambitions, our high ideals and tried to silence our conscience. Perhaps we have attempted to ignore or defy the laws of nature and closed our eyes and ears to the joy and wonder of life. If so, no wonder we feel apathetic, frustrated, discontented; no wonder that life seems heedless and without purpose.

Just as all good housewives undertake the task of thoroughly cleaning their homes in the springtime, so, too, can we make it an appropriate season to give ourselves a complete physical, emotional and mental spring clean.

### Some Practical Suggestions

Let us begin by studying the following questions and reviewing the suggestions outlined:

*Do we get enough fresh air and exercise?* Do we breathe deeply, filling the lungs with fresh air? If we only half breathe, we shall only be half alive. We should also walk at least four miles a day or have some other form of beneficial exercise.

*Do we relax enough, physically and mentally?* In the midst of the most arduous labour we should relax and rest for two or three minutes —physically and mentally. We should shift our attention and think of something pleasant; then we shall return to our work rejuvenated. We should clear out all cobwebs from the mind before going to sleep; take a mental bath and let our last thoughts be happy, constructive and aspiring, so that we awake refreshed and renewed.

*How often do we spend time in quiet meditation?* We need to withdraw from the noise and confusion of our busy, crowded lives, and through the art of meditation become acquainted with ourselves, relight the fires on the deserted altars of our noblest ideals, and enter into harmonious relationships with the divine essence of all life which is within.

*Have we been honest and fair in our relationships and dealings with others?*

*Do we hold grudges?* If we do, these should be cast away. Has someone wronged us? Forget it. Forgive it. Let us show our spiritual supremacy by passing it by. Numerous men and women have lost by storing up bitterness and hate. Grudges gain no good end. They are the rubbish of the soul. Clean them out not only for the other person's sake, but for our own peace of mind and health of spirit.

*Are we using our talents creatively and to the full?* We should find out what we can really do well, develop that ability and bend every effort to improving that talent.

*Are we true to our real ethical selves?* Or have we "watered down" our highest principles and ideals to make material progress more rapidly? Do we conform to the ideas of others or do we follow our own set of ethical principles?

*Are we using our imagination for our welfare and happiness?* Imagination differentiates man from the animal, and the life of dull, drab mediocrity from that of creative, aspiring achievement.

*Do we view life calmly?* Are our minds open to consider the whole facts, free from prejudice? If not, it is rubbish of the mind that needs to be cleaned out. It is a discordant note in the symphony of life. We should cast it forth as a deadly weed from the garden of the soul.

*Do our efforts help to make the world a better place?*

*Have we a sense of inferiority?* Are we in a rut and held down by this depressing feeling? How can others believe in us if we do not believe in ourselves? Do our innate abilities never crystallise in achievement because, doubting our own powers, we fear to initiate the activities which might lead to success? Does inferiority preclude our mixing normally in the activities of business and social life? We should get rid of the paralysing effect of the inferiority complex.

*Are we pessimistic?* If so, here is another habit of mind that should be cast out in this mental house cleaning. It is not an easy task to be optimistic in these troublesome and often depressive times in which we live. But there is no advantage in pessimism. Optimism balanced by a sane appraisal of facts has led thousands through life's trying experiences to ultimate achievement and security. Optimism is constructive—it builds. Pessimism is destructive—it tears down.

We should answer truthfully the above questions and be strictly honest with ourselves. We should not overlook or conceal any of our faults, but openly admit them and set out in earnest to correct them. Then, by following the suggestions made and putting the principles outlined into persistent practice, we shall find our deeper, truer selves and our lives will be filled with new light, new meaning, new power, new poise, new and wonderful possibilities.

# FACING UP TO FACTS

*More people are tired, dispirited, disheartened and disillusioned in trying to run away from life than from grappling with responsibilities. There are more people who give up in despair before trying than there are of those who try their best and meet with set-backs.*

*Millions of people turn away from and are afraid to face reality. Yet those who have the courage to face up to facts are often the happiest and most successful of men and women.*

\* \* \*

IT has no doubt occurred to many of us that those who have least to complain of, grumble the most; that those who have the most advantages misuse them; that those who have every opportunity complain of the hardness of their lot.

The blind and the maimed are traditionally cheerful. Those who are racked by physical defects seem to be the most fervent in counting their blessings, whilst others, who are blessed with health and strength, and some measure of opportunity, often enough rail at life and bemoan their misfortunes.

It would take a whole book to delve deeply into this phenomenon of human behaviour, but a casual acceptance of it as fact should place us on our guard against our own reactions. When we feel weary and dispirited, is it really because we have put everything we have got into the struggle and we feel utterly worn out? Let's be honest with ourselves? Isn't it more often than not because we have only tried half-heartedly, or tried to dodge the issue altogether?

Real effort, though it may tire us, gives us a feeling of *pleasant* tiredness. Running away from things makes us desperately, dejectedly tired.

When we feel depressed, on examining our personal affairs, are we really dejected because, despite our endeavours, we have made but little progress? Or is it because we have expected a benevolent Fortune to smile upon us and give us our heart's desire without any real enterprise or initiative on our part? Are we tired from genuine exertion, or is it our conscience that makes us feel disgusted with ourselves?

When we feel "down in the dumps", we should not accept it as an inevitable, inescapable fact and resign ourselves to its dominion until a brighter hour arrives. We should face up to it! Ask ourselves the cause! We may not find it easy to disentangle the alibis that we sometimes make for ourselves. But honest probing will eventually

245

lead us to the root of the trouble. And in nearly every case, we shall find that this comes from some form of "guilty conscience". We are depressed, gloomy, feel "down in the dumps" because we have not really been trying. Our tiredness is an alibi—not the result of effort.

Let's examine ourselves honestly. We shall be surprised at the self-knowledge we shall acquire, and perhaps more surprised to find that on cool examination our "dumps" will vanish.

## The Lonely Way

There is a phase of human personality which must know loneliness; a phase of the individual which dwells in solitude. A man may mortgage his time to the utmost in social service, in business affairs, or surround himself with friends and acquaintances, but there will come brief periods when his Inner Self withdraws from life around him and he feels completely isolated—tragically alone. The faces around him will mean but little to him; even if he is in the midst of those near and dear to him, loneliness will attack him, because even they cannot enter into that inner chamber of individuality. It is a feeling that comes more often to the contemplative.

Suppose we examine this feeling of loneliness. There are few of us who have not experienced it, when we feel that even those closest to us do not really understand us; that society as such is arrayed against us, is hostile, or, at the least, completely indifferent to our fate; that we are helpless, insignificant specks on the surging tide of life, alone, neglected, uncared for, at the mercy of the elements.

This feeling comes to most of us at one time or another. It comes to the housewife, often bored with her dull, weary routine, alone all day, and when her husband returns, not always able to enter into his sphere of interests. It comes to the man at work, when his efforts meet with misunderstanding rather than with due reward, when he feels that the boss or the management is "down" on him, when his juniors or those who work under him are indifferent, when the problems pile up and the solutions seem to evade him.

It comes to the elderly, particularly, and to us all in some form, when we feel that the changes within society are too quick for us to keep up with, when in a transitional period such as the present, we feel that the changes of environment are inimical to our welfare and well-being.

Every great individual, every truly successful man or woman experiences this loneliness of the soul, much more than the average person. It is, in part, the measure of their greatness and success, the measure of their advance before their fellow-men. The pioneer, the genius is so often ahead of contemporary thought and habit that he is like a man on the hill-top, breathing a rarer air, but at times feeling dreadfully alone.

Anyone who reads Shakespeare with a grain of imagination can understand the haunting echo of his personal disillusionment and aching heart. He had succeeded as no man before had succeeded in the world of letters; he had won the acclaim of his contemporaries, achieved material success, but it was only in his later years that he won through to that calmness and serenity of spirit which he summed up himself in the words: *"Ripeness is all."*

Much the same may be said of all the great souls who have steered perplexed and bewildered humanity down through the centuries. There have been times when they have felt in full the burden of life and the insupportable weight of Cosmic loneliness. We may not feel as they felt in full; but we are likely to taste something of the bitterness of this loneliness. And it is as well to remember that its most poignant moments often come when we are nearest to achieving that contact, that oneness with the Universal Mind. This feeling sometimes precedes the hour of glory; the bitterness becomes the gateway to the life triumphant.

*Let us remember that, when we are most alone, we are nearest to the Universal Mind,* and that when we have exerted the full measure of our strength, there is the all-pervading power of the Infinite to guide us forward to spiritual satisfaction and worthwhile achievement.

## The Dual Danger

We have discussed two of the prime enemies of human happiness and achievement, two dangers which beset us all, that can embitter life and even poison success, that can make living a nightmare and existence a burden. We can call these the terrible twins—*Retreat* and *Loneliness*.

They are quite closely related if we think about them. If we retreat—run away—we are likely to be more among the crowd. We then become ordinary, unenterprising; one of the herd, jogging aimlessly along in the ruts of easy-going mediocrity. But we pay the penalty, for we are pricked by an inner realisation that we could have done better, that we should have tried harder, that we have sacrificed achievement because we did not dare.

On the other hand, if we press on, if we are enterprising, ambitious, courageous, daring and defiant, the other Twin bestrides our path. We may have advanced further along the road of more successful living than the masses. We may be in the vanguard, yet we are so often alone, and the whole weight of life and endeavour seems to fall on us. And so we echo Matthew Arnold when he faced these two alternatives: ". . . *madman or slave, must man be one?*"

Practical Psychology offers the answer. Basically, Practical Psychology affirms that Man alone, with only his conscious powers, cannot fully meet the challenge of life. No matter what mastery we may achieve over environment through the application of science, Man is still the inhibited, fearful, tragic creature at the mercy of, and often fighting a losing battle against overwhelming forces, unless he contacts and uses a power outside of himself.

Practical Psychology teaches men and women to find this Power, to tap the wondrous reservoir of wisdom, insight and energy that can liberate them from bondage, that can give them a strength which makes them all-conquering.

We have referred to Man calling an *outside* Power to his aid; that he had need of a vision and understanding not provided by his Conscious Mind. This may be a little misleading. By "outside" we mean outside the Conscious Mind. The Power we need is not outside of us completely. It is resident in our Subconscious. It is a tiny pocket of power and energy which we all carry about with us, and which is part and parcel of the great Creative Force itself. It is a divine element within us, the spark that inspires our bodies, that can lift us to loftier summits.

Perhaps an anology may make this easier to understand. Suppose we imagine an isolated farm, miles away from the town, buried deep in the heart of the country. Some years ago, the farm was completely dependent upon its own resources, for light and power. Light had to be provided by candles, power by man-power or horse-power.

To-day what a vast difference! At the touch of a switch, every room in the farmhouse and every out-building can be flooded with light! Whatever machinery may be installed in the buildings, there is ample power available to work it—all carried along a thin, almost invisible, electric wire. However lonely the farmstead, it is linked up with the power-house miles away. It has almost unlimited power at its command, drawn from a remote reservoir whose resources are, for practical purposes, unlimited.

Although it may not be wise to carry such comparisons too far, we can be likened to the lonely farm, lacking in power and energy until we connect up with the unlimited power of the great Creative Force. Once we are linked up, the power in the Universal Mind is at our command.

### Press the Switch

If only we could, physically, connect up men and women with visible wires to the Subconscious Mind, show them the switch which would bring a flood of power and energy to help them in their daily lives!

There would then be few mean and frustrated people. We would be like demigods, bestriding our world.

But the connecting link between us and the Subconscious is an intangible thing; we cannot press a switch; it is more a matter of getting ourselves attuned to the Life Force, a mental awakening which illumines for us the almost unlimited treasures of the Inner Sleeping Mind.

This phase of the Mind is the part which is just beyond our reach at ordinary levels of experience. But when we are under the stress of great emotion, when we are uplifted and carried away by the strains of sublime music, when some scenic splendour leaves us almost breathless, or when our lives are in any way transformed by some aesthetic experience—at all these times we are very near to the thrilling experience of drawing upon our inner resources, of contacting the wonderful, inexhaustible Subconscious Power.

"But," some may remark, "all the incidents mentioned are almost involuntary. They come upon us unawares. Isn't there some way of making a direct approach to this hidden force within us?"

For many years *Psychology* has been expounding the methods of getting in touch with the Creative Force within us—the Subconscious Mind. Numerous articles which have appeared have given some suggestions along these lines. However it is worth while mentioning more pointers which can not only assist us to make the first approaches to the Subconscious Mind, but can also enable us to come into harmonious contact with it, in such a way as to enlist its wonderful wisdom and power for our own welfare and happiness.

The law of the Subconscious Mind is suggestion. It does not reason, judge or reject. It simply accepts and unquestionably acts upon the suggestions handed down to it, whether they be good or evil, constructive or destructive.

If we give suggestions to our Subconscious Mind of mediocrity, inferiority or constant fear, we shall become victims of these negative suggestions. If we think in terms of success and achievement, self-confidence and courage, sooner or later we shall objectify our external manifestations of them. This is no mere, idle theory, but sober, scientific fact. Psychological experiments have demonstrated it, while day-to-day experience further proves it to be true.

The Subconscious Mind is affected by predominant mental impressions.

Let us imagine two balls of wood suspended on a string, one a large ball, the other a small ball. If we swing them so that they strike each other, the big ball will move the little ball out of the way as though it were not there at all.

### The Strongest Desire Wins

The larger always dominates. This is true in the matter of attention. When attention is divided between two conflicting interests, the stronger always wins. In the building up of constructive interests, attention should be fastened on to these things.

If, for instance, we are trying to build a good habit, we should make our desire, our interest in that direction, stronger than our interests in other directions. We should think of every reason why we should do this, and every reason why we should not do the other thing; then this will tend to become the dominant interest.

The law of predominant mental impression is, therefore, simply that of two impressions in the Subconscious Mind; the stronger impression ultimately wins and governs our activities and actions.

We must not be discouraged if we cannot, all at once, put this law of mental control into practice. It may take some time before we can do so. This is because we may have been thinking one way for many years—wrong and unwholesome impressions dominating our Subconscious Mind. These impressions are buried deep in the Subconscious and will not be uprooted in a day. But if we persevere, we can replace these old, negative, destructive impressions with new, positive and constructive impressions, and eventually succeed in making them stronger than the old ones. And however long this may take us to do, the results will be worth while, for as soon as we have replaced our old impressions with our new impressions, stronger than the old, the new impressions will prevail.

Then we should use visualisation; form clear, definite pictures in the Subconscious Mind of what we wish to achieve, getting as much detail as possible into the picture.

In order to strengthen visualisation, we should write down on paper, fifty times at least, minute descriptions of these mental pictures. Drive the visualisation right into the Subconscious, through all the different senses! Think it, speak it, write it! And then finally we must act it.

We must live up to what we are impressing upon the Subconscious Mind. We must honestly strive to bring about a realisation of whatever we wish to achieve, and all our efforts must be unremittingly directed towards that end.

An understanding of the Subconscious Mind can give us the will to win, the courage that sustains us when life is difficult, the faith that flames triumphant even in the darker moments of existence, the power that can transform meaningless, purposeless living into lives inspired by lofty achievement and glowing and thrilling significance.

# THE AGE OF LEISURE

HOW many people to-day are frustrated? Would leisure solve the problem? If we were to ask any "man in the street"—or woman for that matter—"Are you frustrated?" I wonder how many could honestly answer "No." Any intelligent thinking man or woman *must*, at some time or other, feel frustrated.

Despite the fact that the world is growing smaller as far as travel is concerned and that opportunities are greater and more numerous, more and more people continue to feel frustrated. Why? Probably because the mind now finds larger scope and travels faster and farther than the body, chiefly through lack of finance or the shortage of time, can take it.

We have, in the far distant past of the world, had the Ice Age, the Stone Age, the Iron Age. Now we are on the threshold of the Atomic Age and if this does not result in the destruction of civilisation it will be linked with the Age of Leisure.

Many of us have begun to see the possibilities of an Age of Leisure and the possibility that it may be within our reach. But there are some people who do not realise that such an Age is possible and others who do not want it and who would not welcome it. For life to then still means work, more work and still more work.

Inventions and mechanisation of industry mean more and more work done by machinery, less by Man. In theory this is good, because Man needs more leisure to recuperate his physical and mental powers; more time in which to indulge his natural bent.

*But*, Man must work to live. At least he must eat and provide for his kind or else leisure time will be as dust in his mouth. Nevertheless, work should be shared among all who are able to work, so that all men and women work to some extent. This is a dream maybe to be fulfilled in the future and for which we need much preparation and education.

The individual on the whole is not ready for leisure. He will have to be trained for it, so that he will know how to direct his leisure time to some constructive purpose satisfying to himself and one which will not be harmful to the community generally. He must learn to *work* serenely and entirely and to *play* completely and wholly. Education lags well behind the needs of the times. Men, women and children have more leisure than ever before, but only a small percentage know what to do with it, or have the means adequately to express themselves. In Western countries particularly, there is quite a large amount of leisure. Does this account for much of the crime existing and growing

251

to-day? Maybe the old adage that "Satan finds some mischief still for idle hands to do" is still true!

## What is Leisure?

Leisure is time to do anything (or nothing) which we are not compelled to do by necessity. It is generally considered to be the time which is our own after working hours—the hours during which we earn our living—are completed for the day. Needless to say, most individuals have other responsibilities which they are compelled to consider and these whittle down the extent of their leisure.

Yet despite the additional leisure we have to-day, the keynote is one of rush. It is an Age of frantic hurry. Meditation and contemplation have but little place in our lives. Gone are the days of easy, relaxed leisure moments or hours when we had "time to stand and stare", to browse through a book while sitting in the sun, or just soak ourselves in its enveloping warmth.

Yes, we have more leisure, but there is so much to do that we are in danger of becoming bewildered and overwhelmed by the multitudinous avenues to be explored, the pleasure to experience. Our recreations and leisure time have become commercialised, so that the majority find themselves herded into uniform recreations or amusements where the character, temperament and natural urge of the individual have little or no chance of expression.

Hurry, hurry, hurry! Yesterday is dead—yes, almost forgotten before the new day dawns, and we hurl ourselves onward with feverish haste—for what? *And we talk about leisure!*

Some of us grow weary of this perpetual rush and bustle. There is too little time for reading and less for dreaming. Gone are the days when we chatted leisurely with friends. A sense of guilt seems to attend such pleasures. There is a restless urge to be in a hurry. We feel we should be working—pushing on to the next job ahead, the next experience or some new form of entertainment, feverishly eager to cram more and more activity into a shorter and shorter space.

## A Comparison

The other day I was talking to an old friend of mine. He was comparing the days of his childhood with those of the present time. Eventually he mentioned the home in which he lived as a child. "There was a garden," he said, "and some iron steps leading down from a conservatory, in one of the then fashionable Victorian houses of a big city. The steps would be hot in the summer sun and it was joy itself to sit and bask in the sun—summers then seemed always hot and sunny and beautiful, with sunny days stretching on interminably, marked only now and then with welcome rain to lay the dust and give drink to the parched garden." He went on to say:

"There was plenty of time to sit and do nothing, except to drink in the surroundings—an hour seemed a day—a day a year! The sun drenched through the leaves of the trees and bathed everything in its enveloping warmth, so that at times there was nothing—only the sun, the garden and me. . . . There was a pear tree," he added, "and I used to watch it with wonder as it blossomed in the spring; my brothers and sisters and myself had tea in its shade in the summer and as autumn came, the fruit having grown and swelled, we then climbed the good old tree to gather the ripened fruit."

My friend recalled the lawn often covered with daisies and butter-cups. "It was not a good lawn," he said, "but ideal for children; we picked the flowers and made chains and bouquets for the weddings we held among the little boys and girls. . . . Then the lawn was cut," he went on to say, "and we played at funerals with no morbidity, only acting out what we saw around us and accepting quite simply the facts of life and death, for death meant nothing to us then. But always there was time—time to do things or do nothing—to wait and watch and absorb."

To-day, life and those riches which my old friend mentioned pass us by in the rush and bustle—for what? True, science has come along with inventions to relieve men of tedious work and drudgery! Yet we appear to have less time than ever before. The housewife, too, is surrounded by mechanical gadgets and devices to make her work easier, yet she rushes around scarcely able to cram her chores into her day.

Before the Second World War there were tea-parties, garden parties, carnivals—"a way of life" which we were supposed to have fought to preserve. But we seem to have succeeded only in losing it, for we have "no time".

### Various Age Groups

The "how and why" of leisure has certainly altered considerably since the last World War. One spends leisure not only according to one's financial means but according to one's time and age group; or maybe, too, it is influenced by one's social group, but then that was always so.

Leisure falls roughly into five groups or ages; they are distinct and are likely to be more so as the century goes on. Let us consider first the teenagers as the first group to spend leisure consciously as apart from the unconscious, spontaneous play of children. The teenagers spend more and more time outside the home in group amusements or occupations of their own age group, free, often irresponsible, bound by their own immediate circle and interests. This tendency seems inclined to spread as time goes on, for the teenagers lead a life apart from the adults of the family.

The next age group are the young married couples with young families. Their recreational interests are mostly in and around the house because they are tied to it by the children. They spend time in the garden, or watching television; knitting or other home occupations and interests.

The third age group is enabled by circumstances to spend more leisure away from home. Home interests, however, still abound, although perhaps on a more ambitious scale. All this is chiefly due to augmented income and the fact of the family becoming more independent physically and sometimes financially. This is the age group of the car users, when the family manages to get an extra holiday, often abroad.

The fourth group is even more financially and physically independent. But in this group, mostly made up of middle-aged men and women ranging onwards from fifty and sixty, physical energies are beginning to lag, so that there tends to be a return to the quiet of the home leisure occupations and to watching television. This group tends to be more home-bound.

In the fifth age group, after sixty-five, leisure activities drop sharply, chiefly on account of lack of physical energy, but partly owing to a tendency to a sharp drop in income and earning capacity. Leisure becomes of the very quiet, innocuous type and rest and dozing take up a lot of time.

So again we come to this question of *Time*. When we have the energy to do things and go places, to have fun or to travel, lack of funds or responsibilities usually tie us down. But with the passing of the years and for a short, brief span of time and provided we are fortunate to have health or funds or freedom, we have time to do those things about which we dreamed when we were young. But there is only such a short time left to us! And that precious time flies by far more quickly than when we were young. By now, nothing seems quite so exciting, so rose-coloured, for as the years go swiftly by, our capacity to thrill to the exuberance of life and adventure begins to fail rapidly. In time we have to face it—we are getting old!

The day when we cease to look forward to spring or thrill to the song of the blackbird is a warning that, no matter what our age in years may be, we are on the very threshold of old age. We should take heed of this warning and try to snap out of it while we can.

### Live Fully To-day

So to those of us who are getting on in years, why not start using *now* what little time we have left to live fully! It's no use saying: "One day I will do this or that," for that day may never come. We are only chasing the sunshine of to-morrow and that we shall never capture. But we have *to-day*! And what we do to-day is what matters.

We should capture it, hold it—squeeze from it all the joy and experience we can. For it will be gone all too soon—never to return!

We have got to-day—*now*! Let's pause awhile and ask ourselves: "Where am I going? What am I doing with my leisure? Am I letting my life and opportunities slip by without making the most of them?"

Time's getting short for many of us. It's slipping by for all of us. And yet we have all the time there is. We may learn from our past, but looking back is of little avail. The future? None of us knows how much to expect. So it is useless to live only for what is to come. We should seize the here and now and drain the cup of the present to its last drop.

Leisure should be a time for relaxing of mind, body and soul; a time in which one may recuperate the body and enrich the mind and spirit. It should involve doing everything at one's own speed.

If necessary or desirable, leisure could mean doing nothing, just relaxing, contemplating, meditating. So we should learn how to do nothing, perhaps with others; perhaps with no one. There are times to be alone, to listen to sounds and let our thoughts wander at will— sounds which are unheard and thoughts which do not come when in the company of others. There are times when leisure should be shared, and there are times when it is better to be alone.

Leisure means getting satisfaction out of life if only for an hour. And this can often be done by looking at life through the trusting adventurous eyes of a child. For as La Bruyère wrote: "Children have no past or future; unlike us, they relish the present."

We cannot relax—we cannot enjoy or benefit by our leisure, whether alone or with others, unless we live in the here and now.

The past is but a shadow, a ghost of faint memories, coloured by the imagination. It seems either much worse or much better than the reality which once was. At any rate the experiences of the past no longer exist—they are gone. The past is dead, so it is better to forget it. And the future? It also does not exist. We cannot live in the unrealities, the shadowy dreams of the unborn "to-morrows".

Yes, much of life's joy can be lost by trying to live in the past or in the future. This is often the tragedy which blights the lives of countless thousands of men and women.

Therefore, if we would get the best out of our lives, we must learn to live fully to-day—*now*. This includes using our leisure wisely and well. We should not allow our leisure to be overshadowed by the worries of yesterday nor by the fears of to-morrow, otherwise leisure will cease to be leisure, in its true sense, for we shall fail to relax. And finally, let us remember that "The supply of time, though gloriously regular, is cruelly restricted." So don't let us dilly and dally over doing those things we have promised to do when we have more time, because before that time comes around, we may have reached the last milestone on life's journey *and realise we have left it too late.*

# THE ENEMY WITHIN

*"What is the course of life*
  *Of mortal men on the earth?*
*Most men eddy about*
  *Here and there—eat and drink,*
*Chatter and love and hate,*
  *Gather and squander, are raised*
*Aloft, are hurl'd in the dust,*
  *Striving blindly, achieving*
*Nothing: and then they die—*

*Perish! and no one asks*
  *Who or what they have been.*
*And there are some, whom a thirst*
  *Ardent, unquenchable, fires,*
*Not with the crowd to be spent—*
  *Not without aim to go round*
*In an eddy of purposeless dust.*
  *Ah, yes, some of us strive*
*Not without action to die."*

\*    \*    \*

DURING the last year or two the number of "jellyfish" men and women seems to have grown by leapsand bounds. There appear to be an epidemic of self-pity and a refusal to accept responsibility for individual endeavour. There's a danger of our becoming a race of State spoon-fed individuals, incapable of individual initiative or self-expression.

There has always been, of course, a great number of people with abnormally large wishbones and remarkably flabby backbones. But it is only in recent years that the lack of backbone appears to have become almost fashionable—a symptom to parade as an excuse for failure rather than a weakness to be regretted and to be overcome.

Years ago, the self-conscious, the timid, the weak used to approach Practical Psychology with a view to finding concrete help in overcoming their shortcomings. But the trend to-day is for the approach to be made in the spirit of receiving confirmation that they are handicapped by an incurable affliction. Once, they came for assistance; to-day they come for sympathy; previously they retained some consciousness of an individual responsibility, but now they regard themselves as martyrs to a malignant Fate.

We should be gravely perturbed by this trend; we can find confirmation of these misgivings in the news reports, in the philosophical temper of the age. More and more we appear to be tending to the belief that men and women are not responsible for their actions, that vices, weaknesses, sloth, indulgence—all vices of the personality—are factors beyond the control of the individual. The view is taken that these faults arise from heredity or environment, with society responsible for misfits, the individual being incapable of improving his lot.

This is fatalism at its worst. *If we accept this philosophy, as individuals we shall be damned—as a Nation, we shall perish.*

I do not write these words lightly. I believe, very sincerely, that the individual is more or less responsible for his own success or failure. Admittedly, environment, upbringing, social status, heredity—all help or hinder him. But in the last resort *a man makes himself*. And he cannot palm off the responsibility for a shoddy product on the shoulders of Fate, nor attempt to proclaim that it is the fault of society that he is—what he is.

*We make ourselves*. Let us remember that, then act on it!

We are responsible for our actions and what we make of ourselves and of our lives. The choice is ours—whether we wallow in the gutter of self-pity or march with self-respect along the high-road of endeavour.

It is not the purpose of this article to trace in any detail the growth of this defeatist attitude to life. The falling off in religious belief has played no mean part in this; the "determinist" basis of scientific thought has led to its acceptance; the science of psychology—*misunderstood*—has contributed to the fallacious belief.

A number of people assume that psychology encourages the belief in a fatalistic attitude. According to them, we are at the mercy of subconscious forces which the conscious mind is unable to control. They say that even free will is an illusion; that we make our choice, not in any degree of freedom, but merely following the dictates of the dominant instinct.

If we take this argument to its conclusion, then we are mere puppets dancing on the strings of Fate. Everything that occurs to us, according to the fatalistic theory, is the result of forces beyond our control; our characters are moulded by subconscious forces which we can recognise but cannot divert—the best we can do is to live for the moment, allowing to-morrow to take care of itself; our best philosophy is that which accepts good and evil as serenely as possible, knowing that there is nothing we can do to affect the issue. Those are the logical conclusions derived from the acceptance of the fatalistic attitude. What a gruesome, melancholy and devastating philosophy of life!

But let us see how easy it is to prove that it is false! Suppose we take, for instance, an ambitious young man, faced with the choice of going to a dance or of staying at home to study a subject that will help him in his work. Inclination—instinct, if we prefer to call it so —urges him to be gay, carefree, to go out and enjoy himself. But— despite the struggle between inclination and duty—he stays at home and puts in three or four hours of honest study. Will, determination —call it what we will—has triumphed; the young man has enhanced his stature by becoming responsible for his actions. He did not succumb to the urge of inclination; he made a free choice—he chose the path of endeavour rather than the easy road of non-resistance.

A similar choice faces us every day. Men and women, emancipated from the toils of self-indulgence, make their choice wisely and with reason. "Jellyfish" men and women take the lines of least resistance.

### The Inner Forces

"But," some people will say, "what a very simple example to give! What happens in the case of men and women dominated by sub-conscious urges they do not understand and cannot control?"

We are not overlooking such cases. They do exist in larger numbers than many people imagine—men and women driven by inner forces in spite of themselves—driven to ruin, desperation and despair.

*What has psychology to say in such cases?* Only this, that such men and women are often ignorant of the workings of mind—that self-knowledge frequently would enable them to control, to sublimate and harness the inner forces, now driving them to destruction, to re-create and re-shape their lives.

To sum up, men and women often are at the mercy of environment, heredity or their baser selves as long as they prefer to be puppets rather than realised personalities. Life can be strengthened and enriched by substituting knowledge for ignorance.

We must not, however, pass lightly over the problem of psychological maladjustments, because we are only too well aware of lives made miserable and ineffective through psychological ill health. But proper treatment can do a great deal for such people and will help them to lead fuller and more satisfying lives.

Practical Psychology can give men and women a clearer picture of the make-up of their minds and enable them to use its forces for progress instead of destruction.

### The Enemy Within

Neurotic maladjustments usually are the symptoms of mental unrest, of inner conflicts, of repressed instincts. Let us take a typical example.

Mrs. X is an unhappy, irritable, depressed woman, finding no joy in her home, her friends, or any comfort in the fact that financially she is moderately well-off. She is "nervy", cries for no reason at all, is haunted by some nameless fear she cannot define, sleeps badly and exhibits other symptoms of a nervous disorder. The doctor assures her that there is no physical foundation for her malaise. What, then, is amiss?

Mrs. X has been married for fifteen years, but is childless. Most of her unhappiness arises from the fact that her mother instinct has been repressed. She has not realised that her life is incomplete without children, that inwardly she feels herself a complete failure because she is not a mother. She does not face up to that fact but thrusts every idea connected with it deep down into her Unconscious. The result is—the symptoms enumerated and a miserable, ineffective life.

If Mrs. X realised the cause of her complaint, she would be able to tackle life more realistically; she could become a "mother" to children not her own, she could express her maternal instinct in social work and find contentment and happiness.

We have dealt in very simple terms with this case and left out a number of complicating factors to demonstrate our point more clearly —that ignorance of the way the mind works was Mrs. X's worst enemy.

Let us glance briefly at another case—a man this time—and again look at it in the simplest possible terms. Mr. Z was a young man of great promise, did exceptionally well at school and college, but now that he has been earning his own living for a few years, has seriously deteriorated. He gives scant attention to his work, indulges in frequent bouts of intemperance, is unreliable, careless about his person and seems to have lost that brilliance which earned him a high place in his school.

What has happened? How is it that the young man is drifting so rapidly and becoming a drunkard—a ne'er-do-well? Can he help himself?

Here is the answer. Mr. Z achieved an easy success at school and college. He had the "examination mind" and he gained rewards with very little labour. But he found matters entirely different in the outside world. There were responsibilities to face, problems to be solved and difficulties to be overcome. He had to concentrate, to work —if he was not to fail.

So Mr. Z retreated into his shell—he was afraid of being a failure —and provided an alibi in advance as to why he was not successful. What he was saying, in effect, to the world at large, was "I could have succeeded as well in business life as I did at school except for the temptations of drink. My failure is not due to any lack of brilliance, but to weakness."

If Mr. Z could be brought face to face with the real reason for his present state, there is little doubt that he would make an effort to lift himself out of the rut. His self-esteem had been wounded in some way; once let him see this, once let him tackle his life with fresh determination and courage and he would become a new man. Here again it was more or less ignorance that had made a man into a "jellyfish".

## Man Set Free

We have outlined these two cases briefly in order to show how self-knowledge can help people to overcome their "last enemy"—the weakness within. The men or women set free have rid themselves of the last trace of the "jellyfish" in their make-up and can advance boldly and with courage into the worthwhile life.

So far we have dealt only with knowledge—with an understanding of ourselves that leads to freedom—to a new chance. But we should emphasise, too, that in the process of re-making ourselves, we can draw upon a vast, Creative, Healing Power within the Subconscious Mind. It is not knowledge alone that we secure when we learn about our minds —there is also a curative, Creative Power that can energise all our actions, step up our abilities and make new people of us.

Men and women are not slaves—either to circumstance or to their selves. But they are in bondage as long as they prefer to be ignorant.

It is the failure to accept responsibility for our lives, that tendency to blame others, fortune or fate, that drags us down to the level of the jellyfish.

If there are some people who still believe that men and women are mere puppets—helpless playthings of Fate—then here is an experiment for them to make. Just for one day, let them discard that belief. Just for one day, let them think and act as if they were entirely responsible for their own lives; think and act as if they were the architects of their lives and fortunes. For one day, they should refuse to accept the idea that their chances haven't been good enough, that luck plays a dominating role in human life and that heredity is a bar to real progress.

Before nightfall, these people will have abandoned the false philosophy. They will have realised what a tremendous change can be effected in one day by an individual who believes in himself, what a transformation occurs when a person holds his head high, and with courage marches on towards a worthy purpose.

Many of us may stress the fact that we are not of the "jellyfish" type. But the truth is that there is something of the "jellyfish" in all of us. We so often prefer to ascribe our failures to ill-luck rather than admit that they may be due to lack of judgment; we sometimes prefer to consider ourselves unlucky rather than admit we may have been unwise. It is not easy—except to the realised personality—to admit that all we are to-day, including our successes or failures in our chosen fields, is very often the direct *result* of *past* thoughts, habits and actions.

We mould our characters, our very lives, from day to day, but do not always like to accept the responsibility.

### Moral Courage

How can we discover how much of the "jellyfish" there is in us? By answering the following questions.

Do we believe, consistently, that we are the product of what we have thought, what we have done, what we have attempted to do over the past five years?

Do we ascribe our misfortunes to ill-luck or to lack of foresight? Do we consider our failures to be partly due to circumstance or entirely to our ignorance or insufficient endeavour?

Do we believe that we can succeed, live effectively, achieve our ambitions entirely by determination and endeavour without the intervention of luck?

If we answer the questions honestly, there may be the need for some of us to take ourselves in hand.

So very often we make ourselves and our lives. If our lives are a mess, then we should blame no one else but ourselves. We are in charge. We are the bosses. If we are brave enough to accept responsibility and discharge it well, then we will know the meaning of vibrant living.

One of the main essentials of the full life is—*courage*. It was when the Ape-man first stood erect that Man emerged; it is when we have good backbones that we can make our lives fuller, more successful and more worth while.

" But if I lack courage, what can I do about it?" That is a question that often confronts us. Courage, like any other virtue, has to be cultivated. We cannot have courage merely by wishing that we possessed it—*we must act courageously*.

There are times when we are confronted with a situation that we can either avoid or with which we can deal. We are tempted to run away from it, instead of forcing ourselves to face up to it. What matter if our knees do tremble and we feel we can never go through with it? We have got to go on trying—and trying hard—if we wish to build up courage.

Physical courage is often a question of lack of imagination but the courage we are seeking is of the mind—moral courage. It is not dependent upon our physiques; it is something we can cultivate. It is not a virtue given to us at birth; it is something we build up over the whole of our lives.

"Jellyfish" men and women can be transformed into new and vibrant personalities by arousing themselves from their lethargy and buckling on the armour of action. Then they would find joy in accomplishment, reach the summit of successful living by pursuing their way unrelentingly, unwaveringly and undauntedly.

# LET'S FACE REALITY

*"And you all know, security*
*Is mortals' chiefest enemy."*

\* \* \*

WE seem to hear a lot these days of cases where there is a lack of responsibility, lack of enterprise—a spirit of wanting something for nothing—on the part of individuals and groups. Apart from examples that we hear of, hardly a day goes by without newspapers publishing accounts of such conduct. This could become a serious matter, for it proclaims a spirit that could result in national degeneration, social stagnation and could shatter our high ideals of a nobler way of life.

The increasing frequency of such incidents suggests that there is a rot within the community that we would do well to try and stop before it undermines the structure of our way of life and blights our hopes of the better land for which we strive.

This degenerate spirit takes many forms: the "couldn't-care-less" attitude, the general indifference to things that matter, the discouraging of the "go-ahead" spirit by the "can't-be-done" brigade. It is not confined to one section of the community, nor is it a phenomenon of any particular age group.

In industrial affairs it is often blamed upon the Communists and their desire to undermine the national prosperity as a whole.

But the baleful influence of Communism seems only to flourish where the degenerate spirit exists. Strikes over trivial pinpricks, "go-slow" methods for no apparent reason, the refusal to adopt new and better methods of production, "sending to Coventry" those who put their backs into their jobs. Ostensibly these un-British and un-adult actions may appear to be the work of a handful of agitators. But such deplorable actions are possible only because a section of the people obey unworthy impulses, are immature, lack the optimistic fighting spirit that is essential to individual well-being and social progress.

## Generally Recognised

*Psychology* does not intend to take a narrow, restricted or party view of our industrial and commercial troubles. It merely asserts that our salvation, nationally lies in more "productivity", that is, more production per man. In old-fashioned terms, we must work harder. In more scientific terms, we must work more effectively.

262

*Psychology* does not necessarily assert that this means longer hours or more drudgery. It believes in the adoption of better methods and techniques, in planned management, in the efficient selection and handling of the human factor. The ideal is that every man should be "on his toes" to do a better job, to work more effectively. Nor does it apply only to the workers. Management, too, must be alive and enterprising. Only by such action can we ensure that the standard of living we have achieved will be maintained and improved.

But—and let us make no mistake about it—our standard of living is beginning to decline. It may not be very obvious, just at the moment, but the slide downhill has already started, and will continue with increasing momentum unless the country as a whole rolls up its sleeves in earnest and really goes to work with a will.

All this is generally recognised in principle. Yet what do we find? A clamour for larger rewards without reference to greater production. A general indifference to the implication we have outlined and a spirit that seeks to get everything without giving anything— a tendency to shirk and to slack.

Right at the outset let us make it clear that this is not a sweeping condemnation of all the working population of the country. Far from it! Rather do we seek to pin-point what appears to be a growing tendency that we must arrest—or take the calamitous consequences.

Why is this spirit so prevalent?

There are several answers. A higher standard of living tends to make many people more indolent and unenterprising; the richer life in terms of material things is apt to encourage sloth and idleness; prosperity seems to beget vices rather than virtues. And the social upheaval of the last decade or two may have unsettled men's and women's minds and confused the national aim.

Then there have been "prophets" who have seen visions of a new Utopia where work was unnecessary and effort not required—a brave, new world that could be achieved merely by clamouring for it, without the necessity of work or endeavour.

All these, and many more, have played their part in sapping many people's will-power, in weakening their resolution, in undermining their faith in the doctrine of self-reliance.

But the basic factors are psychological. And it is only individual psychology that can revive the fighting spirit, the sense of enterprise, of activity and effort that will make the social body well again.

### The Nobility of Work

Let us look at the plain facts!

We must, all of us, work more effectively, produce more, give more of ourselves to our jobs, whatever they may be, must find a joy and a pride in our daily routine, take a greater interest in the means whereby

L.C.—18

we earn our daily bread. Only thus can we secure the necessary productivity that will enrich our nation and give us the golden opportunities which we desire.

There are some people who consider their labour as a necessary evil, the only available means of keeping food in their stomachs and a roof over their heads. But work is not a curse—it is a blessing. For work can become the opportunity of leading a fuller life. A job well done ennobles man. Working with a will, giving of our best, taking an interest and a pride in our jobs, can bring an unfailing sense of satisfaction that can enrich our lives. It is when we try to shirk that the devils of dissatisfaction and doubt prey upon us. Work provides us with a stepping-stone to self-realisation.

The "nobility of work" is not a catch phrase. It is essential to human well-being. It affords an opportunity for man to find himself; to lift himself above the petty irritations and accidental annoyances of the lazy life, to sweeten the hours of leisure, to find a greater purpose in existence.

> *"This is the gospel of labour,*
> *Ring it ye bells of the kirk,*
> *Heaven is blest with perfect rest,*
> *But the blessing of earth is work."*

It is a pity that the slackers and grumblers of our day couldn't be inoculated with the bracing philosophy of work. Then we should see disappearing the side-street loungers, the shamefully work-shy, the pitiful spectacle of people trying to kill time; no longer should we see the tragic sight of men and women bored with work, tired of simple recreation; dissatisfied, half-hearted and half-alive.

If only a new and virile force could electrify our nation, clear the air of this fog of indifference and apathy, give to men and women the eager eyes of adventure, a zest for life, an active, enterprising appetite for living, with eyes lit up with faith and hearts made steadfast by resolution.

Although such a reformation cannot be fulfilled by accident, it can be accomplished by Practical Psychology. But the reformation, as always, must start with the individual. If men and women in general could see this light of truth, could appreciate it to the full, then a tremendous force would be released that could transform our society. We should as a nation breathe an air of optimism and faith, a new spirit would possess our people and a new era of golden opportunity would be open to all.

We cannot wave a magic wand and say, "Let this be!" But we can, individually, become one of the new crusaders to try and bring this about. We can change our lives by the light of Practical Psychology, so that we shall be beacons unto others. And, in so doing, we may inspire them to see a better way of living.

We do not need riches or social position, a lavish education or great influence to do this. All we need is to learn to smile where previously we grumbled, to see our disadvantages in true perspective and try to turn them into advantages, to greet each day as one of boundless opportunities, to endeavour to appreciate the simple joys and common pleasures of life. In all this, Practical Psychology can help us and teach us, too, the wisdom that will enable us to meet misfortune with courage, defeat with the resolve to succeed; it will give us the light of wisdom to pierce the darkness of doubt and send us forth in search of the fuller and larger life.

This is a part we can all play in helping to banish the fog of doubt and the mist of indifference which clouds our generation, and, in doing so, we shall also be exerting a splendid influence upon our fellow-men.

### Mr. Can and Mr. Can't

Mr. Can and Mr. Can't were well-known advertisements before the war. With due acknowledgments to the proprietary product which they advertised, we can very well use them as an object-lesson in the way of more successful living.

Mr. Can and Mr. Can't are more or less in the same station in life; their opportunities have practically been equal; fortune does not seem to have favoured one more than the other.

But Mr. Can't always looks on the dark side and magnifies his troubles tenfold. He greets every trivial difficulty with a groan. Every simple set-back to him is the forerunner of impending disaster, every daily incident is perceived through the glasses of deep, disgruntled pessimism. His face never lights up with a smile.

Mr. Can is an optimistic type. He gets up in the morning with a smiling face. No doubt he feels as tired as Mr. Can't, but he shakes the feeling off with a laugh. Things are not always easy for him; they often go wrong, but he sets about cheerfully to put them right.

These two are not comic figures presented for amusement. They represent the extremes of psychological types.

To which type do we belong? We can belong to one or the other. It's up to us.

Suppose we check up on ourselves. Do we get irritated easily? Then we should get out of the habit; force a smile instead of the normal whine—there's magic in a smile. Are we nursing negative thoughts? We should substitute positive ones for them; fill the mind with pleasant, agreeable and relaxing thoughts.

When we leave home in the mornings, we should put a spring into our gait, force a more cheerful note into our greetings with acquaintances.

When we arrive at work, let us get down to things right away; don't dawdle on the brink but jump right in; take a lively interest in what we do and a pride in how we do it. We should refuse to join the grumblers; and not be influenced by those who moan about the weather, the cost of living or other negative factors. We can force ourselves to be cheerful, refuse to let our spirits droop and take an interest in all around us.

When work is done, we can find something creative to do. We can be active, thereby preventing all thoughts of gloom and despondency from entering our minds.

### Decision and Action

Each one of us should decide right now to live the fuller life; try to be more friendly and thoughtful in our daily actions, to cultivate a more optimistic and cheerful frame of mind, to live more vitally.

Suppose, for a start, we try this for one day only—then ask ourselves at the end of that day, "Does it work?" If we have been sincere in our efforts we know what the answer will be. And the success of such a short experiment will inspire us to carry on and each day's success will hearten us for further effort.

Some of us by now may be saying to ourselves: "Yes, I must give this a fair trial—some time. I've nothing to lose, but I'm tired just now. I'll wait till to-morrow." But *to-day* is the day to act—not to-morrow. *Now* is the time to get started.

The act of "putting it off" is one of the greatest of all brakes upon individual and human progress. Whatever circumstances hold us back from *action* to-day will be just as valid to-morrow—more valid, indeed, because they will have given us an excuse that seems to work without entailing a surrender of our resolve to get started eventually. It is only by making an immediate start that we will ever get started at all!

Inertia is a very potent force in the human make-up. Men and women tend to remain in a groove, to dislike change, to put off and keep putting off any kind of action.

Inertia is the first obstacle we have to overcome in our endeavours to live more successful lives. So let us start to-day—*now*—to become more cheerful, optimistic, forward-looking, positive, forceful, vibrant personalities. Difficult? Of course it is! But everything worth while is difficult at first. Yet it eventually will pay rich dividends, life will become more meaningful, opportunities previously missed will again come our way, and we will get a far greater share than ever before of the joy and fragrance of life.

# HIGH-PRESSURE LIVING

*"We are all of us dealers in Time . . . Time is one thing we all possess. Our success depends upon the use of our Time, and its by-product, the odd moment."*

\* \* \*

DURING the last few years, there has been a definite trend towards making people equal—a movement towards equality—which is considered by so many people as being the ideal state of existence. But such an ideal is a useless dream, for by the very nature of humanity and individual make-up, absolute equality would never last more than a day, if even as long as that.

Yet in certain things we are all equal. The most important, vital and necessary possession we all have is time! We cannot buy time. We cannot make it or save the wasted or unwanted moments for another day. Every individual, be he high or low, at the head of State affairs or but a sweeper of the streets, has exactly the same amount of time at his disposal—twenty-four hours to the day, sixty minutes to the hour.

But there it ends—the individual, with his varying abilities and interests, decides what he shall do with that twenty-four hours, and by their use he becomes richer or poorer. Did I say richer? Yes, but that does not necessarily imply financial riches, although later it may lead to them. It means spiritual or mental riches, the acquiring of knowledge, an improved skill, an enriching experience; it implies the fullest use of every minute as against their wanton waste, for never, having failed to use them to-day, can we use them instead to-morrow —they are gone for good.

## Harvest of Haste

This desire to utilise time to its utmost limit has, during the past fifty years, become an obsession in civilised countries—an obsession that has become almost a fetish. Nations and individuals have become possessed with a feverish desire to save every second, chiefly in order to cram some other experience into an already overcrowded existence. Like all actions, all possessions, this craze for speed will bear, and has borne, a harvest—and all the harvest is not good. We have but to read the daily papers to realise a little, but only a very little, this dreadful harvest of haste. Accidents on the roads are a shame and disgrace to any civilised community. We are far from being sufficiently

267

conscious of this dreadful toll, or we should, as individuals, work towards lessening these accidents.

An old man is knocked down and killed—a young couple, involved in a motor crash, die on the threshold of their married life—a father is killed on his way to work—a child lies dead in the road. But it does not end there—the suffering, the loss, the sorrow remain with those who are left behind.

Then there is the more individual cost of haste—the child, eager to get home from school, to play his favourite game, inculcated with the modern urge to save a few moments—and those few moments hurl him into eternity and his parents into the depths of sorrow.

The workman, his day's work done, hurries home to feed his pigeons or his dogs, to attend to his garden or build a shed—home to his wife and family. Yes, he must hurry, for he hasn't much time; he can save twenty minutes if he catches that early bus. And another sacrifice is made to the god of speed—the family is left without the father, the hobby without the worker.

The person in haste to catch bus or train, or whether on foot or in a car, is gambling with eternity—life against a few moments' saving of time.

### Hurry! Hurry! Hurry!

Less obvious, yet far more insidious, is the harvest of "nerves" resulting from this urge for haste. Hurry, hurry, hurry! ! Life is one mad, ceaseless whirl of activity. From the moment one wakes in the morning till sleep comes to silence it at night, a little demon in the mind whispers these words: "Hurry, hurry, hurry!" No respite—hurry and get up, throw on your clothes, gulp down a hasty breakfast, never mind your health or your digestion. Hurry to work—risk your neck as you cross the road; raise your blood-pressure, strain your heart as you run to catch the train—hurry! Hurry through the hustle and bustle of the city streets, with their ceaseless roar of passing traffic.

The day's work starts—hurry, hurry—all the day long. Work to a clock, machines driven at dizzy speed to push up production, the feverish activity for bigger turnover and increased sales.

You rush out to swallow a quickly served lunch, often made up of indigestible food, and race back to join the swift pace of the afternoon work. Then another rush home by crowded train or bus. No time to spare. Save those few moments! What for? A dance, a dinner, a visit to the cinema or to the "local", or just a hobby at home. But whatever it is, we must hurry. Even the housewife hurries about her work—she must get in an extra job before they all come trooping in for an evening meal. Perhaps the tempo slackens a bit with the coming of evening. But those who venture out for their leisure are still often driven by the demon of haste, and hurry they must, so that accidents continue and the strain on the nerves goes on until sleep calls a halt.

This habit of rushing and hurrying gradually wears out the human machine. Youth with its resilience often shows no sign, *but it is there and will take its toll later on in life.* Men and women rush about their work and their leisure with all too often insufficient time for food, rest, quiet or adequate sleep. The art of relaxation is almost forgotten, so that books have to be written to tell people all about it, its place and value, and how to practise it. Relaxation disappeared with the Second World War—we were all keyed up and we've stayed that way; the younger generation has inherited the atmosphere. We are living at much too rapid a tempo. We have lost our sense of poise and tranquillity.

## Modern Day Tension

Tension is one of the greatest troubles of our time. And tension is just as catching as calmness and harmony, it will spread as the circles spread outward when a stone is dropped into a pond. And what do they gain for us, these few extra moments? Yes, a little more done maybe, but do we ever weigh the gain against the loss?—the strain on the heart, disordered nerves and the human machine's resistance lowered?

Business men collapse—why? That is the price they pay for the grinding strain and the rush and bustle of competitive effort. Others suffer from nervous exhaustion or various physical ills—victims of an over-speeded mode of living.

We give a car an overhaul—a rest, a refuelling, but the finer, more complex machine of the human mind and body, when does it get so much consideration? We take our minds and bodies too much for granted, and expect them not only to work for us for ever, but to submit to abuse and neglect without rebellion.

This is where Nature steps in. Just as a car breaks down under stress of perpetual wear and neglect, so in time will the human mind and body rebel against the perpetual demands made upon them. Nature cries halt; something refuses to work harmoniously and the individual, at last, is compelled to rest and repair the much-abused machine. Lucky is he who heeds Nature's warning and, by complete relaxation, rest and treatment, helps the human machine again to function properly. Fortunate is he who learns the lesson during the days of illness and convalescence, learns to respect the mind and body that have worked so hard for him, learns to treat them in future with care and consideration, not pushing them to their maximum speed. A wise man should learn through accident and ill health the high cost of haste, not only from his own experience, but from those around him whose health has been permanently impaired or whose life has in some cases been cut needlessly short.

## Leisure and Relaxation

Much stress is laid to-day on the need of holidays. Yet very often the average holiday does more harm than good. There are many people who return to their work almost worn out by two weeks of over-tensed, hectic pursuit of pleasure during the holiday period. It may well be asked—do people understand the purpose and use of holidays? Although life to-day is one of rush and bustle, individuals should learn to slow down in leisure hours and during holidays.

Surely the main purpose of shorter working hours, more leisure, annual holidays should mean a relaxation of mind and body, a temporary retreat from the stress and strain of ordinary life, a rest, a pause in the perpetual hurly-burly of modern living, a halt to recharge the human batteries, a break to get "second wind"?

Slowing down and relaxing do not mean going to the other extreme of wasting time. There is a certain type of individual who talks glibly of "killing time". A happy, successful person has no time to kill, for his days are always too full of something useful to do. Relaxing does not mean doing nothing; holidays and leisure time are not meant for rushing about or for wasting one's time, but for leisurely doing those things which interest and give us pleasure, and for which we have little or no time during the normal working day.

Slowing down does not imply wasting time, but the organised and wise use of a twenty-four-hour day, filling in, without rush, fuss or worry the odd half-hour, the ten minutes before or after breakfast, the twenty minutes we may have to wait for a client, an appointment or a train; then we may read or figure or think or observe instead of fuming or fretting.

## Value of Meditation

To-day's idea of the wise use of time needs to be revised. Meditating, observing, thinking is not wasting time. In the rush of practical affairs, enervating pleasures, of doing things and going places, most of us have lost the ability to stay still, to think or truly observe and absorb what is going on around us. We are children of a machine and speed-ridden age with minds and souls atrophied by our dependence on machinery. We drive ourselves in top gear from morning till night.

Meditation has become a lost art. Yet meditation is to the soul what food and rest are to the body. The storage battery of the soul is recharged, during meditation, with cosmic energy. When, in meditation, the soul of man communes with the Infinite, some of this divine energy, which is God, is being absorbed. Thus, man can come forth charged with godlike power to function victoriously in the world of human activities.

We can learn much from the older philosophies and religions in which meditation played a large part, and still does, for those who still give religion an important place in their lives.

Jesus felt only too well the urgent need to withdraw from the rush of his busy life of preaching and healing. He frequently withdrew from the noisy world, in order that he might meditate and commune with the Source of all the wisdom and power, the Source of all life and all being.

The Christian Churches, both Anglican and Roman, encourage periods of meditation. The Quaker religion is largely based on silent meditation, seeking wisdom and knowledge from the greatest Source of all wisdom and knowledge. Even the non-Christian religions place great importance on meditation.

### Spiritual Nourishment

We should ask ourselves—is this almost insane urge for greater and greater speed resulting in spiritual under-nourishment? Let us by all means have speed if it will lead us to greater knowledge of the wonders of the Universe, *but* let us not become *slaves to speed*, making needless sacrifices of human lives on its altar. Let us rather cultivate the mental and spiritual gifts in any spare time, in order that we may fully benefit by the advantages of speed.

We spend time and money on achieving greater speed, on striving to penetrate outer space and solve the secrets of the Universe, but in the end we must come back to the individual. And the individual, in order to survive in sanity, to grow in knowledge, to develop spiritually and mentally, needs to cultivate the art of meditation.

The human race seeks to unlock the door of the Universe, yet we tend to-day to neglect the key which lies at our hand. The Universe is the abode of God—yet in searching for knowledge we ignore the very means placed at our disposal—meditation, which will unlock the doors to a knowledge of the Universe, which is God. There can be direct communication between ourselves and God, but these lines of communication are too often blocked by the rush and roar and the distracting noises of a speed-ridden world. Meditation alone can clear the line and enable us to communicate with the Source of all wisdom and knowledge, and help us to find spiritual tranquillity, inner calm and mental peace.

# ARE WE WISHFUL THINKERS?

*A discussion about facing facts—boldly and honestly*

\* \* \*

HOW many of us, who may be physically courageous, are afraid of facts? How many of us have the courage to ask ourselves this question and answer it truthfully? If we are sufficiently courageous, each one of us will probably answer, "Yes, I *am* afraid of facts, just as a child is afraid of the dark."

Why are we afraid of facts? It is because there is something in our consciousness which is cowardly. It constantly pushes out of our minds, and keeps out of our minds, numerous things which we do not like to think about, because for various reasons they are unpleasant.

Psychologists have called this cowardly mental mechanism "repression", which is especially connected with sexuality. But there is not only a mechanism of repression in sex, but in all the disturbing and embarrassing facts of life.

However strange it may seem, it has been found that it is usually the men and women who are most courageous in facing physical dangers, who are most cowardly in facing facts.

For instance, there is the case of the man who, during the war, was decorated for bravery in battle. But if someone began a discussion about lax morals, the number of illicit love-affairs, infidelity and divorce, he became very much ill at ease and would blush profusely.

## Facts are Realities

It seems that the cowardice which troubles most of us is not the fear of things. Physical danger comes to us only on rare occasions, and then it usually comes unexpectedly and too quickly for us to fear. Even death most of the time seems too far off for us to fear it. Physical cowardice appears to be limited to those periods when we face a crisis in the objective world which impinges upon us with a menace extraordinary and unprecedented.

Yet the fear of facts is not conditioned by any such unusual collocation of things in the outer world. A fact is not a thing, an object. We would not call either a man or a tree a fact; we would call a fact the association of man and tree, inasmuch as at one time, in his early development centuries ago, Man did climb trees like an ape. Facts are realities, and yet, strangely enough, we fear them. How can we fear immaterial entities? It is becuse we can be hurt not

272

only by enemies who do violence to our bodies, but also by facts which come into conflict with our prejudices and so cause us emotional pain and distress.

In other words, we fear that which is unpleasant to think about, whatever the reason may be that causes the unpleasantness to arise. The unpleasantness of thinking of certain things is as much of a nervous shock as any painful physical impact on our bodies. Indeed, with certain types of people it is even more so.

For instance, to those who believe in evolution, the proposition that primitive Man was a gorilla-like being, more beast than man, and once climbed trees like an ape, is an accepted fact. But to many people it is highly unpleasant. There is something in the conception which outrages their sense of personal dignity.

It would seem that the reason these people become all seethed up about the teaching of evolution is not that they are convinced it is untrue, but that they fear it might be true. It is because they are actually afraid of being convinced of its truth that they close their minds to anything concerning evolution, refuse to face facts which are at variance with their own theories, and very often denounce and attack it. They are afraid of evolution as a fact, even though as a fact it is something quite immaterial.

### Egotistical Desire

There is nothing which is so harmful to an individual as regards his character and personal advantage, as a blind subservience to certain conventional or repressive dictated standards which brings about a fear of facts. Yet practical and applied psychology has not given this matter the amount of attention it surely deserves. A great deal has been said against cowardice, but it has been assumed that cowardice is only fear of the objective.

Now the fear of facts has no biological purpose because, as we have already discussed, facts do not harm us in any physical sense at all. So it would seem that the fear of facts arises only out of our egotistical desire to think only of the pleasant, to have a mental view of the Universe which coincides entirely with our infantile desires.

Apart from serving no biological utility, the fear of facts can do us practical harm. For facts are what we *must* know if we are to live and to adapt ourselves. When we refuse to face facts, it certainly does not safeguard us from coming up against them—often to our detriment.

Let us now deal with the actual facts of which people are afraid. And among "people" we must also include ourselves. Practically all of us in one way or another are afraid of facts—"Thus conscience does make cowards of us all."

We could no doubt, by following this theme of the fear of facts, make a good diagnosis of the majority of the spiritual ills of society.

But the theme in its entirety is too wide and varied for us to deal with in the space available. So we must content ourselves with a quick survey of some of the principal forms of this fear of facts.

We have already discussed the fear of evolutional facts which many people consider are injurious to their "dignity". There are certain scientific facts which lower Man not from any inherent dignity, but from a false dignity which is claimed for him by those who would be little lower than the angels.

In this connection we must consider not only the scientific discoveries about Man's relation to the anthropoid ape, but the old scientific theory of the Universe. This is a theory which has displaced Man from the central and titanic role which is given him in the pietistic account of the history of life. These scientific discoveries reveal not only that Man was not first upon this planet, but that the planet itself is an insignificant point in the immense plurality of orbs which we envisage in the innumerable stars.

The facts of physical science not only rob us of a romantic dignity, but they also push us into insignificance. And because these facts do reveal these things, they hurt. They hurt so much that we greatly fear them.

### Scientific Investigation

It may seem to some people that the struggle to look scientific facts in the face ended years ago, after being waged under the banner of Huxley and Darwin. In those days the evidence of science was ridiculed, reviled, denounced and bitterly attacked. Since that time, however, many cherished convictions have vanished under the searchlight of scientific investigation. It may be true that for the majority of civilised people scientific facts no longer have such an alarming aspect and that much of the evidence of science is now accepted. Nevertheless, there is still a great deal of pervasive ignorance in regard to the matter. Why is this? The reason why ignorance can persist in the face of such a diffusion of scientific knowledge is that there is something more than simple ignorance with which to contend. It is the dynamic emotion of fear, which actively fights against being educated because education will destroy the sense of cosmic security.

People fear not only the truth about their physical past; they fear also the truth about their mental past. They look upon and fear as a personal assault such truths about their sentimentalised childhood as are imparted by Freud in the mental sphere. The teachings, such as those about the sexual urges of childhood and the affective basis of our consciousness, had to contend against, and still have to contend against, a veritable storm of prudish denial.

The same fear of facts crops up in regard to the psycho-analysis of our contemporary sexuality. It is not so very long ago since there was a conspiracy of silence about sex; social proprieties enshrouded the whole subject in the taboo of silence. Trivialities were freely discussed, and matters of no concern filled innumerable volumes, *but the subject more essential to racial health and happiness than any other was avoided as one might avoid coming in contact with smallpox.*

## Personal Analysis

To-day, the imputation that sexuality is the *leitmotiv* of our conscious and unconscious processes in adult life arouses even more hostility than the discovery of the sexuality of childhood. We are afraid to have the mirror held up to our sexuality because of a sense of shame and false modesty, and because we have imagined ourselves pleasurably to be something we are not.

It is, however, in the specific cases of personal analysis that the fear of facts connected with sexuality comes to the forefront. Psycho-analysis reveals that innumerable experiences with unpleasant or unhappy associations are repressed, pushed out of consciousness, because as facts they are distasteful or painful to contemplate. There is fear of the facts of childhood and fear of the facts of the present.

In order to escape the painful consciousness of some fact a whole neurosis of *evasion* will be built up, which puts one type of fact in place of another to distract the attention. Or a flight from reality to a world of fantasy—anything so as not to hear the insistent knock of some unpleasant fact at the threshold of consciousness—even the mental deafness of amnesia.

It is not only the psycho-analysts who point out facts about us which we are afraid to know. The psychologists of literature—the realists—turn their keen microscopes on numerous little bacteria of the soul, fungi of egotism, of malice, of pettiness.

While the real purpose of these authors perhaps is to create, through satire, a greater integrity, many reviewers of their works pounce upon them as though they had invented human sins rather than observed them.

## Bold and Honest Facts

It is probably in war-time that the fear of facts best demonstrates itself in the autocracy and officiousness of national authorities. It is then that we get a censorship which suppresses ruthlessly any uncon-forming facts which cast any doubt upon the absolute rightness of the nation's purpose and method in the clash of arms.

The fear of facts is dominant as long as war lasts, but once it is over it relaxes its dictatorship. Historians who proceed to search into the true complexities of the entrance into war, arouse an anxiety which can best be described as an expression of a bad or guilty conscience.

It is almost unbelievable to realise that all the titanic expenditure of national strength, accompanied by untold misery and sacrifice, should now be attacked in regard to the purpose of the war and on the grounds that it appears to have been all futile.

To-day, once again, the international scene is seething with unrest, with nation at the throat of nation, with fear, hatred, prejudice and intolerance rampant, with truth pilloried and propaganda used as a terrible weapon in a horrible war of nerves.

Nations shy from facing real facts and make biased and almost hysterical statements in support and defence of their different ideologies, over which such bitter conflict now rages.

There seems to be a powerful resistance to the publication of facts which indicate that nations are heading for economic ruin in the race to build up armaments.

Facts reveal that nuclear warfare means the end of civilisation. Isn't it time that these facts were faced boldly and honestly—now before it is too late? Isn't it time that there was a general awakening to the fact that the secret of atomic power was not revealed to Man for the purpose of destroying the earth, but for the purpose of building upon earth a new order of undreamed-of blessings for the good of all humanity?

# MEN, WOMEN AND NATURE

THE last fifty years have witnessed revolutionary changes in the habits and behaviour of men and women. The relationship between the sexes has altered even more. Many factors have led to the present status of each sex, but in this article we shall examine the changes themselves and their impact upon society.

Owing to lack of hygiene and to strictly limited medical and scientific knowledge, human society was based upon the survival of the fittest. Infantile mortality was very high, for the weaklings died off early, and only those of sound constitution remained to do the world's work and to reproduce themselves. So, a tough race was bred by Mother Nature.

This was particularly evident among the male population. We have only to imagine those rugged seamen of the sailing era; the early explorers; the pioneers; the buccaneers; the weather-beaten, horny-handed farming and peasant community. As a modern quip reminds us, those were the days "when men were men and women were glad of it!" We may chuckle at this, but it can be a sound psychological truth!

In the old days this was indeed a "man's world". Men asserted their superiority over the female sex. Men were the acknowledged leaders, providers and protectors. Theirs was the voice of authority. Women accepted a dependent and inferior role, and it must be admitted that most of them had a very rough deal, in many respects.

Education, as we know it to-day, was not considered very important for girls. Those who worked at all were domestic servants, nursemaids and the like. Their training was directed towards their natural destiny in marriage, housekeeping and motherhood. There was practically no opportunity for freedom of expression, and certainly no hope or intention of competing with men in business or professional life. The daughters of well-to-do families were not expected or even *permitted* to earn their own living. No self-respecting young lady would dream of doing *that*!

At home, the girls of "yesterday" remained under the strict supervision and control of their parents, guardians or chaperons. Ideas of sex equality and sex freedom had not even dawned. Indiscriminate love affairs were comparatively unknown. Divorces were rare and frowned upon.

"Father knows best" was the family motto, with the eldest son second in command. Wives and daughters were hardly given credit for possessing any *intelligence*—still less any authority.

To-day the pendulum *for both sexes* has swung to the other extreme.

For example, our grandfathers and even the fathers of many of us, often had to rise at the crack of dawn and perhaps walk miles to their daily toil. They worked for more hours each day than is now necessary, and the work was much harder, with less mechanisation. By the time those young men had walked back home and had their evening meal, they were ready for bed. Even at week-ends there was little time for recreation and little spare cash for what entertainment existed. The physical energy of our fathers and grandfathers in their youth was used to the full in the process of earning a living. They had no time, desire or surplus energy left to roam the streets in gangs, getting up to mischief.

### Remarkable Contrast

The contrast to-day is remarkable. A large proportion of modern youths earn big money. They travel to work by train, bus or on motor-cycles. Their work is far less arduous than it was in the old days. They have plenty of leisure, plenty of surplus energy to use up and ample spending money.

Modern girls are in a similar position, and the emancipation of women has transported them into a totally different world to that of their mothers and grandmothers. There is even more difference between the young woman of to-day and her counterpart of previous generations, than there is between the modern young man and his predecessors of years ago.

Women to-day compete with men on almost equal terms. Boys and girls are often educated in "co-ed" schools. The sexes are in very close contact. Women are entering almost every business and profession that exists, and they are conscious of their ever-growing freedom and social equality. Sexual equality and freedom is now the generally accepted state of affairs. The age of chaperons is in the dim and almost forgotten past. Young couples to-day frequently spend their holidays together even before they become engaged to marry. The ambition of many eligible young spinsters is to have their own bachelor-girl flat where they can entertain friends of both sexes—especially their male admirers. In fact, nowadays, any handsome young man is as likely to be seduced as a pretty girl. In the relationship of the sexes, the pendulum has swung with a vengeance, and with a mighty crash to the other extreme.

This modern phenomenon is evident even in dress, fashion and mannerisms. Girls are wearing slacks and sweaters and short hair styles, while young men sport fancy waistcoats, gaudy shirts, suède shoes and individual hair styles. Most young wives go out to work, women have their own clubs and organisations, and sometimes the whole world seems to be turned upside down.

Is there any connecting link between the remarkably changed status of the sexes and the apparent revolt of modern youth? We believe there may be.

So much has been said about modern youth that we are heartily sick of the subject. Yet to-day's youth must be given their place in the picture of modern sex relationship and its impact upon our lives.

### Are the Signs Symbolic?

A refreshing light has been thrown upon the teenage problem by Dr. John Burton, of the World Health Organisation. Having taken many other factors into consideration, Dr. Burton regards the violent tendencies of some Teddy boys, for example, as *an assertion of their masculinity*, which may be an early sign of a new biological situation.

The fact is that the lower infantile mortality rate in progressive countries is changing the sex ratio among youth. In the future it is estimated that there will be considerably more men in the world than there are women. Although men are increasing in number, however, they are fast losing a great deal of authority. Women are encroaching upon what used to be solely a "man's world", and men now find fewer opportunities of *expressing their manhood* adequately. Less still can men prove and maintain the superiority over women they have hitherto claimed.

Now this is a most interesting and maybe somewhat disturbing situation. It represents an increasingly difficult psychological problem for both sexes, which probably is already being sensed by our young people, even if they don't understand what is happening to their world.

Thanks to the advance of medical science and vastly more healthy and comfortable living conditions, the old law of the survival of the fittest no longer applies to the same extent that it did. Even the weaklings of this modern age have a much greater chance of survival. They also share almost unlimited freedom to express their individualities.

There are many young people nowadays who seem to have more surplus energy than they know what to do with. Some of them have little inclination to expend their abundant energy in sports, games, walking, climbing, and other outdoor activities. They prefer to spend their leisure hours in milk bars, cinemas, clubs, pubs and cafés. Is it any wonder they turn to mischief? Some of these young people also possess excessive, undisciplined emotional energy. The boys often appear to expend it in gang fights, petty crime, police-baiting and sexual adventures; the girls seem to find emotional outlets by shrieking and squealing at their favourite "pop-singer", or by defying conventions and seeking more promiscuous sexual excitement.

*These, boys and girls alike, are inexperienced young people who are*

L.C.—19

*trying to grow up in their own way, in a precarious environment.* They may have accepted wise guidance from their parents, had they received it early enough. But by the time they are teenagers they resent any good advice from their elders.

Fortunately, the majority of young people are more reasonable and level-headed, and the violent type of Teddy boy is still only a minor blot on our social landscape. We must deplore and condemn his acts of violence, brutality and stupidity, but is this another sign of the times? For all we know to the contrary, the "rough-stuff" Teddy boy may be symbolic of Man's fight against encroaching feminine domination. They may be trying to show us—in a pathetically twisted way—that *there are still a few he-men around*, and that they are not going to become as soft as so many of their contemporaries. For however much we may try to wriggle out of it, our boys seem to be growing softer as our girls are becoming more precocious and daring. If the pendulum swings too far back it is possible that we may find ourselves living in a woman's world.

Perhaps Dr. Burton can see this situation looming ahead, for he says: "It is not impossible, therefore, that we will witness outbreaks of seemingly purposeless male exhibitionism and aggressiveness on an increasing scale."

If this modern tendency of feminine domination is to be halted, then men must behave and *act* like men.

### Lingering Doubts

For many years Man seems to have been surrendering his former authority and leadership to Woman, and she has, perhaps reluctantly, taken advantage of his weakness and seized the reins of control to some extent. Most men believe this to be wrong and unnatural. Many women—even those who would not readily admit it—have lingering doubts about the wisdom of usurping the male prerogative of leadership. Women are *not* happy in a dominating role, but what are they to do when so many men no longer behave like men?

No fair-minded person can begrudge Woman her present freedom, security and social prestige, but feminine domination isn't good for any of us. There are mothers whose possessive domination robs their sons of much manly initiative, enterprise and self-confidence. Such boys, when they marry, are ripe for continued domination by their wives, if they are that way inclined. Even if these wives never intended to become "the voice of authority", they are often forced into it by their spineless husbands.

No matter what "equality" women may claim, how can they have any love or respect for the man who meekly submits to their domination? Why is it that many men fail to realise this simple fact of feminine psychology?

*Why* do some women attempt to boss their husbands about, often against their own better nature *and true desire*? It may be a sheer feminine trait, but aren't there deeper reasons than this? Couldn't some of these reasons be, that a wife wants to feel *secure* in her husband's love and protection; that she wants him to be a *man* in the real sense of the word? But if she suspects he is a weakling, isn't she likely to get a bit scared and want to *test out* his manhood? And maybe she does this by attempting to dominate him. Yet in her heart, she probably hopes that he will rise to the challenge and *prove* to her that he is a *man* and not a mouse. If she is disappointed too often, isn't it then that trouble may begin and the marriage is apt to deteriorate rapidly?

In modern marriage, women expect to be treated as intelligent equals in the partnership. Most of them *deserve* to be regarded by their husbands with respect and due consideration. But the woman who persistently tries to dominate her man, does so, not only to her own detriment but also to the detriment of other members of the family.

### Intelligent and Mature Co-operation

Modern girls mature early. They leave school at a later age than their mothers did, and the modern way of life brings them into earlier and closer contact with the opposite sex. A headmistress was recently lamenting the fact that girls are marrying so early in life, many of them step almost straight from school into wedlock. There are some girls of eighteen who imagine they are "on the shelf" if they have not yet started courting.

Girls of that age are often attracted to much older and experienced men. Why? Is it because they want *men*—not pampered mother's darlings or swaggering bullies?

The violent type of Teddy boys maybe are trying to be men, but they are on the wrong track. Many of them have not been properly trained for manhood. Some of the "mother's darlings" *want* to be men, but their potential manhood has very often been seriously undermined by their doting mothers.

Women have fought a long and tough battle for sex equality. This emancipation of women can be a distinct personal and social gain provided that it does not degenerate into the misuse of their emancipation.

It is ironic that, although there is a natural attraction between the sexes, there is also a certain antipathy. Under various guises, this battle of the sexes is a continuous operation, usually hidden beneath the surface of conventional politeness and outward respect.

There is no point in either sex claiming superiority, or even equality in all things. Men and women each have their own natural part to fill; their roles are complementary. The destiny of Man is to lead, to take the initiative, to decide, to provide and protect. The complementary functions of Woman, apart from motherhood, are to comfort, sympathise, respect, co-operate. She has to be—or try to be—a wife, mother, sister and daughter in her relationship with her husband. Her best qualities are in her affections.

This ideal in which men are men and women are women, each playing their own respective parts in everyday living, can only be brought about by intelligent and mature co-operation between both sexes. And the realisation of such an ideal is the only way to the most natural and satisfying way of life.

# THE ART OF DECISION

*Never before have there been so many wonderful opportunities*
*for men and women of decision.*

\* \* \*

HOW many people find it extremely difficult to make a decision?
Nothing appears to be harder for them than to give a straight
"yes" or "no". Are there ways and means that will help us in making
decisions? Let us probe into the matter and see.

Animals and plants are controlled by Nature. But Man can
control himself as far as making decisions is concerned. He is the
decider. And he knows instinctively that he should make his own
decisions, carry them out in his own way, and not obey and follow
the directions of others.

Yet there are so many people who either cannot or will not make
decisions for themselves. They drift along with the crowd. They
allow themselves to be led or pushed. They are guided by herd
instincts and let others make decisions for them. Those who become
"herd men and women" rarely reach any worth-while decisions;
they merely drift along a dead-end road—a road that leads to *nowhere*.

The men and women who do big things, who succeed and make the
best use of their lives are those who do their own deciding, who break
loose from the rank and file—those who often decide to do something
that has not been done before.

Suppose we now try to analyse this matter of making our own
decisions. How can we make them promptly, independently, vigorously
and confidently in such a way that we do not have to decide all over
again—differently? Can we make our decisions produce good results
for ourselves and for others?

## Dare to Decide

The first step in decision-making is self-reliance—to be determined
that we are going to make our own decisions, place our trust in them
and *act* on them. We must acquire *freedom* in making decisions.

After this freedom, the most important factors in our lives are
their principles and purposes. What are we living for? What do we
believe in? What are our ambitions? Have we set a goal?

If we have no definite aims, if we are not trying to reach a definite
goal, to achieve a specific thing, then we shall make a queer series of
inconsistent and fruitless decisions.

When we are confronted with a problem we should ask ourselves: "Which decision will bring us nearer to our goal?"

When making important decisions we should review these main principles and purposes of life and try to analyse them. Are they the same as they used to be? Or have they changed? Are they as sound as they were previously? Are we as certain as we used to be that the direction in which we are going and the things we are doing are taking us just where we want to go? It is important that we answer these questions in arriving at our decisions. We should have a clear understanding with ourselves concerning these deep principles and vital purposes of our lives.

We should take into consideration our inclinations, our preferences. The free men and women will, of course, do as they like, other things being equal. And they are quite right to do so, provided what they like does not interfere with the welfare of others and does not detract from their own best and deepest purposes.

Life is so difficult to-day and human beings are such complex entities, that it is often difficult to be sure just what we desire most. Perhaps a few tests, therefore, will help us to solve this section of the decision problem.

Suppose we check what we want to do now with what we know we shall wish we had done some time later on? It is not very wise to do something now because we happen to wish strongly to do it, when we know we shall regret the choice to-morrow. Here again, the recognition of the principles and purposes will help.

We should acknowledge frankly that here is something we would like to do now. Then we should analyse it by asking ourselves if it will really push us forward towards our goal, or whether it will hinder or turn us away from it.

There is another check we can make, and that is whether the wish arises from our better or worse selves, from our deeper or shallower selves. This matter, however, is too intricate and far reaching for us to dwell upon at great length during this Chat. Most of us know, more so since psycho-analysis revealed it to us, so much about the often mysterious behaviour of the Subconscious Self, that men and women often find themselves with desires and emotions which do not seem to fit into the general plan and pattern of their lives. There are many lives that lack unity. How we may discover which are our real selves and what are our superficial or artificial selves has been dealt with in previous Chats.

What we are concerned with in this discussion is to learn how to make the proper decision after we have found out all about these two selves and the general direction of our life purpose. We also want to discover whether the carrying out of the considered wish will hinder or harm other people. Keeping these guides in mind, we can go ahead and do as we like or, at least, as we believe we really want to act. Is it in accordance with our main purpose? Is it our better or worse self that wants it? Will it be detrimental to other people's welfare? After we have answered these questions satisfactorily then we should go ahead.

## Desire for Self-expression

The desire for self-expression is a simple *human* demand that should not be denied. This persistent urge to do as an individual pleases is one of Nature's noblest demands. Life is full of tragedies because men and women have denied themselves or been forbidden by others the delight and right of self-expression.

There are, of course, some people who think they were born to do some artistic or creative work, or fill a job that calls for outstanding merit but for which they have not the necessary capabilities. But even such yearnings should be taken seriously. They should be tried out. After all, the majority of eminent people are very much like the rest of us.

We can, at least, become great in the art of making helpful and sensible decisions. We can try out the things of our choice. Even if we fail, we can take up the duller routines and make artistic work of them.

So very often the discontent that men and women feel about their daily work means that there is some other more congenial job they could do and ought to do—tasks that would satisfy this urge for self-expression.

If we are not happy at work or at home, we should not unduly blame ourselves or be filled with self-pity. Rather should we face the problem realistically and calmly. Then let us make a decision about it. Tests can always be applied that will make reasonably clear the wisest course to follow.

So far we have discussed matters that concern the individual himself. But every decision is composed of two sets of factors, one inside the individual and the other one outside.

When we are called upon to make a decision on some problem, we should make carefully written notes of the relations and values of the courses of actions which are open to us. Then let us study the notes and estimate the value of each of the items involved, first in regard to the inner facts—our principles, desires, purposes and the demand for self-expression—and then the other facts.

Strange as it may seem, the first of these outward facts may look like another inner fact. But this is not so, for it concerns our capabilities. If we have a tenor voice we should not try to sing bass, because our voices are not part of our inner minds but part of the physical machine with which we do our work.

## Stick to Facts

Now let us deal with a problem which is common to many people —that of changing one's job. Should a person leave his present occupation and connections and try to take up a different type of work? Is this other form of work suitable to the individual concerned and could he do it? Here is a case where the person must be frank with himself and sensible about the matter before making his final decision.

Again, let us take a business proposition. We should consider our resources, the money available, our experience, our interest, time and any assistance which may be available to us. Can the proposition be put into operation? If so, has it a reasonable and sensible chance of success? In all such problems we must stick to the facts, write them down, appraise them. Then let the facts decide.

After we have given every consideration to capabilities and resources, all the circumstances must be taken into account. We should give a great deal of thought to the facts and persons that will be involved in the decision to be made. Like the skilful player of chess, who sees every piece and all the moves that are open to each piece, both those of his opponent and his own, we should try to miss nothing.

If it is a matter of purchasing certain commodities, we should find out what they are actually worth. We should not move into a new town or city without first of all visiting it and finding out everything we can about it. In other words, we should not make decisions with our eyes shut.

# CONSIDER, DECIDE AND ACT!

*(Concluding the previous article on The Art of Decision)*

IN making decisions there is one group of circumstances of such importance that it should be given special consideration. This is in connection with one's personal relations with others. This group may be classified as:

(1) Those who are dependent upon us—our family, etc.; (2) people associated with us at work; (3) our competitors; (4) those whom our work influences or affects.

The next step, sometimes difficult, is to form an estimate, not of *known* facts but of the *probable* ones. We should make a written list of the different courses of action that are open to us and the relation of each course to our principles, purposes and desires.

Then, in connection with each course of action available to us, let us carefully study the whole list again and make notes about the probabilities in each case. All this may seem to be very tedious, but it is far more tedious to undo mistakes or to put up with mistakes that cannot be undone.

Now we should answer fully and frankly the following questions: Will the step we propose to take bring us nearer to the goal to which our principles, purposes and desires point? What will be the probable effects of each course of action on our *entire* work? What will be the probable effects on our dependents, our associates, our competitors and on other people our work affects?

We now come to the analysis of the problem we may be considering. We should:

(*a*) Make a choice from two or more courses open to us in connection with the action we propose to take.

(*b*) Consider the principle involved in the decision, the pros and cons, the greater or lesser value in relation to the principle.

(*c*) Consider the purposes from a similar angle as in (*b*). What purposes are involved? What relation have the courses under consideration to these purposes?

(*d*) Next deal with all the desires to which the courses of action can be related; desires of the present, of the future, of our better selves for self-expression, of the various individuals who will be affected by our decision.

(*e*) Make a note of all the facts—our resources, capabilities, money, health, influence, circumstances, etc.

(*f*) Consider the probabilities, weighing up for or against the factors in their relation to the items already considered under desires and facts.

The course of action that is the most favourable gets the *decision*.

## Do "Hunches" Count?

Where do "hunches" fit in when making decisions? There are some successful individuals who seem to rely upon some sort of inner, instinctive illumination when making their decisions rather than upon cool reasoning.

There is something deep within every thoughtful person that corresponds to this yearning for a sort of "inspiration". What is this "something" and what should the mature modern-minded person do about it?

Perhaps it may be sufficient to call it a sense of universal *harmony*. Many of us feel that our lives are related not only to a lot of other lives but to a huge infinite scheme of things. But there are others who seem to give the impression of being "out of tune". They seem to lack inward *unity* and so fail to fit into any unifying plan of social and cosmic organisation.

So it would seem that after all we have discussed in regard to making decisions, it would perhaps be as well if we paused and pondered on these high and deep considerations. If we try and see our individual lives as they are related to the infinite mysteries, we may perhaps receive some sort of answering echo or gleam of light that will assure us that the course we have decided on will add to the ultimate values and finest harmonies.

## What about Taking Risks?

Let us now consider risks in connection with decision-making. It must not be taken for granted, from the suggestions we are about to discuss, that it is better always to avoid risks—to remain "safety-first" men and women all our lives. Some people who live daring lives often find life most worth while. Daring decisions sometimes count the most.

Nevertheless, daring decisions should be made with the greatest possible care. There is a difference between daring and recklessness. The reckless individual does not reckon. He plunges into a scheme without thought or preparation. The daring person makes reckoning carefully, considers the details and the risks, weighs up all the pros and cons. He is both cautious and daring; cautious without being afraid and daring without being foolhardy. He is not like the individual who leaps without looking and lands in a bog, nor like the person who looks and never leaps.

We should neither sit still and do nothing nor should we plunge into schemes without thought and preparation, without considering the details and the risks. We must not jump to conclusions. We must separate facts from opinions and carefully analyse the facts. Are the desires and ambitions really worthy ones? Are they in accordance with the best principles and purposes? Is there every possibility that they will bring good to other people? Has all the evidence that has been collected, for and against, been carefully scrutinised? Is what will be gained worth the risk? The two sets of answers to these questions should be weighed on a pair of scales, so to speak, and notice taken of which set is the heavier. In the majority of cases this will enable a decision to be made that will not be regretted, and prevent foolish decisions being made on the spur of the moment. We can never eliminate risk altogether, but we should eliminate it as far as possible.

What do we do about mistakes? There are people who become totally unfit for efficient work because they cannot forget the mistakes of the past. They let these mistakes destroy their faith in themselves. And, what is more important, by holding mental images of past mistakes they are apt to make the same error again.

The sensible thing, of course, to do about a mistake is to forget it. But not before we have learned a lesson from it. We should study and analyse why we made the mistake and learn all we can from it; keep specially in our mind how and why we made the blunder and the results that came from it, so that we do not make that particular mistake again.

### Face the Future Resolutely

We should keep resolutely to the plan of facing the future. Our goal lies ahead, not behind. There is nothing to be gained, and much to be lost, by brooding over past failures and mistakes. If we worry and fret about these past mistakes, and let them dominate the present, our mind will be filled with thoughts that will clog to-day's activities, weaken, obstruct and unsteady us in making to-day's decisions.

Let us try to cultivate the habit of making our decisions promptly. Admittedly, it is better to make the right decision later than a wrong decision earlier; nevertheless the capacity for quick decision is of the utmost importance.

If two persons make equally wise decisions, the one who arrives at the wise decision first will win. There are some types of work where it is absolutely necessary that decisions be made quickly. Hesitation and procrastination can become bad habits and are detrimental to progress.

We should not be afraid to change our minds, but once having made a decision, we should not hesitate or draw back unless the evidence is overwhelming that it is better to do so. It is often better to go ahead with a mistaken choice and connect it up later with the main line of right choices than to turn back.

We should form the habit of action, strong action that seems, in our best judgment to be the right action.

Finally, we must learn to distinguish between what is important and what isn't. For there are many trivial matters of life that are too small to be made the subject of much conscious consideration. Life can become petty if too much attention is given to petty things. We should fix a regular programme and form sane, healthy, efficient, productive habits. Then we can live more or less automatically as far as the petty details of daily living are concerned, leaving our mind and will free for the big problems and the big tasks of life.

# TIME—FRIEND OR FOE?

*"As every thread of gold is valuable, so is every minute of time."*

\*     \*     \*

TIME is extremely important, if only because we have a limited and unpredictable supply of it!

Young people, especially, may be lured into a state of foolish complacency by the thought that they have a "whole lifetime" in front of them, during which they can do all that they wish to do at a leisurely pace. Well, how long is a "lifetime"? It *may* be seventy to eighty years, or even longer. Or it may be only thirty years or even less. We just don't know how much time there is ahead of us. Yet one thing is certain. During the span of our lives, Time treats us all alike. It has no favourites. Twenty-four hours are a day to both king and peasant. No more. No less. And the utilisation of Time is the determining factor upon which the successful life is built.

The utilisation of Time—"managed minutes"—is of vital importance to everyone. It may be difficult to realise that the "wastage" of to-day will be a drag upon to-morrow and that each passing minute is a tool with which to fashion the future. How many men and women who have frittered away Time down through the years look back upon life with sadness and regret, thinking, "If only I had done this," or "If only I hadn't done that, how different things would have been to-day." It is the old story of "what might have been".

When we are young, Time passes slowly but as we grow older, it passes with frightful swiftness. Some of us would, if we could, wander back over the path we have trod and take advantage of the opportunities we missed to do those things we ought to have done. But we cannot turn back the relentless tide of Time. Time Policies cannot be renewed —they are not like Insurance Policies.

### Life's Greatest Asset

Time is one of our greatest assets. It is indeed very precious. Each minute is a golden treasure and the way we spend it moulds our very lives.

We have all heard business men declare that "time is money"— and so it is, in an indirect and strictly material sense. One writer was so conscious of the value of Time that he said we ought to count Time by our own heart beats. This appreciation of the value of Time suggests the purpose of this article—to emphasise the fact that although

291

we may accept the materialist's view that "Time is money", we shall do well to realise that Time is Life itself. *This* is the conception of Time that we should embrace and always hold in our thoughts.

We should have no difficulty in treating Time with a healthy respect. Those of us who are in employment sell not only our labour and skill to our employer, but also our time, and that time represents a substantial part of *our lives*. Our employer himself has to devote a considerable portion of *his* time to his business affairs, or he may soon find himself in trouble.

A reliable and efficient wife spends most of her time in running the house, planning and cooking meals, shopping, mending and performing countless other tasks which her duty demands. If she is also a mother she has to devote a lot more of her time to the needs of her children as well. Indeed, she then has so little, if any, time left for herself alone, that time to her is more precious than gold.

An ex-soldier once remarked to me that a former C.O. of his was what he called "a stickler for time". If that C.O. ordered anything to be done, however trivial, *by a certain time*, it had to be done "on the dot". Otherwise he would create an awful scene about it, no matter if he had merely requested a cup of tea at "15.00 hours" precisely.

The fact that the cup of tea might not arrive at the exact moment he ordered it, could not have been all that important to him, but— as he frequently reminded his men—Time *could* be a matter of life or death. This is true enough, and that C.O. knew that if his men were trained to complete even *unimportant* tasks at the time ordered, they would certainly act "on the dot" when a highly important order was given. In short, he knew he could always *rely* upon them to do their duty without hesitation or question, when *lives* were at stake. Moreover, no doubt, when the men under his command returned to civilian life, the *habit* of punctuality stood them in good stead. Then they were likely to be more efficient in this respect in their daily work. Good time-keeping suggests general efficiency.

### Scheduled Time

A simple example in daily life is offered by the railway time-table. The travelling public expects to be able to rely upon the departure and arrival times of trains as published in the time-table. Otherwise, how can travellers plan their own appointments? Suppose we wish to catch a train scheduled to leave the local railway station at 10 a.m. If we are wise, we are there on the station platform a few minutes before the train is due to leave, and we rightly expect to catch the train. What would we say if we were then informed that the train left at 9.45 a.m.? We should have every reason to complain to railway officials about such lack of consideration.

Fortunately this situation is not at all likely to occur, but *late* trains can and do cause no end of inconvenience to those who use them, or wait for passengers to arrive on them. Most of us are reasonable enough in such matters. We realise that many unexpected and unpredictable circumstances may delay the journey of a train, but when trains are *persistently* late, the public understandably begins to lose its patience. Soon the whole railway service and everybody connected with it comes under adverse criticism. They are labelled "inefficient"—and that label sticks fast for a long time to come, unless the service is quickly and satisfactorily improved. Time must be respected, if only as a mark of efficient service.

## A Wealth of Meaning

Now let us look at Time from another angle. Consider the old adage: "Time will tell." This saying alone conveys a wealth of meaning.

Time will tell *what*? Many things are revealed to us by the passage of Time, not only concerning that indefinite period "from the cradle to the grave", but even before and after that! One or two examples will suffice.

An expectant mother begins to wonder many things about the child she hopes to bring into the world. Will she be able to carry the unborn child for the full term? Will it be born alive and without complications and possible danger to it and herself? Will it be a boy or a girl? Will it be perfectly formed at birth? Will it grow to manhood or womanhood? What will the child's future be in terms of health, happiness and success? *Only time will tell*, and the mother has to wait and see, with whatever patience and faith she can muster.

On numerous occasions throughout life we have to wait for a period of time to elapse, before we can know the effect of some action we took, perhaps years before.

Then, towards the end of our earthly life, when we know there may not be many years ahead of us, we have ample time to sit and think. We shall probably turn over in our mind the eternal question: *Is* "death" the end of our individual, personal, conscious existence? Or does a spiritual body within us release itself from our mortal frame, to live an eternal life in a spiritual Utopia called heaven? We hope to discover the answer to these questions—*in time*.

Coming back to our workaday existence, imagine a business management deciding to change its policy in some respect, or its production methods. Will this change produce the results hoped for and expected? Time alone will reveal the answer.

It has been truly said that Time makes more converts than Reason. Many people don't even bother to reason things out, but even if we permit reason to be our guide, we must admit that the reasoning powers of the human mind are often faulty. Or, rather, we may easily base our reasoning upon a false assumption. We can, however, usually rely upon Time to provide the correct answer to any doubt. More problems are solved by Time than by brains. Many of life's problems are solved by waiting. When at times we may be worried because we don't know what to do, it is often best to wait. Time will often provide the solution.

Time also brings many changes. Opinions, fashions, morals, standards, living conditions—everything, in fact, changes with the passage of Time. Some things improve, some things degenerate, some things merely age, rot and disintegrate. In all cases Time means change, for nothing pertaining to this world remains static. Generally speaking, Time brings maturity, then antiquity, then destruction.

### Human Relationships

Time takes on another important significance when we associate it with personal, human relationships. For example, an employer engages a new man, probably an absolute stranger. He may be a good, conscientious worker, of unimpeachable integrity and capability. Alternatively, he may turn out to be idle, incompetent, or even a downright rascal. Time will test him. In time, the employer develops confidence and trust in the new man, or he is disappointed to discover that he would be far better off without him.

An inspiring fact about Time is that it permits acquaintanceship to ripen into friendship, with all the pleasures, advantages and opportunities to serve, that true friendship provides. Between persons of opposite sex, Time can allow friendship to develop into love, and love into the intimacy of marriage. In such cases Time is the most valuable ally we can have.

Time also hides life's many scars. It is a wonderful healer. The heartbreak that follows a shattered romance; the grief of a bereaved wife, mother, husband or child; the shock of a great injustice; the pain of a physical sickness or injury; the shadow of international misunderstandings, disagreements, threats and hatreds; the horrors of war; the fear of the unknown and of death itself. All these things are healed with the passing of Time.

There is also a right time and a wrong time for many of our activities. A time to work and a time to relax; to speak or to remain silent; to go forward or to hold back; to sow and to reap; to praise or condemn; to fight or submit. If we dare to ignore the existence of these right and wrong times we shall make a shocking mess of our own affairs and shall probably involve others through our stupidity or thoughtlessness.

There are further fascinating and thought-provoking aspects of Time. The meaning of Time has baffled scientists and philosophers.

Time cannot be explained nor can its source be found or its end foretold. Time stretches away into the illimitable. Yet Time must have existed at least as long as Life itself. Time is, and always has been with us. We are chiefly conscious of the present period of Time, but we remember something of the past and we can project our thoughts and dreams into the future. When we sleep, we lose all sense of Time, yet the seconds, minutes and hours by which we attempt to measure Time, are ticking away, relentlessly, shortening the remainder of our earthly lives. When we are bored, lonely or unhappy, Time seems to walk with leaden feet. Yet, when we are particularly happy or busy, Time has wings. It flies away so quickly, we hardly believe that so much Time has flashed past. Truly, grief counts seconds and happiness forgets hours.

Time creeps up on us, silently, remorselessly. We are powerless to halt its progress, even if we would. Yet once a period of time has passed, it has gone for ever. We cannot recapture it to use again. Although Time destroys so much it also creates one thing as it destroys another.

In this modern age many of us have more leisure time than we have ever had in our lives. Yet we never seem to have *enough* time to do all the things we wish to do. There are so many ways of using our leisure time to advantage.

Yet we still hear some people talk about "killing time". These are usually the aimless, unsuccessful individuals. They apparently do not realise that by killing Time they are often really killing their own opportunities in life. The individual who succeeds is the one who makes Time live by making it useful.

## The Pattern of Life

Having discussed all these points concerning Time, let us retrace our steps to draw our own conclusions. We have gathered the following thoughts about Time.

Time is limited *to us*—as our lifetime. We do not know how much of it we shall be able to use, yet it has no beginning and no end. Time is Eternity. We can restrict our *attitude* towards Time, by thinking of it in the strictly narrow and material sense as representing money. Or we can regard Time as our Opportunity—to acquire knowledge, to perform useful service, to reach maturity, to gain a certain amount of wisdom. We can use a lot of Time as we wish. We can make it our friend or our enemy. We can enjoy the present or be miserable in it; we can dream about the past or plan hopefully for the future. We can be punctual or dilatory. We can make good use of our time or waste it.

Due regard for time is a mark of efficiency. The more goods we produce in a given time, the more valuable that time has been to us.

L.C.—20

We have realised that "Time will tell"—it can settle doubts and solve many problems. The passing of Time brings many changes. Time helps to establish friendships or love. Time is also a great healer, yet it can destroy as well as create. It is silent, remorseless, inevitable in its passage.

Whatever we may think about Time, and however we use it, we dare not *ignore* it. It represents invincible power for good or ill—largely depending upon what it means *to us* and how we use it.

Surely we must realise and remember that Time is indeed a very precious thing—Life itself. Unless we respect Time to this extent, it can't be worth much to us. We need leisure, relaxation, rest, as we need mental and physical exercise. But when we merely "kill time" we are, as it were, shortening our own lives.

Time, *wisely* occupied in work and leisure enriches life considerably. If we could imagine an hour-glass or an egg-timer filled with gold dust instead of sand, we should more easily be convinced of this vital fact, as we watched the gold dust trickle away. One thing we should never forget. We can turn an hour-glass up the other way and let the contents trickle back again. But we cannot do that with Life. Every minute is a "thread of gold" helping us to weave the pattern of Life itself.

# RELIABILITY—A WORTHY ASSET

A S we endure the cold, damp gloominess of winter every year, we are cheered by one thought above all else—the Promise of Spring. Fortunately for us, Nature is governed by reliable laws. From past experience we *know* that each winter, however unpleasant it may be, will be followed by the glorious spring. Our faithful old friend, the sun, will climb higher in the heavens, to warm a grateful earth. The naked trees will soon be clothed by fresh, green foliage. Flower bulbs, long hidden in the damp soil, will send up green tips to greet the spring sunshine. All Nature will awaken from its winter sleep, and take on a new and more beautiful life, as it does every year with unfailing regularity.

In the same way if in less spectacular fashion, we can rely upon day following night, and we can regulate our lives accordingly. If we were unable to *rely* upon this pattern set by Nature, life would be absolutely chaotic.

As always, Man can learn a lot from Nature—if only he puts his mind to it, and one lesson we should take to heart is to appreciate the value of *reliability*. It is true that the day-to-day British climate is notoriously erratic, but this is an incidental and comparatively unimportant inconvenience. The course of Nature itself remains constant and reliable in all major respects.

Reliability is one of the finest and most vital attributes any person can possess. It is an additional sign of efficiency which stamps our every thought, action or intention. Without reliability we are as straws in the wind, and everything we touch becomes tainted and practically worthless.

## An All-embracing Necessity

Let us look around for convincing examples. Newspaper reporters are often criticised for snooping into other people's business. Some are accused of sensationalism, ruthlessness and other unpleasant characteristics. Often these criticisms are justified. But there is one basic, unwritten law among news reporters, and that is *never let the Editor down*!

When a good reporter is sent out to get a particular story, rest assured he *gets it*. If necessary, he will not bother about the number of hours he works at a stretch, his personal comforts, or even food or sleep until he has fulfilled his mission, and his story is ready to go to Press. Occasionally we do find an unreliable news reporter, but his journalistic career is cut woefully short. Even his former colleagues will have no sympathy for him, for an *unreliable* reporter is worse than useless—he is a constant source of anxiety, even a menace to his editor, his colleagues, his newspaper, the police and other official bodies, and to the general public. He is liable to let anybody down, possibly with far-reaching consequences, and he lets himself down with an almighty bump. Reliability is the watchword of journalists. It *has* to be, or they are very soon in serious trouble.

Most of us have to rely upon watches and clocks to measure the hours each day. Is there anything more annoying and confusing than an *unreliable* timepiece? If a watch or clock fails to keep correct time and cannot be repaired, we might as well throw it away. It is not difficult to imagine circumstances in which a knowledge of the correct time could be a matter of life or death.

Now let us consider professions such as surgery and medicine. What would happen to an unfortunate patient in the hands of an *unreliable* surgeon, anaesthetist or physician? Suppose an unreliable chemist put a lethal dose of poison in our medicine? Even an unreliable nurse could place a patient in grave danger, to say the least.

In this mechanised age we have to depend increasingly upon the efficient performance of all kinds of machinery. An aircraft is flying overhead as I write. The safety of the crew and passengers depends upon the reliable functioning of the engine and other mechanical devices, the accuracy of navigation, the sound construction and design of the aircraft, the general efficiency of the crew, accurate information and advice from ground control, and probably upon other factors not mentioned. A typical example of reliable teamwork. One blunder could easily jeopardise the safety of all concerned.

The same high standard of reliability is necessary for safe travel by sea, rail or road.

In factories and workshops throughout the world, millions of workers are using machines of all descriptions. Unless those countless machines are reliable, they can cause serious faults and delays in production. They might even endanger the limbs or lives of the men and women in charge of them. Here again, reliability is essential.

We must also remember that all these mechanical devices have to be invented, built and tested. This demands reliable information and deduction; reliable scientists, engineers, and mechanics as well as reliable operators. In fact, no matter where we search in industry, business or professional life, reliability is indispensable to efficiency and progress.

### Dependable Human Relationships

So far we have touched upon the importance of reliability among professional men, craftsmen and machines, referring chiefly to instances where unreliability can cause serious accidents or other forms of disaster. Many of us may not be engaged in such responsible work. This may tempt us to minimise the importance of reliability in our particular field of activity. We may think reliability is essential in selected cases, such as those mentioned, but is it so important for the rest of us? The answer is "Yes." Reliability is very important in all human relationships, especially in unexpected circumstances.

For example, representatives of the Law, whose duty it is to apprehend criminals and to protect decent society, depend upon accurate information and witnesses to help them draw criminals into their net. But they must be *reliable* witnesses, otherwise they are more hindrance than help. It is no use any so-called witnesses imagining they saw what they did not. It is no use a "witness" describing what he "saw", when and where, and then changing his story because he is in doubt. *Reliable* witnesses are the only ones worth listening to, even during preliminary enquiries. In a Court of Law the unreliable witness is soon "tied up in knots" and rightly discredited.

I once heard a witness in Court declare that he saw a collision between a bus and a private car. During cross-examination he was asked, "Are you quite sure you saw this collision?"

"Most certainly, I did," he replied.

Next question: "Very well, exactly which part of the car struck which part of the bus?"

"It was impossible to see that, from where I was standing."

So the cross-examination proceeded, the witness becoming more and more uncertain in his replies, until in the end he didn't seem sure whether he had seen the collision at all! An unreliable—and therefore worthless witness. It could have been you or I. Just how reliable would *our* testimony be if we were questioned closely by a clever lawyer?

Now let us refer to business relationships. Nobody is in business merely for the benefit of his health. Businesses exist to make profits, and to achieve this they must offer reliable goods and reliable service. Yet, without exaggeration, observation and experience indicate that good, solid reliability in business is fast becoming the exception rather than the rule.

### Criticise Where Necessary

We do not wish to be unduly critical, but where criticism is rightly deserved we should not hesitate to criticise. For it is only by recognising the faults and weaknesses in ourselves and in others that we can hope to eradicate them and bring about an all-round improvement. No one is perfect. We all have faults and weaknesses. We are all *unreliable* at times. But we should avoid being habitually unreliable, and also *refuse to endure* persistent unreliability in others.

In these days, for some odd reason, many of us have grown too soft and timid. We put up with too many glib excuses. We have been let down so many times—by unreliable tradesmen, for example—that we are inclined to accept this off-hand treatment as a matter of course. Why *should* we accept it? By doing so, we are only encouraging this pernicious habit of unreliability in others.

How many times have some tradesmen *promised* to deliver goods at a certain time on a certain day, and then failed to keep that promise? Even if the goods do arrive on the *day* they are promised, they are seldom delivered at the time stated!

Of course, these unreliable tradesmen usually attempt to give a convincing reason (real or imagined) for the delay, but this is poor compensation for the inconvenience and trouble caused to the customer.

There are decorators, builders, chimney-sweeps, taxi-proprietors, dry-cleaners, shoe-repairers, and scores of others whose business it should be to give *prompt and reliable service*. Most of us have been let down by many of these, not once, but many times. There are notable exceptions, such as gas bills, electricity accounts, tax demands, which arrive with monotonous regularity and promptitude. But many of those from whom *we require* a service for which we are ready and willing to pay, too often disappoint us. Why are these people so unreliable—and why should we be expected to put up with this shabby treatment indefinitely?

### Encourage Dependable People

Suppose we all decided from to-day to *insist* on reliable service from all with whom we have dealings? What good would it do? Quite a lot! It would cause a minor revolution—and about time, too. These unreliable people would soon feel the pinch. They would have to smarten themselves up without delay—or else! Even more important, it would give the conscientious, dependable business man, worker or other person the opportunities he so richly deserves.

One keen housewife tried out all the tradespeople in her district in her determination to receive the best values and most reliable service obtainable. One by one the unreliable people were eliminated. They would all be out of business by now if every housewife adopted the same tactics.

Tradesmen are not the only unreliable people by any means, but they provide useful examples. The same technique as used by the housewife can be used in various spheres by every one of us to encourage this attractive human quality—reliability.

So urgent has this need for reliable service become, that those who place this attribute at the top of their list of business and personal assets to-day, will go far in promoting their own success and self-development.

*Psychology's* own thriving business was built up from almost nothing to its present world-wide status and prestige, only because we have always striven to provide *reliable service* in all respects.

Those of us who are determined to demand reliable service from others must be sure that we build up a reputation for reliability ourselves. We can do this in many ways, in our private and business lives.

The first thing to remember is never to make a promise unless we are reasonably certain of our intention and ability to fulfil it. If by any chance our good intentions appear to be going adrift, the least we can do is to notify others concerned in time for them to make alternative arrangements. This is common courtesy as well as sound business, and it will enhance our good reputation considerably. Too many people make *idle* promises to create a favourable impression at the time, or in their anxiety not to lose an order. Why not be honest and admit it, when for any reason we are unlikely to be able to keep a promise or carry out a responsibility? This is far more sensible than taking on more than we can handle, and then disappointing a customer or a friend.

An acquaintance of mine happened to mention that he was about to lay a concrete floor for a new garage. A neighbour, who was in the building trade, offered to do the job for him in his spare time, and arranged to start work on the following Saturday. The cement and other materials were ordered and delivered in readiness—but the neighbour failed to arrive on the day arranged, and *nothing was seen or heard of him for a fortnight.* Eventually he arrived at a most inconvenient time, with a flimsy excuse for the delay, and started work. He vanished again, leaving the work half-finished, and without any explanation. He never did return to finish the job and my acquaintance had to complete it himself. He could have done the whole job himself in the first place, without delay.

Later, another person *promised* to deliver and fit some guttering to the garage roof—"*to-morrow*". That was *six weeks* ago, but there is still no sign of the man or the guttering, and no explanatory message has been received.

This kind of thing is happening every day, everywhere. It just isn't good enough. These unreliable people are a constant source of annoyance and inconvenience. The best thing to do is to *cancel* any order not fulfilled, unless some reasonable explanation is offered at once. Why should any of us be pushed around by people who "couldn't care less"? Let us encourage the all too few *reliable* folk.

Then there is the matter of private or business appointments. There is nothing more annoying than to arrange an appointment with someone who arrives late. If an appointment is for ten o'clock it *means* ten o'clock—not half-past ten.

Again, how many times have we spent a most unreasonable time *waiting for service* in a restaurant? How often does a firm's telephonist forget that phone call? Is coal delivered to us as promptly *as ordered*? Did the TV mechanic arrive to repair the television as *promised*—or did he make us miss our favourite programme? These are just a few examples of unreliability that happen every day, and could be multiplied a thousandfold.

Yes, there is plenty of room for improvement towards reliability in all our lives and affairs. It is up to each one of us to help the wheels of industry, social and private life, to turn more smoothly.

Reliability also helps the individual to build up a good and strong character; it gives him a reputation for integrity, uprightness, trustworthiness and dependability. The reliable person stands head and shoulders above the majority of his fellows. He attracts friends, commands respect, improves business, satisfies his employers, maintains goodwill. In fact, he is the "salt of the earth".

# THE FOLLY OF REGRET

*"The present only is a man's possession; the past is gone out of his hand wholly, irrevocably. He may suffer from it, learn from it— in degree, perhaps, expiate it; but to brood over it is utter madness."*

\* \* \*

WHEN we are young, virile and ambitious, we stand sturdily and erect, as upon a mountain peak, surveying the world around us to the limit of our vision. Behind us, in the shadows of the past, there is only history—an indelible record of the triumphs and failures of our forefathers. Our present circumstances, which we take for granted, we believe are the result of the inspiration and the colossal blunders of those who trod Life's path before us. When we are young we can be forgiven for not feeling particularly grateful for our heritage, for we do not realise and cannot appreciate all the past faith, effort, courage and heartache of our fathers and grandfathers and generations before them, who were responsible for the majority of the good things that we have to-day.

Of course, in those early days of our lives we can see clearly enough what is wrong with the world and whose fault it was, and is; but now it is *our* turn. We have no time for the old-fashioned twaddle of our elders. Directly we get half a chance, we'll soon sort things out and put the world to rights. We have the whole future before us, with countless opportunities, some of which we can still only dream about. If we fail—but it is impossible for us to fail. Surely we shall not be stupid enough to repeat the same mistakes that we read about in history! So we believe, as we stand on our private "mountain-top" and survey the future, spread out as far as our youthful eyes can see —and even into the misty distance beyond.

Were it not for the incurable optimism of Youth and the inspired visions of alert young minds, the world would stagnate. Let us, then, be eternally grateful for the blessings of Youth, bestowed upon the world by the wisdom and benevolence of Nature.

Youth sets forth to battle its way through a harsh world. Some of us realise most of our ambitions and reach the topmost rung of our particular ladder. Others reach the top by middle age or even long before, and then tumble down again to the bottom. Many of us stick half way towards the realisation of our youthful dreams. Some of us have our youthful ambitious urges silenced by the clash and clatter, the din and confusion of life, until we are content to wander along in an endless, aimless rut. It takes all sorts to make a world,

and here again we see the wisdom of Mother Nature. Heaven knows
what would happen if we all aimed at the same target and jostled
each other along exactly the same path—or huddled together in a
gloomy pit of despair, or adopted a "couldn't-care-less" attitude
towards our individual problems and those of the rest of mankind.

### An Inescapable Fact

In considering the eternal cycle of life, with its myriad, ever-changing
patterns, its centres of interest and its diverse paths into the boundless
future, we are conscious of at least one inescapable fact. No matter
who we are, what sex or age we are, or how far we have journeyed
through life, we are all getting older every day. The younger we are
the less troubled we feel about the advancing years. We are gaining
valuable experience, approaching maturity, claiming more independence, building up a clearer picture of our final goal. Although we are
in such a hurry, we expect to have plenty of time ahead of us in which
to achieve our hearts' desires.

By the time we reach middle age we have already travelled half way
along the road to Somewhere, and instead of reading ancient history,
we have a considerable past of our very own to review. As we look
back down the years of our own lives, we make several remarkable,
and often humiliating discoveries.

### Unrealised Youthful Dreams

There are always outstanding exceptions, but for the majority of
us the picture of the past is something like this.

We remember ourselves as the bold and headstrong young man
or the romantic teenage girl. There we were, standing on the summit
of our individual and very private mountain. We knew just where
we intended to go, even if we were not quite sure how to get there.
But somehow we got lost. Perhaps we misread a signpost, 'way back
along Life's road; or we encountered an almost impenetrable jungle
of trouble, or a soul-scorching desert of despair, or the road became
filled with sharp and treacherous "rocks". We stumbled and fell,
hurting ourselves so badly that some of the wounds have not yet
healed. Perhaps we were misdirected by other travellers, or the fickle
winds of chance blew us off our course. Whatever the reason or
combination of mishaps, we now find ourselves heading in a quite
different direction to the one we intended to travel. The boy who
wanted to be an explorer and discover buried treasures may now find
himself exploring nothing more exciting than columns of figures, in
his job as an accountant. The romantic girl who had visions of
marrying a rich and handsome film director—or at least of becoming
a famous film star herself, is now living in suburbia with an ever-
demanding family, having married one of the local postmen.

## Life is Unpredictable

Strangely enough, although so many of us end up in a totally different situation to the one we saw in our youthful dreams, we admit that we might have done a lot worse for ourselves. Indeed, in many instances we may be better off, or at least far happier in our present circumstances than we might have been had we been able to follow our youthful inclinations. We could go further and realise that had Fate (if we believe Fate was responsible) not pushed us into a different path than the one we originally selected, we might not be still *alive* to-day.

We think, for example, of all those intrepid young men who were anxious to become pilots or members of an aircrew during the last war. Many failed to make the grade, because of physical defects or educational deficiency. They had to accept less exciting tasks among the ground staff. How many of these "unlucky" ones who are fit and active to-day would even be alive now, had they realised their ambitions? We just don't know.

We consider the boy who yearned to be a ship's radio officer but became a television engineer. He is now earning a good living and is a happy husband and father. Had he become a ship's radio officer he might well be lying at the bottom of the sea by now. Who knows? Life is so strange and unpredictable. What is the use of imagining what *might* have been, and having regrets because we did this instead of that? We simply don't know what would have happened to us had we been permitted to go our own way. Of course, if we regret a certain mistake in the past, we can and should learn an important lesson from it, but we should let it go at that. It is senseless to brood over the past and dwell upon all the wonderful things that might have happened to us if only circumstances had been different or if we had only made a different decision. It might have been much better for us—but again, it might have not.

Some of the happiest people are those who sincerely believe that there is a Guiding Providence in life—a Divine Power that helps to shape our destiny—a Power that knows better than we do, what is best for us. Some psychologists keep telling us that we shape our own destinies. This is partially true, but is it the whole truth? From whence do we derive the necessary aspiration and inspiration to select and decide which way we shall go? Are we not being too arrogant in assuming that we shape our destiny all by ourselves? We should consider this question very deeply.

With regard to regrets, one writer has put it this way: "We often regret we did not do otherwise, when that very otherwise would, in all probability, have 'done for' us!"

Hope helps to keep us going when the present is grim and the future looks foreboding. Happy memories of the past can often sweeten the present—but vain regrets and anguish concerning the past, disrupt our inner calm and are useless burdens. We should cast out these devils of blistered memories, those haunting, ghostly visitants that leer at us from the mystic shadows of long past experiences. For we cannot be happy while constantly pursued by futile, bitter memories of past transgressions, errors and failures.

### The Future Still Beckons

Consider the life story of one of the most famous of film stars as published in a leading daily newspaper recently. He was born and reared in one of the roughest parts of New York, known as "Hell's Kitchen". He refers to himself in those days as "a hungry kid chasing a fast buck" by delivering bootleg liquor. He came to England in 1926 as the highest-paid dancer in the country, and was presented with a gold cigarette-lighter by the then Prince of Wales, for teaching him to dance the tango.

This famous film actor became one of the greatest of the film gangsters, and he made *ten million* dollars. By 1933 he was the highest-paid film star. He owned a string of racehorses, a night club on Broadway, a gambling ship outside New York harbour and a club in Havana.

If ever a man was "sitting on top of the world" this film celebrity was, in his heyday, but it didn't last. He lost most of his fortune for various reasons, including his own misjudgments. "Mistakes? My life's full of them," he confessed to the reporter who interviewed him. Looking back over his life, he knows now what he should have done and what he should not have done. As always, it is easy to be wise *after* the event. Here is a man who could be thoroughly bitter and miserable with his load of regrets. After years of fame and glory this once-famous star has now become what he terms "a lonely legend". Yet this former idol of the silver screen is something of a philosopher. He doesn't cringe in a corner licking his wounds, and he hasn't allowed vain regrets to defeat him. He is now, at sixty-five years of age, the director of a chain-store, and he has an interest in an air-line. "Who knows what I'll do next?" he asks. "Who knows?"

### Make the Most of To-day

This famous actor of the past is right enough there. Who knows what lies ahead for any of us? "While there's life there's hope" may be a trite saying, but it is true and worth remembering. We have all transgressed, made mistakes and lost opportunities. Every life has known its failures. But let us not forget that the path to victory is ever lined with failure and that failures can be used as stepping-stones to success. We can profit by our mistakes and learn important lessons from our failures. Every to-morrow is a new day, with fresh opportunities, new ideas. Inspiration often comes when we least expect it. So we should cast away the haunting memories of the past —that we have tried before and failed—otherwise they will rise up to paralyse our efforts and defeat our hopes. Only when we give up hope and stop trying are we finally beaten—and unavailing regrets are like so much dead wood hindering our progress as we try to climb uphill again towards more success and greater happiness. The past is dead and gone. To-day alone is ours. Let's make the most of to-day and have no regrets about any of our yesterdays.

> "Weep not o'er precious chances past away,
> Wail not o'er golden ages on the wane.
> Each night I burn the records of the day—
> At sunrise, every soul is born again."

# THOUGHT—THE VITAL FORCE

ABUNDANCE is the natural law of the Universe. The evidence of this law is conclusive; we can see it on every hand. Everywhere Nature is lavish, wasteful and extravagant. Nowhere is economy observed in any created thing.

The millions and millions of trees, flowers, plants and animals, and the vast scheme of reproduction, in which the process of creating and re-creating is for ever going on, all indicate the lavishness with which Nature has made provisions for Man.

It is evident that there is an abundance for everyone, but it is also evident that a great many people seem to have been separated from this supply. What is the reason for this state of affairs? Could it be that the majority of men and women have not yet come into a realisation that there is a universality of all substance, and that mind is the active principle which starts causes in motion whereby all are related to the things they desire?

It would seem that in order to control many circumstances, a knowledge of certain scientific principles of mind-action is required. And such knowledge could become a most valuable asset. Can this knowledge be gained by degrees and put into practice just as quickly as it is learned?

Admittedly, power over certain circumstances seems to be the fruits of such knowledge; harmony and prosperity assets in its balance-sheet. And it would appear that the only cost is the labour of harvesting its great resources.

If we probe deeper into the matter, we find that all wealth is the offspring of power; possessions are of value only as they confer power. Events are significant only as they affect power; all things represent certain forms and degrees of power.

The discovery of a reign of law by which the power could be made available for all human efforts marked an important epoch in human progress. It is the dividing line between superstition and intelligence; it eliminated the element of caprice in men's lives and substituted immutable, universal law.

A knowledge of cause and effect as shown by the laws governing steam, electricity, chemical affinity and gravitation has enabled Man to plan courageously and to execute fearlessly. These laws are called Natural Laws, because they govern the physical world. But all power is not physical power, for there is also mental power as well as moral and spiritual power.

Thought is the vital force or energy which is being developed.

308

It has produced such startling results during the last half-century as to bring about a world which would seem inconceivable to an individual living only fifty years ago. If such results have been obtained by organising these mental power-houses in fifty years, what may we expect in another fifty years?

Some people may say, if these principles are true, why are we not demonstrating them; if the fundamental principle is correct, why do we not get proper results? We probably do, for it seems that we get results in accordance with our understanding of the law and our ability to make the proper application.

We did not obtain results from the laws governing electricity until someone formulated the law and showed us how to apply it.

Mental action seems to inaugurate a series of vibrations in the ether, which is the substance from which all things proceed, and they, in their turn, induce a corresponding grosser vibration in the molecular substance, until finally mechanical action is produced.

This puts us in an entirely new relation to our environment, opening out possibilities hitherto undreamt of, by following an orderly sequence of law which is naturally involved in our new mental attitude.

## Thoughts of Abundance

It is clear, therefore, that thoughts of abundance will respond only to similar thoughts. Affluence within is found to be the secret of attraction for affluence without.

Thought is the energy by which the law of attraction is brought into operation and which eventually manifests abundance in the lives of men and women.

The source of all power and all weakness is from within; the reason for success as well as failure also comes from within.

All growth is an unfoldment from within. Nature provides evidence of this; trees, plants, animals and human beings are living testimony to this great law, and the error of the ages is in looking for power and strength from without.

So it would seem that a thorough understanding of this great law, which permeates the entire Universe, leads to the acquirement of that state of mind which develops and unfolds creative thoughts that can produce some amazing changes in life.

Men and women who understand the working of this wonderful law find golden opportunities strewn across their paths, and the perception and power to utilise these opportunities spring up within them. Friends and popularity seem to come to them almost unbidden; circumstances seem to adjust themselves to changed conditions— these are the people who have indeed found the "Pearl of greatest price."

Wisdom, strength, courage and harmonious conditions are chiefly the result of power—the power within. Likewise, limitation, lack, and many adverse circumstances would seem to be the result of weakness. And as weakness is the absence of power, the remedy is simply to develop power.

This is the key which many have used to unlock the door to the fuller life, to convert loss into gain, fear into courage, despair into joy, and hope into fruition.

All this may seem too good to be true. But we should remember that within a few years, by the touch of a button or the turn of a lever, science has placed almost infinite resources at the disposal of Man. Is it not possible, therefore, that there are other laws containing still greater possibilities?

## Invisible Forces

Let us look at some of the most powerful forces in Nature. In the mineral world everything is solid and fixed. In the animal and vegetable kingdom there is a state of flux, for ever changing, always being created and re-created. In the atmosphere we find heat, light and energy.

Each realm becomes finer and more spiritual as we pass from the visible to the invisible, from the coarse to the fine, from the low potentiality to the high potentiality. When we reach the invisible we find energy in its purest and most volatile state.

And as the most powerful forces of Nature are the invisible ones, so do we find that the most powerful forces of Man are his invisible forces—his spiritual force. And the only way in which the spiritual force can manifest is through the process of thinking. Thinking is the only activity which the spirit possesses and thought is the only product of thinking.

Addition and subtraction are, therefore, spiritual transactions; reasoning is a spiritual process; ideas are spiritual conceptions; questions are spiritual searchlights and logic, argument and philosophy are parts of the spiritual machinery.

Thought brings into action certain physical tissue, parts of the brain, nerve and muscle. This can produce an actual physical change in the construction and harmony of the cells of the body, and a number of thoughts on a given subject can bring about a complete change in the physical organisation of an individual.

This is a process by which failure is often changed into success. Thoughts of courage, power, inspiration and harmony are substituted for thoughts of failure, despair, lack, limitation and discord. And as these thoughts take root, the physical tissue can change and the individual sees life in a new light. He seems to be born again, this time of the spirit; life has a new meaning for him; he is reconstructed and is filled with confidence, hope and energy. He sees opportunities which previously he missed. He recognises possibilities which before had no meaning for him.

The thoughts of success with which he has been impregnated are radiated to those around him, and they in turn help him onward and upward. He attracts to himself new and successful associates and this in turn changes his environment. And so it is, by this simple exercise of thought that an individual may change not only himself but his environment, circumstances and conditions.

Can it be that we are at the dawn of a new day with wonderful and fascinating possibilities, perhaps so limitless as to be almost bewildering?

A century ago, a man with an aeroplane or even a machine-gun could have annihilated a whole army equipped with the implements of warfare then in use. Likewise to-day, the individual with a thorough knowledge of practical psychology and metaphysics has an inconceivable advantage over the multitude.

### The Law of Attraction

Mind is creative and operates through the law of attraction. Men and women should not, however, be influenced to do what others think they should do. Each individual has a right to choose for himself. But apart from this, to influence other people means operating under the laws of force, which are destructive in their nature and just the opposite of the law of attraction.

A little reflection will no doubt convince us that the great laws of Nature operate in silence and that the underlying principle is the law of attraction. It is only destructive processes such as earthquakes and catastrophes that employ force. And nothing good seems to be accomplished in that way.

To be successful, attention must invariably be directed to the creative plane, but there should be no exploitation. There's no necessity to take from one person to give to another, for the supply for all is abundant. Nature's storehouse of wealth is inexhaustible, and where there is a lack of supply, this is because the channels of distribution are as yet imperfect.

Abundance chiefly depends upon the recognition of the laws of abundance. Mind is not only the creator but the creator of all there is. Certainly, nothing can be created before we know that it can be created, and then follows proper effort.

There is no more electricity in the world to-day than there was fifty years ago, and until someone recognised the law by which it could be made of service, we received no benefit. Now that the law is understood, practically the whole world is illuminated by it. And so it is with the law of abundance. For it is only those who recognise the law and place themselves in harmony with it who share in its benefits.

A recognition of the law of abundance develops in the individual certain mental and moral qualities, among which are courage, loyalty, tact, sagacity, individuality and constructiveness. These are all modes of thought, and, as all thought is creative, they manifest in objective conditions corresponding with the mental condition. This is because the ability of the individual to think is his ability to act upon the Universal Mind and bring it into manifestation; it is the process whereby the individual becomes a channel for the differentiation of the Universal Mind. Thought is a cause and condition an effect.

This principle seems to endow the individual with apparently transcendental possibilities, among which is the mastery of conditions through the creation and recognition of opportunities.

This creation of opportunities implies the existence or creation of the necessary qualities or talents. These are thought forces and result in a consciousness of power which future events appear not to disturb.

It is this organisation of victory or success within the mind, this consciousness of power within, which constitutes the responsive harmonious action, whereby we are related to the objects and purposes which we seek. This is the law of attraction in action. And it would appear that this law, being the common property of all, may be exercised by anyone having sufficient knowledge of its operation.

Courage is the power of the mind which manifests a fondness for mental conflict; it is a noble and lofty sentiment; it is equally fitted to command or obey; both require courage.

### Valuable Assets

Courage often has a tendency to conceal itself. There are men and women who seem to exist only to do what is pleasing to others. But when the time comes and the latent will is revealed, we find under the velvet glove an iron hand.

Real courage is cool, calm and collected. It is never foolhardy, quarrelsome, ill-natured or contentious.

Accumulation is the power to reserve and preserve a part of the supply which we are constantly receiving, so as to be in a position to take advantage of the larger opportunities which often come as soon as we are ready for them. Has it not been said: "To him that hath shall be given"?

James J. Hill, a wealthy industrialist, once said: "If you want to know whether you are destined to be a success or failure in life, you can easily find out. The test is simple and it is infallible: Are you able to save money? If not, drop out. You will lose. You may think not, but you will lose as sure as you live. The seed of success is not in you."

This is very good so far as it goes, but anyone who has read the biography of Mr. Hill knows that he acquired his great wealth by following the methods we have been discussing. In the first place he started with nothing; he had to use his imagination to idealise the vast business he built up. He then had to come into a recognition of the law of abundance in order to provide the ways and means of materialising it; unless he had followed out this programme, it is very doubtful whether he would have had anything to save.

Accumulativeness acquires momentum. Usually, the more we accumulate the more we desire, and the more we desire the more we accumulate. So that it is but a short time until the action and reaction acquire a momentum that is difficult to stop.

Accumulativeness should, however, not be confounded with selfishness, miserliness or penuriousness, for they are perversions and will make any true progress impossible.

Constructiveness is the creative instinct of the mind. Every successful business man must be able to plan, develop or construct. In the business world it is usually referred to as initiative. It is not enough to go along the beaten path. New ideas must be developed, new ways of doing things must be devised.

Constructiveness manifests in building, designing, planning, inventing, discovering, improving. It is a most valuable quality and should be constantly encouraged and developed. Every individual possesses it to some degree, because he is a centre of consciousness in that infinite and Eternal Energy from which all things proceed.

Water manifests on three planes, as ice, as water and as steam; it is all the same compound. The only difference is the temperature, but no one would try to drive an engine with ice. But convert it to steam and it easily takes up the load. So it is with our energy. If we want to act on the creative plane, we should begin by melting the ice with the fire of imagination. The stronger the fire, the more ice we melt, the more powerful our thought will become, and the easier it will be for us to materialise our desire.

Sagacity is the ability to perceive and co-operate with Natural Law. True sagacity avoids trickery and deceit. It is the product of that deep insight which enables one to penetrate into the heart of things and understand how to set causes in motion which will create successful conditions.

Tact is a very subtle and at the same time, a very important factor in the achievement of success. It is very similar to intuition. To possess tact, one must have a fine feeling, must know instinctively what to say or what to do.

In order to be tactful one must possess sympathy and understanding, the understanding which is so rare, for all men see and hear and feel, but how very few "understand"?

Tact very often enables one to foresee what is about to happen and calculate the result of actions. Tact enables us to feel when we are in the presence of physical, mental and moral cleanliness, for these are to-day invariably demanded as the price of success.

Loyalty is one of the strongest links which bind men and women of strength and character. It is one which cannot be broken with impunity. The individual who will never betray a friend will never lack for friends. The man who will stand in silent guard beside the shrine of confidence or friendship of those who have allowed him to enter, will find himself linked with a current of cosmic power which will attract many desirable conditions.

Individuality is the power to unfold our own latent possibilities. Strong men care nothing for the flock of imitators who trot complacently behind them. They derive no satisfaction from the mere leading of large numbers or from the plaudits of the mob. For this appeals only to petty natures and inferior minds. Individuality glories more in the unfolding of the power within than in the servility of the weakling.

Individuality is a real power inherent in all, and the development and consequent expression of this power enables one to assume the responsibility of directing his own footsteps rather than stampeding after some self-assertive demagogue.

Inspiration is the art of imbibing, of self-realisation, of adjusting the individual mind to the Universal Mind. Inspiration is the art of attaching the proper mechanism to the source of all power, of differentiating the formless into form, of becoming a channel for the flow of Infinite Wisdom, of visualising perfection.

Truth is the imperative condition of well-being. To be sure, to know the truth and to stand confidently on it, is a satisfaction beside which no other is comparable. Truth is the underlying reality, the condition precedent to successful business or social relation.

Every act not in harmony with truth, whether through ignorance or design, can cut the ground from under our feet, lead to discord, inevitable loss and confusion. For while the humblest mind can foretell the result of every correct action, the greatest, most profound and penetrating mind is apt to lose its way hopelessly and can form no conception of the result, if it departs from correct principles.

## A Storehouse of Mental Wealth

Those who seek to imbue themselves with the requisite elements of true success should establish confidence and organised victory. It then remains for them to take such steps from time to time as the newly awakened thought force will direct. This is one of the secrets of all power.

It is said that only 10 per cent. of our mental processes are conscious; the other 90 per cent. are subconscious and unconscious.

So that the person who would depend upon his conscious thought alone for results is only 10 per cent. efficient.

Those who accomplish anything worth while are those who are enabled to take advantage of this greater storehouse of mental wealth. It is in the vast domain of the Subconscious Mind that great truths are hidden, and it is here that thought finds its creative power—its power to correlate with its object, to bring out of the unseen, the seen.

Those who are familiar with the laws of electricity understand the principle that electricity must always pass from a higher to a lower potentiality, and can, therefore, make whatever application of the power they desire. Those not familiar with this law can effect nothing. And so it is with the law governing in the mental world; those who understand that mind penetrates all things and can be responsive to practically every demand, can make use of the law and can often control conditions, circumstances and environment. The uninformed cannot use this knowledge because they are unaware of it.

The fruit of this knowledge is often looked upon as a divine gift to all humanity. For the law to which we have referred is no respecter of persons; it makes no difference what our habit of thought may be, the way has been prepared.

When it is realised that this mental power controls and directs every other power that exists, that it can be cultivated and developed, and that there is little or no limitation that can be placed upon its activity, it will become apparent that it is the greatest fact in the world. For it would appear that it is the remedy for almost every ill, the solution for practically every difficulty, the gratification of almost every desire; in fact, that it is the Creator's magnificent provision for the emancipation of all mankind.